Senate Elections and Campaign Intensity

Senate
Elections and
Campaign
Intensity

MARK C. WESTLYE

THE JOHNS HOPKINS UNIVERSITY PRESS
Baltimore and London

© 1991 The Johns Hopkins University Press
All rights reserved
Printed in the United States of America

The Johns Hopkins University Press
701 West 40th Street
Baltimore, Maryland 21211
The Johns Hopkins Press Ltd., London

∞ The paper used in this book meets the minimum requirements of American National
Standard for Information Sciences—Permanence of Paper for Printed Library Materials,
ANSI Z39.48–1984.

Library of Congress Cataloging-in-Publication Data

Westlye, Mark Christopher.
    Senate elections and campaign intensity / Mark C. Westlye.
        p.   cm.
    Includes bibliographical references and index.
    ISBN 0-8018-4102-X
    1. United States.   Congress.   Senate—Elections.
    2. Electioneering—United States.   I. Title.
JK1965.W47   1991
324.7'0973—dc20   90-46421
                                                          CIP

Contents

Acknowledgments

I am grateful to many people for their support and assistance throughout this project. I would particularly like to thank Raymond Wolfinger and Nelson Polsby, who have guided my understanding of congressional elections. For his insightful counsel throughout the project, I am indebted to John Zaller. Steven S. Smith offered invaluable suggestions for final revisions, and Allan Sindler and Larry Bartels generously commented on drafts and offered methodological suggestions throughout the project. Christopher Achen, Henry Brady, Jack Citrin, Dennis Chong, David Glass, Donald Green, J. Merrill Shanks, and Eric R. A. N. Smith also provided valuable assistance.

I would also like to thank Eugene Lee, who, as Director of the Institute of Governmental Studies at the University of California, Berkeley, secured funding for the purchase of several state-level surveys used in this study. The acquisition of state-level survey data could not have been accomplished without the cooperation of numerous state data organizations, sitting and retired senators, professional polling firms, and university archives. I am grateful to the following individuals for providing survey data used in this book: Bill Gunter, William Hamilton, and Betty Ryner for 1980 Florida data; Birch Bayh, William Hamilton, and Betty Ryner for 1980 Indiana data; John Blydenburgh and John J. Coleman for 1978 Massachusetts data; William Bradshaw and Michael Traugott for 1978 Michigan data; Stephen Salmore and Rod Forth for 1976 and 1978 New Jersey data; F. Chris Garcia for 1976 and 1978 New Mexico data;

vii

Kathy Frankovic for 1976 New York data; Boyd L. Wright for 1974, 1976, and 1980 North Dakota data; Harry Sharp for 1964 Wisconsin data; and Kendall Baker and Oliver Walter for 1972, 1976, and 1978 Wyoming data. In many instances, these individuals assisted in rendering their data compatible with the computer system to which I had access. For the time and effort they generously extended I am very grateful.

I would also like to acknowledge the dozens of political scientists, pollsters, data archivists, and public officials who took the time to respond to requests for help in locating data. Because state-level survey data on Senate elections are not systematically archived, the task of hunting down data consisted largely of following their leads.

For their crucial technical assistance in converting data for analysis at Berkeley I would like to thank Margaret Baker, Christine Day, Ilona Einowski, Alistair Fyfe, Ellen Liebman, and Peter Linquiti. Newspaper coverage of Senate campaigns was researched with the invaluable aid of Mary Lavender and Venita Jorgensen, of the Library at the University of California, Riverside, and Jo Lynn Milardovich, of Berkeley's Doe Library. Thanks also to Evelyn Westlye for commenting on the manuscript.

The data utilized in this study from the University of Michigan's Center for Political Studies National Election Studies were made available by the Inter-University Consortium for Political and Social Research. *Los Angeles Times,* California Poll, CBS/*New York Times,* ABC News/*Washington Post,* and Roper Center surveys were provided by the University of California State Data Program, Berkeley. Neither the original sources of any of the data nor the organizations that provided them bear any responsibility for the analyses or interpretations presented here.

Senate Elections and Campaign Intensity

1. Patterns and Anomalies in Senate Elections

Every two years, after election day, news commentators and columnists are called upon to explain congressional election results. They take notice of the fact that almost all members of the House of Representatives were returned to office and then turn to the year's thirty-three or thirty-four Senate races. In years when most incumbent senators have been reelected as well, explanations tend to center on the public's desire to "stay the course" or on the extraordinary insulation that the powers of incumbency provide members of Congress. But in years when a number of incumbent senators have lost, discussion revolves around the relative electoral vulnerability of senators owing to their high political profile and the controversial issues from which they may find it difficult to hide. In years when one party makes big gains in the Senate, the economy or the popularity of the current president is often cited as the cause, even though in other years similar circumstances may yield no such gains. And every four years, Senate election outcomes are tied to (or contrasted with) the fate of the presidential candidate: in 1980 challenger Ronald Reagan's success was said to have helped many Republican senators into office, whereas the unpopularity of President Carter was viewed as having hurt Democratic senators' chances; in 1984, when Democratic Senate candidates did quite well despite Walter Mondale's dismal showing against President Reagan, there was discussion of incumbent safety in both houses and of voters' differing agendas in presidential and in congressional elections.

General explanations of Senate election outcomes, however, rarely account for the invariably large number of anomalies that contradict the prevailing theories of the year. In 1980, for example, Reagan was elected by a large margin, and the Republicans also won control of the Senate, with Republican challengers from around the country defeating liberal Senate opponents. A triumph of conservatism, aided by Reagan's pull from the top of the ticket, was declared. But there had in fact also been numerous easy Democratic Senate victories, notable among which were landslide victories by three liberal Democrats, in California, Hawaii, and Ohio. In 1984, when President Reagan won reelection by a landslide in a political climate not unlike that of 1980, it was the Democrats who gained seats in the Senate. Democratic incumbents defeated Republican conservatives by landslides in Georgia and Alabama, where the Republicans had defeated Democratic incumbents four years earlier; a Republican incumbent was defeated in Iowa, where a Democratic incumbent had lost in 1980.

A complex interplay of influences in Senate election campaigns continually produces unexpected sets of election-year outcomes. In this book, therefore, I identify general patterns of behavior by candidates, the news media, and the electorate that explain these diverse outcomes both across states and across time within the same states. I examine such questions as whether challengers' success in reaching the voters is a function of their own campaign decisions and activities or is mediated significantly by decisions made by news organizations; when and to what extent Senate candidates' issue positions affect voters' decisions; how much the size and partisan slant of a state affect the outcome of a Senate race; and whether divisive primaries affect the general election results.

The campaign strategies senators pursue and the effectiveness of those strategies differ remarkably. Among the campaigns analyzed in depth are that of a candidate who made every effort to appear with candidates at the top of his party's ticket and that of a candidate who persistently criticized his party's top standard-bearers, appearing to hope that they would not actively support him. In one campaign, a major city's newspaper devoted 122 stories to the race, while the most attentive of its television news programs gave it less than 11 minutes of coverage during the entire last month of the campaign. Some challengers took every opportunity to attack their incumbent opponent, while others chose never to do so. In one Senate election campaign several issues debated by the candidates affected the voters' decisions, while in another race the issues debated by candidates had virtually no impact on the voters' choices. The campaign strategies of some of the challengers whose races are studied here seemed

2

to produce pretty much the response they had planned for, while the strategies of others produced almost the opposite of what was intended: in one case a candidate walked all around his state in an effort to drum up statewide recognition but was able to attract almost no media coverage, while in another state a challenger was extensively covered on an issue that he never expected would make the news while receiving almost no coverage on the issue that he had expected would be his ticket to Washington. One challenger spent 89 times as much money as his incumbent opponent and lost by a landslide; another spent $1.7 million less than his opponent and still won. The same state elected, by a landslide margin in each case, first a conservative Republican and then two years later a liberal Democrat and subsequently returned them both to office, again by a large margin.

Patterns that help to make sense of such diverse Senate election outcomes may be found in the behavior of candidates, the media, and the voters, and in exploring them I take as a point of departure existing research on House elections. They resemble Senate elections in many respects and differ importantly in many others.

Comparing House and Senate Elections

Most scholarly research on congressional elections has focused on the House. In large measure, this is because House elections are easier to study systematically than Senate elections: all 435 House seats come up for election every two years, and a randomized national survey of voters yields a reasonably representative sample of House voters. The first systematic research on House elections, undertaken by scholars at the University of Michigan, concluded that the key to explaining the vote for Congress was party identification. Looking at the 1958 electorate, Stokes and Miller (1962)[1] found that voters' level of information about House candidates was so low that it was impossible for most people to choose between candidates on the basis of issues or personal characteristics. Knowing little more about the candidates than their party affiliation, voters tended to cast a party-line vote.

Of fundamental interest to scholars studying House elections has been the fact that so many congressmen win reelection year after year; this percentage has hovered around 90 percent for decades. One contributing factor to the high reelection rate is that the distribution of voters' party affiliations within congressional districts is often skewed in favor of one party or the other; voters from the dominant party usually elect a member of that party, and with substantial party-line voting the incumbent

3

is repeatedly reelected. Scholars have also found that for a variety of reasons the magnitude of incumbents' electoral advantage has increased since the 1950s. Explanations for this incumbency advantage are legion; indeed, a large proportion of the congressional elections research in the last fifteen years has been devoted to this topic. Foremost among these explanations is congressmen's increased attention to constituent casework and other district service, their use of more frequent and improved mailings, and more time spent in the district.[2] In general, voters identifying with the incumbent's party have been found to be as loyal as ever to their party when it comes to casting a vote for Congress, but increasing proportions of "out-party" identifiers now defect from their party to vote for incumbent candidates.[3] The twin considerations of *party identification* and *incumbency* have been invoked innumerable times by journalists and other analysts of particular elections, and in numerous American politics texts, as the key to individual voting decisions and to overall patterns of congressional election outcomes.

In 1978 the University of Michigan's Center for Political Studies National Election Studies (CPS/NES) greatly increased the number of its survey questions on congressional elections and included a battery of new items exploring respondents' familiarity with and opinions about both House and Senate candidates. Research coming out of the 1978 survey began to change the focus of explanations for voting behavior in House elections. Where party identification and incumbency-related advantages had been seen as key to an understanding of the vote, the new research tended to emphasize the quality of the candidates. Most House challengers, it was noted, were ill-equipped to put up a viable campaign against incumbents: they could neither raise money nor gain name recognition. Not only were challengers unable to win, they could not even come close.[4]

Senate races received considerably less attention throughout this period.[5] The inaccessibility of useful survey data collected in individual states precluded efforts at analysis of the vote decision process in these elections. While national voter surveys are available, they are of little use in studying Senate elections, since only two-thirds of the states elect senators in a given election year; the number of respondents in a national sample who are voting in Senate elections is therefore considerably diminished. In addition, most respondents in any nationwide survey are drawn from the larger states, with the majority sometimes coming from just the three or four largest states.[6]

There was good reason to study Senate elections, to be sure: while senators and representatives have been seeking reelection at the same high rate over the last several decades,[7] senators running for reelection lose more often, and those who win do so by much narrower margins than do House incumbents. In the period 1960–84, an average of 94 percent of House incumbents won reelection; this rate dropped below the 90 percent mark only three times during this thirteen-election period. The proportion of Senate incumbents who won reelection over the same period, however, averaged 83 percent. The rate topped 90 percent only twice and dipped below 65 percent three times.

The average margin of victory in Senate reelection campaigns has also differed from that of the House over this period. House incumbents are typically reelected by very large (and increasing) margins; the close House race has become a rarity (Mayhew 1974b; Cover and Mayhew 1981). In the period 1960–84, 70 percent of House incumbents won reelection with at least 60 percent of the two-party vote; however, only 44 percent of Senate incumbents won by this margin over the same period. Not only do representatives win reelection more readily than do senators but the proportion of House incumbents holding "safe seats" is considerably greater than that of senators.[8] Speculation on the reasons for these differences has focused heavily on the nature of the office of senator as well as on aspects of Senate and House constituencies. One explanation holds that because senators supposedly receive greater and "feistier" media coverage than do members of the House (Hershey 1984, 166), voters hold senators individually more responsible for government policy (Hibbing and Alford 1982, 506). Senators are thus said to be more vulnerable to attack for unpopular views or legislative actions. As Hershey argued, "Coverage of a senator's actions puts more emphasis on national policy issues; thus senators' stands on controversial issues are likely to be better known, and to be a factor in their public images. House members are less visible in the media; there are more of them, and their office is less 'elevated.' . . . House members can hope to become known to their constituents primarily through the pork barrel projects they bring home and the constituent services they provide" (1984, 166).[9]

Sundquist and Scammon (1981, 23), too, asserted that "senators, after all, are national figures, identified with the making of national policy," whereas congressmen "are associated more with district matters and constituency services." They attributed the Democrats' sizable loss of Senate, but not House, seats in 1980 to this difference (ibid). Jones (1981, 100) made a similar point:

> If the voters are in the mood to "throw the rascals out," then it appears that senators are right out in front as visible targets for the expression of voter dissatisfaction. . . . Apparently, [voters] don't connect House

members with the "mess in Washington." . . . It is another story for
senators, however. . . . Ironically the greater resources available to senators no doubt contribute to more notoriety that, in turn, encourages
the voter to identify the incumbent with national politics. . . . the reason
senators lose sounds very much like what many describe as good old
responsible democratic politics. Voters are aware of both candidates,
they hold the incumbent accountable for what happens in Congress,
and they support the challenger if they are dissatisfied. Meanwhile,
House incumbents can count their blessings as they seek to control voter
awareness of themselves and their potential challengers.[10]

Uslaner (1981) argued that the greater vulnerability of senators may
come from an inclination, not shared by House members, to downplay
constituency services in favor of seeking national forums for the purpose
of "position-taking." Asserting that "most Senators would prefer to appear on 'Meet the Press' or 'Face the Nation' than to address a garden
club or listen to a constituent's personal problems in some remote 'district office' in their own state" (107), Uslaner suggested that "voters may
become so accustomed to seeing their Representative that they expect
similar attention from their Senators—and want to see the latter members in person rather than on television from Washington" (109). The
implication is that senators could improve their electoral chances by following the example of members of the House and spending more time in
their states looking after constituents' needs.

"Constituency-based" explanations have been offered by scholars asserting that House members' greater incumbency advantage is more a
function of district structure than of members' inclinations. Several point
to congressional district size: House members are in a better position to
make effective use of perquisites and the prestige of the congressional
office to keep in touch with a constituency that is manageable in size.
Richard Fenno (1982, 12) noted that the smaller size of House districts
allows for an emphasis on the "personal touch" in House campaigns:
"Most campaigning House members make some . . . effort to present
themselves, in the flesh, to the largest possible number of voters. They
tend to cultivate small spaces very intensively, even in rural districts,
where they saturate each community with their physical presence. They
believe that 'the best way to win a vote is to shake hands with someone
. . . by looking individuals in the eye one at a time and asking them.' . . .
And they believe that the voters they reach personally will talk to other
voters about them."

Along these lines, Hibbing and Brandes (1983, 810) suggested that
"representatives, because of their smaller constituencies, are able to meet

personally virtually every politically significant person in the district, while senators have no similar opportunity." Jewell and Patterson (1977, 91) claimed that the typically larger size and greater heterogeneity of states makes it "more difficult for a senator to build a secure political base by assiduous attention to the needs of his constituents." Making much the same point, Jones (1981, 98) concluded that the congressman's electoral environment, unlike that of the senator, is "typically one which can be managed by the member."

The nature and composition of a given constituency, in addition to its size, have been seen as affecting election outcomes as well. First, if House districts are more homogeneous than states, congressmen may be better able to identify and champion dominant interests in a district and, conversely, to avoid taking legislative positions that might not please voters. Senators, on the other hand, are "not only . . . expected to master a wider range of issues, but they normally also have larger and more diverse constituencies to please" (Bibby and Davidson 1973, 26). A senator thus runs a greater risk of alienating conflicting interests somewhere in his larger and more diverse constituency, interests that might back a challenger in the next election.[11]

House districts are also more likely to be dominated by one party, while a senator's state is likely to comprise a more diverse mixture of constituents and to have a more balanced distribution of partisan loyalties.[12] Accordingly, to the extent that people tend to vote for the candidate of their party affiliation or registration, House incumbents are more likely, on average, to win by larger margins than Senate incumbents.[13]

Constituency-based explanations of the differences between House and Senate outcomes form a basis for an investigation of voting in Senate elections; clearly, the dynamics of Senate elections differ from those of House elections. Moreover, Senate elections differ *from each other*. Different outcomes result from a host of factors—who the candidates are, how they become candidates, the resources and strategies they employ, the intensity of their campaigns, the partisan distribution of voters in the voting "district," and the roles played by national and local issues. Some differences in Senate election outcomes can undoubtedly be explained by state size and constituency characteristics. For example, a state that is chiefly Democratic, agricultural, or oil-producing might favor the election and retention of a certain type of candidate (in the first case a Democrat, in the second an advocate of farmers' interests, in the third an advocate of the oil-depletion allowance), while states whose composition is mixed would not consistently elect any one particular type of candidate. A senator from a more homogeneous state might find it easier to champion the

7

dominant interest of the constituency than would a senator from a more heterogeneous state, who by taking any stand on an issue would risk alienating some part of the electorate. And senators who represent states in which the party distribution is skewed in their favor might be seen to win by larger margins than senators from states where party identification is balanced.

There is a problem, however, in concluding that the diversity of Senate election outcomes is caused by difficulties senators may have in appealing to different elements of their constituencies. By definition such an explanation cannot account either for different election outcomes in states of similar size (of which there are many) or for different outcomes in the same state over time (of which there are also many instances). In fact, over the last nine election years every one of the fifty states has had one closely contested Senate race back to back with a Senate race that was not at all close. Even more striking, in eighteen states over the same period Senate incumbents from both parties have been elected by large margins. Consider the following examples:

- In North Dakota, conservative Republican Milton Young defeated Democratic opponents in 1962 by 21 points and in 1968 by 31 points. Meanwhile, Quentin Burdick, who was known as a moderate Democrat and whose Americans for Democratic Action and American Conservative Union scores showed him clearly to be a liberal, defeated conservative Republicans in 1964 and 1970 by 15 and 24 percentage points, respectively.

- In South Carolina, conservative Democrat–turned–Republican Strom Thurmond won elections in the period 1966–84 by 24, 26, 12, and 35 points, respectively. In 1968–80, moderate South Carolina Democrat Ernest Hollings defeated his conservative Republican opponents by 24, 41, and 40 points.

- In 1968 liberal Democrat Frank Church was elected by 20 percentage points to a third term as senior senator from Idaho. In the election for Idaho's other Senate seat in 1972, conservative Republican James McClure defeated by 6 points a Democrat whose views were close to those of Church. In 1974 Church won reelection by a 14-point margin, and in 1978 McClure was reelected by 36 points. In 1980 Church was narrowly defeated.

In these and other cases like them, voters from the same state elected senators from opposing parties, sometimes with opposing ideologies, both by large margins. Constituency-based explanations cannot account effectively for such occurrences, since they would predict that in the ho-

TABLE I
Number of States with Senators from Different Parties, 1968–1988

Congress	Following Election of:	Region* NE (N=10)	B (N=5)	S (N=11)	MW (N=11)	W (N=13)	Total (N=50)	Percentage
91st	1968	4	2	4	5	6	21	42%
92d	1970	5	1	3	5	5	19	38
93d	1972	5	1	5	4	7	22	44
94th	1974	5	0	4	4	7	20	40
95th	1976	7	2	5	5	5	24	48
96th	1978	7	3	6	5	5	26	52
97th	1980	6	3	8	3	5	25	50
98th	1982	6	3	7	3	5	24	48
99th	1984	6	4	6	3	4	23	46
100th	1986	6	2	4	3	6	21	42
101st	1988	5	2	5	3	6	21	42

* NE = Northeast: Connecticut, Delaware, Maine, Massachusetts, New Hampshire, New Jersey, New York, Pennsylvania, Rhode Island, Vermont
B = Border: Kentucky, Maryland, Missouri, Oklahoma, West Virginia
S = South: Alabama, Arkansas, Florida, Georgia, Louisiana, Mississippi, North Carolina, South Carolina, Tennessee, Texas, Virginia
MW = Midwest: Illinois, Indiana, Iowa, Kansas, Michigan, Minnesota, Nebraska, North Dakota, Ohio, South Dakota, Wisconsin
W = West: Alaska, Arizona, California, Colorado, Hawaii, Idaho, Montana, Nevada, New Mexico, Oregon, Utah, Washington, Wyoming

mogeneous states Senate election results should be one-sided and that in heterogeneous states Senate races should be closely contested. Are there other explanations that can augment the fixed-constituency idea and the notion that senators are simply more nationally prominent than congressmen? Let us look more closely at what appears to be happening in the seemingly odd cases listed above and others like them.

It is clear that in these cases many people vote in one year for the Senate candidate of one party, for the other party's candidate in the next election, and still later return to the first party.[14] As table 1 shows, voters' switching from one party to the other appears to be quite common. Since 1968, an average of 45 percent of states have had senators from both parties in Washington at the same time. This proportion dipped below 40 percent only once—to 38 percent after the 1970 elections—and reached at least 50 percent in 1978 and 1980. As the regional breakdown in table 1 shows, this pattern of electing one senator from each party holds in all sections of the country; it cannot be explained merely as a temporary condition created by sectional realignment in which voting patterns once favoring one party slowly change to favor the other. First, regional distributions of split states in 1968 resembled those in 1984. Second, with the possible exception of the South, regional party distributions have not changed much since 1968.[15] In many cases, the pattern derives from the fact that one party consistently won one Senate seat and the other party won the other.

To be sure, the split-state pattern is in some cases the result of two very close races in states in which party affiliation is fairly balanced.[16] But in a considerable number of states the pattern is much closer to the three examples above—senators from opposing parties are both elected by a wide margin. In such instances large numbers of Democrats and independents are voting for Republican candidates, or Republicans and independents are voting for Democratic candidates. In some cases, liberals and moderates are voting for conservative candidates, and in others conservatives and moderates are voting for liberal candidates.

Why, then, do senators from different parties, often with diametrically opposed ideologies, win elections back to back in the same state time after time? Since one or the other of them in such a situation has to be at odds with some segment of the electorate, why does this seem to pose no danger at the polls? Jacobson and Kernell (1981, 14–15) have observed that "what matters most to voters is the choice offered by the particular pair of candidates. . . . Voters' assessments of the two candidates are at least as important as party attachments in determining how people vote and . . . these assessments are vastly more important than any other factor." They also observed, as have others,[17] that voters are influenced not only by the direct effect of presidential popularity and the prevailing economic conditions on election day but also by the effects of these national factors on decisions by political actors. Jacobson and Kernell have argued persuasively that

> politically active elites—candidates and those who recruit and finance them—provide a crucial connecting link between national-level phenomena and individual voting decisions. National political conditions systematically shape elite decisions about running for office or contributing to campaigns. These decisions determine the alternatives presented to voters. Voters who must choose between two candidates will favor attractive candidates who run well-financed campaigns. In this way, even those voters who are blissfully free of any concerns with national political issues may, in voting on the basis of bumper stickers and billboards, contribute to a national electoral swing by reflecting in their votes the advantages that accrue to the political party favored by national political conditions. (1981, 2–3)

10

Voters' assessments of political candidates are to a great extent shaped by the information they have about the candidates. Campaign news coverage and advertising convey such information by bringing the names of previously unknown challengers before the electorate, as well as by illuminating the personalities or issue stances of better-known candidates. These processes occur in Senate election campaigns in so many combinations that it is not unusual, in a given election year, to find some Senate incumbents battling in hard-fought races while other incumbents coast in low-key ones. As a result largely of analyses using the 1978 CPS/NES survey, however, the widespread assumption arose that in Senate elections challengers are nearly as well known as incumbents. As Jones (1981, 99) put it, "Senate races are between the known and the slightly better known." This assumption is inaccurate, however, and has led to a number of other erroneous conclusions and generalizations about Senate elections.[18] In fact, not all Senate campaigns are highly visible, hard-fought affairs merely because they involve senators. Indeed, in a given state—that is, a single constituency with a given mix of party identifiers— one year's Senate race may be a hard-fought race between equally well-known candidates, while the next, just two years later, may be a low-key campaign involving a nearly invisible challenger. The advantage of incumbency, the extent of party-based voting, and the influence of national factors on the vote are therefore most usefully considered *within the context of campaign intensity,* and in view of the amount of information voters receive in individual Senate campaigns.

In many hard-fought races voters receive enough information about both candidates to be able to make judgments about specific aspects of their candidacies. But in low-intensity campaigns voters may receive little or no new information. It is in the latter type of race that voters end up basing their evaluations of the candidates on other, more obvious cues (party labels) or on information acquired prior to the campaign (which leads them to favor the incumbent). Very generally, as level of information (which is a function of the intensity of a given campaign) increases, the influence of party and incumbency decreases, while that of ideology, issues, and other campaign factors increases. So incumbency can be a significant advantage in Senate elections, but campaign-specific factors can also play a central role; if they do, the incumbent may only squeak by, or even lose. A great deal depends, therefore, on whether a challenger can put together a viable campaign and get his message across.[19]

Operating on the premise that the amount of information voters acquire during a campaign, and not just the content of that information, is

11

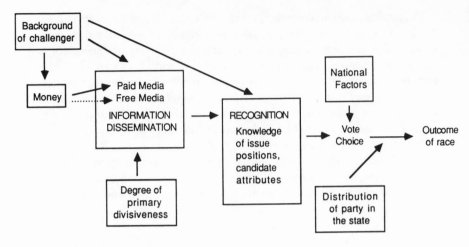

Figure 1. Influences on Senate Elections.

key to the choices voters make between candidates, we will look at the way information is disseminated in both hard-fought and low-key Senate campaigns, mainly through news coverage.[20] The amount of information conveyed by news organizations is inextricably linked to the intensity of a political campaign and thus to the way the campaign influences voters' decision making (see fig. 1).

As the schematic in figure 1 suggests, candidates must be known before they can expect to attract votes on the basis of their own merits (rather than simply on the basis of party identification). Whether people vote by comparing personal attributes of candidates, issue positions, general ideology, or anything else (other than national conditions), they must first know something about the candidates. So if one of the candidates— most often the challenger—is not known at the start of a campaign, he must become known, and he must do so in a few months by using paid media and attracting news coverage. Campaigns direct varying amounts of information at voters; on their end, voters receive varying amounts of information, which leads to differing levels of candidate recognition. When voters are aware of both candidates, they can choose on the basis of factors such as issue positions, personality attributes, or past performance. When they are aware of only one candidate, whether because only one candidate is running hard or because they are not personally paying much attention, they are more likely to choose on the basis of party identification or incumbency than on any other basis. This distinction has been described by Hinckley (1981, 10–13), but only in terms of differences between House and Senate elections. In Senate elections, depending on the level of intensity of the Senate campaign, either of these voting processes may occur; moreover, one or the other can occur in the same state from one election to the next.

Analyzing Senate Elections

Most races fall clearly into one of two categories: "hard-fought" and "low-key." Whether a campaign is hard-fought or low-key is influenced by initial factors such as the political experience of the challenger. Challengers who have a background in politics, who have proven that they can win elections, and who are tied to the political infrastructure of a state are more likely to be able to put together the funding and organization needed for a highly visible statewide race. Potential contributors are more likely to risk their money, volunteers are more likely to give their time, and other politicians are more likely to offer their endorsements when the challenger has a proven political record. The more political experience a challenger has, the more likely he is to command the publicity and other resources necessary to conduct a hard-fought campaign and to achieve a high level of information dissemination.

The news media have a special role in the dissemination of campaign information, and levels of information disbursement depend heavily on candidates' ability to attract free press coverage. The attraction of news coverage derives from candidates' ability to convince the press to take them seriously. A close look at news coverage of a number of hard-fought and low-key races reveals that candidates must engage in activities that will attract news media attention and must be aware of the norms of the news media, especially the need of reporters and editors to find controversy in, and to make a horse race out of, a political campaign.

Any study of Senate elections must include in its focus the voters and must investigate links between the extent of campaign news coverage and the information voters acquire about the candidates—especially the challenger—in a given race. While simply achieving a high rate of recognition is not the ultimate goal for challengers, it is a crucial first step toward getting people to vote for them, since a candidate's level of recognition among voters greatly affects overall defection patterns on Election Day. If one party's candidate is not widely recognized, many of the voters affiliated with that party will vote for the known candidate instead (the incumbent), but voters of the other party remain loyal to the known (incumbent) candidate. Of course, specific issues and short-term forces of a campaign may also affect such voter defection levels, but when voters

13

can recognize only one candidate, they have little alternative but to vote for the one they know (if they vote at all); the result of this dynamic will be massive voter defections in the direction of the better-known candidate, who is almost always the incumbent.

Figure 1 also suggests that the amount of information voters possess may affect the incidence of ideological or issue voting in Senate elections. If a voter does not recognize a challenger, it is difficult to weigh his issue positions against those of the incumbent, and it is difficult, by the same token, for the voter to cast a vote on the basis of political ideology. Thus policy and ideological voting are impossible if the challenger never succeeds in becoming known. News coverage of candidates and campaigns not only affects candidate recognition rates but also determines whether voters have enough information to base their decisions on issue positions or general candidate philosophies.

Senate election outcomes are also an area to be investigated, as they reflect not only individual-level vote decisions but also the aggregate effect of constituency-related factors beyond the candidates' control. Among these are the size of a state's population and the partisan distribution of voters within a state. These factors affect Senate election outcomes, viewed both in terms of winners and losers and in terms of margin of victory, though they are possible mediating effects of campaign intensity on the party distribution variable. In addition, divisive primaries, a phenomenon sometimes singled out as particularly damaging to the prospects of Senate candidates, especially challengers, may affect Senate election outcomes.

The central proposition of this study is that what causes divergent outcomes in Senate elections within the same constituency is variation in the amount and quality of information available to voters. Patterns of information dissemination, candidate recognition, and subsequent voting behavior are quite different in hard-fought and low-key elections, and when they have little or no information about one candidate—usually the challenger—voters opt for the candidate they know. If hard-fought campaigns actually do get through to the voters, voters receive information about both candidates; conversely, if candidates in low-key races really do fail to get their message across to voters, the acquisition of information by voters about both candidates in a Senate race is precluded.

2. Hard-fought and Low-key Senate Races

Because variation in the intensity level of campaigns is central to this analysis of Senate elections, I will first define "intensity" and determine how it can most usefully be measured. Some have claimed that Senate elections are generally energetic, high-visibility contests between two well-known candidates,[1] and indeed, a close look at Senate races since 1968 shows that many certainly were extremely intense and hard-fought. Candidates often spent millions of dollars, and reports of their campaign activities appeared prominently in newspapers and on television news around their states (occasionally drawing even national network news attention). However, there were also many low-key, nearly invisible Senate races in which neither the incumbent nor the challenger generated much activity or interest during the campaign.

To assess the intensity of Senate campaigns, and especially to do so systematically and across many election years, is not a simple matter. Such an assessment is crucial to this study, however, because variations in the intensity of Senate campaigns—the degree to which they were "hard-fought" or "low-key"—form the basis of subsequent key assertions about the vote decision process in Senate elections. For example, voters who gain considerable information about *both* candidates in a high-intensity Senate race behave differently from voters who gain limited information about only *one* candidate in a low-intensity race. The extent to which voters are able to recognize only one of the candidates is especially important in light of their tendency to vote for candidates they

15

recognize, regardless of party affiliation. In addition, issue voting, and voting on the basis of candidates' ideologies, takes place more often among voters who have information about both candidates as a result of exposure to a high-intensity campaign and less among those who have information only about the incumbent. Therefore, I begin by considering not only what is meant by "campaign intensity" but how best to measure the concept.

The Concept, Measurement, and Significance of Campaign Intensity

In any campaign, what voters know about the candidates is in large part a function of information imparted, either directly (person-to-person) or through the news media via news reports or paid political advertising. Incumbent senators have the opportunity to develop and then maintain a flow of information to their constituents during six years in office by traveling in their states, using their mailing privileges, and transmitting reports of their accomplishments to the news media. Senate challengers rarely have these advantages, and because their campaigns must reach so many people in so little time, they must rely on mass media rather than face-to-face, press-the-flesh campaign techniques. Thus, most actions and activities in a Senate campaign are undertaken with the direct or indirect intention of imparting information, via either free news coverage or paid advertising.[2] Our task is to devise a way to distinguish between campaigns that succeed in disbursing information widely during the course of a race and those that are less successful in doing so.[3]

Many of the terms describing campaign activity in a given race— "energy level," "noise level," "volume," "intensity"—can be assumed to reflect the level of information dissemination via the mass media. However, these kinds of terms can be used to describe a number of other things that candidates do that are not actually related to the direct disbursement of information. For example, a candidate may travel extensively around the state or spend twelve hours a day, seven days a week, campaigning. In one sense this is an intensive effort; it is certainly energetic. But if the state is a large one and the sum total of this effort is that the candidate logs hundreds of miles driving between small towns in a pickup truck, talking to people on the streets, or just "watching a lot of antelopes," the actual amount of information dissemination the candidate achieves is likely to be negligible. There are numerous examples of campaign energy being expended by candidates with very little payoff. In 1976, while incumbent Senator Hubert Humphrey jetted from one location to

16

another, his little-known opponent drove around Minnesota in a pickup truck. In 1974 in California, the challenger to incumbent Alan Cranston flew or drove hundreds of miles to address small groups of voters who already supported him. During the 1978 Senate campaign in Wyoming, Democrat Raymond Whitaker scoffed at candidate Alan Simpson's many trips to small towns around the state, during which, he said, Simpson doubtless encountered more antelope than voters.[4]

Similarly, if a candidate raises a great deal of money but spends very little of it either on paid advertising or on efforts to garner press coverage, it is likely that very little information about the campaign is disseminated. The same may be true if a candidate makes the effort to attract media attention but finds that news organizations are not receptive. In any of these situations, with very little information about the candidates being disseminated, all the candidates' efforts may fail to generate "high-intensity" campaigns even though the candidates themselves may be very active. Throughout this study, therefore, the term "intensity" will be employed with reference to the *level* of information disbursement in a given Senate race, and not with reference to the absolute number or nature of candidates' activities per se. Races of greater or lesser intensity will be classified as either "hard-fought" or "low-key," with the aim of distinguishing high-intensity races—in which a great deal of information about both candidates is made available to, and presumably reaches, the electorate—from low-intensity races—in which very little such information is produced. Hard-fought campaigns are those in which challengers conduct strong, highly visible campaigns, managing to attract the media attention that is necessary to make their state's voters aware of them. In most (but not all) such races, both sides raise comparable amounts of money. Occasionally the challenger will already be familiar to voters, either through having held prominent public office or by being a celebrity from another walk of life.

Low-key races, on the other hand, are those in which one of the candidates—by virtue of an inability to raise funds, to attract media coverage, or both—is unable to mount a forceful, stimulating campaign. This is often the case in House races in which an incumbent seeks reelection; it is characteristic of many Senate contests. A low-key race might result from choices made by one or the other candidate; for example, incumbents sometimes wish to draw as little attention to themselves as possible on the assumption that they have a large lead in the polls and their generating any news will only provide the challenger with valuable publicity. Challengers may attempt to mount a high-intensity campaign but fail to achieve it because of insufficient funds for advertising, travel,

17

or the staging of media events. A low-key race may also occur as a result of candidate ineptitude, or because (despite candidates' energetic efforts) the press simply does not see a particular campaign as worthy of a great deal of attention. And some challengers may never intend more than just a token campaign effort.

MEASURING CAMPAIGN INTENSITY

Quantifying campaign intensity in a single valid measure, in order to assess its impact, is a complex task. There are a number of possible options, each with its own assets and liabilities.

Margin of victory. Perhaps the simplest way to assess a campaign's intensity would be to look at the election's final outcome and make the necessary inferences from the size of the winner's margin of victory. If the race was a lopsided rout, it might be assumed that the challenger was unable to get his campaign off the ground and that the winner probably managed to avoid an ordeal of debates, attacks, and counterattacks which might have drawn the attention of an otherwise inattentive public. One might even assume that such a lopsided race provoked scant press coverage and that the challenger probably spent very little money.

By the same token, if an incumbent was defeated, or won only by a slim margin, it might be tempting to assume that the race was hard-fought. After all, incumbents have the advantages of office (direct, free access to voters through newsletters, large staffs to take care of constituents' needs, opportunities to impress voters by claiming credit for federal projects or other improvements in the state), networks of political contacts and contributors, and ties to state party organizations (where such organizations exist). All of these resources imply that for a challenger to have come close or to have defeated an incumbent, there must have been a high-intensity campaign.

In many instances, a close margin of victory does accompany a high-intensity campaign, and vice versa. But the two concepts are theoretically distinct, and it would be a mistake to characterize the intensity of a campaign solely by the margin of the outcome. For example, a Republican challenger in a solidly Democratic state (such as Rhode Island, Hawaii, or many southern states) might wage a high-intensity, very visible campaign but still fall far short of victory because too many Democrats, while they came to know the Republican challenger, remained loyal to the candidate of their party. Or, to turn the example around, an incumbent from the minority party in such a state might win by a very small margin even though the challenger (from the state's majority party) ran a lackluster

18

campaign and many voters of the challenger's own party eventually defected to the incumbent.

It is also possible in any Senate race, no matter what state or distribution of party identification or registration, for there to be a very hard-fought campaign—in which there is heavy news coverage of both candidates, large amounts of money are spent, and the voters become well aware of both candidates—where the margin of victory for one candidate is nevertheless enormous. This may occur because most voters simply prefer the views of one candidate over the views of the other or because of some scandal or other form of negative perception affecting one of the candidates, or it may be related to the difference between attempting and achieving—one candidate's best effort may simply surpass his opponent's. A striking example of this phenomenon is the 1978 race in Minnesota between David Durenberger and Robert Short. The campaign was hard-fought and extremely expensive for both sides, but Durenberger still won by 61 percent to 35 percent.

Margin of victory, then, is at best a problematic measure of the intensity of a given campaign.[5] And since achieving a high level of intensity is essential in terms of a campaign's purpose—conveying information to voters—it makes more sense to use a measure that directly taps activities designed to reach voters. As mentioned above, there are many ways that Senate candidates can try to reach voters, but not all of them are fruitful in dealing with constituencies as large as entire states. Personal communication via speeches and meetings can serve to mobilize campaign workers and encourage contributions, but as Hershey (1984, 169) put it, "Senate candidates normally cannot expect to contact more than a small part of their big constituencies without the use of television and radio and the attention of newspapers." The "use" of television, radio, and newspapers falls into two areas: news coverage and paid advertising.

Quantity of news coverage. Measuring news coverage is difficult for several reasons. Assessing television or newspaper coverage of Senate elections is theoretically possible, but to do the job completely would require that all television news programs and newspapers be monitored for all Senate races during a given time period—assuming that such sources have been archived. One could count the number of stories (in minutes or in newspaper column-inches) or candidate mentions and evaluate the substance of each news item. To tap the likelihood of newspaper articles' having been read, one might also distinguish between front-page stories and those appearing on inside pages, between stories appearing above or below the fold on the front page, and between various headline sizes. A

19

measurement scale could then be established in which campaign intensity would be calibrated in terms of amount of newspaper coverage. Television news coverage of Senate campaigns, on the other hand, cannot be reliably monitored unless analysts make their own videotapes of news broadcasts, since the only television news programs that are systematically archived are national network nightly news broadcasts. Some, but by no means all, local television news organizations archive past broadcasts, but news segments are generally stored by subject matter, thus precluding any monitoring of overall news content, and television news stations generally do not make such archives available for public use.

Quantity of paid advertising. Measuring the number and frequency of paid ads is even more difficult. Since there is no collection of local television or radio broadcasts from which to monitor such data, one would need to rely on candidates' records and on television stations' logs. Such documents are unavailable in most cases (especially for past years); and even if the necessary film could be obtained, systematic counting or content analysis of all the political ads broadcast in a state would be an enormous task.

Candidate expenditures. In view of such difficulties, a surrogate method for measuring campaign intensity must be found, one that most closely taps the quantity and character of information emanating from Senate campaigns. One alternative would be to assess a representative and manageably sized sample of newspapers and local television news broadcasts. With an archive of local television news broadcasts currently unavailable, this remains a task for the future. An analysis of the coverage given by a sample of newspapers would be possible, but any study of all Senate races across even a few elections would be a herculean effort. Another, far more workable alternative is to use candidates' own campaign expenditure data as a surrogate for the quantity and frequency of actual paid political advertisements. Jacobson (1980, 1984) and others have demonstrated that the amount of money spent by challengers is an important factor in the outcomes of Senate and House elections. Unquestionably, a candidate needs money to have any hope of running a viable campaign, and given incumbents' initial advantages with respect to organization and public recognition, it is reasonable to assume that challengers need even more money than the incumbents they take on. Generally speaking, the more money challengers raise, the more advertising they can buy on television, radio, in the newspapers, and on billboards. Advertising is not the only use for campaign funds. It also takes money to travel widely and efficiently; the high cost of flying around most states not only cuts down

20

on the number of appearances candidates can make but forces them to take up valuable time by using slower means of getting from place to place. And of course the more money candidates have, the more campaign workers they can employ.

However, spending figures are not always a reliable measure of the level of intensity of a Senate campaign. Per capita measures of spending allow one to control for the enormous population differences among states; for example, a candidate in Vermont who wanted to send each eligible voter a letter in 1980 would have had to spend (at 20 cents per letter) $80,000, while to send all eligible voters in California a similar letter would have cost a California candidate $3,391,200. But even in states with similar populations the same amount of money can buy a candidate much more visibility in one state than in another. Suppose candidates in Utah and Nebraska, states with approximately the same number of voters, want to cover their states with a thirty-second television ads (at a cost, say, of $1,000 per ad). Broadcasts from Salt Lake City stations are within range of almost all of the state's population, so a Utah challenger could be seen on all three network stations every night during the last week of the campaign for $21,000. However, all of Nebraska can be reached only through four media markets, not one, so the cost for a Nebraska candidate to run an ad reaching an audience of similar size would be $84,000. A Texas candidate trying the same tactic would have to buy time in twenty-three media markets. But that does not mean that the Texas candidate would necessarily have to spend twenty-three times what the Utah candidate spent to reach the statewide population, since several of Texas's media markets have relatively few people, and it would cost less to buy air time in those smaller markets than in major metropolitan areas such as Dallas or Houston. On the other hand, the same amount of air time costs more in Dallas than in Salt Lake City.

There are other problems inherent in comparing dollars spent across elections. For one thing, inflation during the 1970s affects year-to-year comparisons, since dollar costs were higher in later years for the same services. Correcting for inflation is relatively simple, but it is still difficult to establish what proportion of any candidate's expenditures is actually devoted to the goal of getting his message directly to the voters. In some cases, candidates recycle much of the money they receive into additional fund-raising efforts. Others may devote their resources less to advertising than to traveling over long distances to address small groups of already committed voters. Still other candidates receive contributions in the form of campaign services instead of in the form of funds. According to Herrnson (1985, 4), such "'in-kind' contributions often include mass media advertisements and campaign polling services, which the parties and candidates frequently report at well below their true monetary value. Utilizing the in-kind approach to contributing enables party committees to circumvent the FEC's $5000 contribution limit and to maximize the amount of input they have into the conduct of a particular campaign." For these reasons, at least for House races, the figures reported for the parties' financial activities understate the significance of party contributions. Since this practice undoubtedly occurs unevenly across campaigns, some candidates' reported campaign expenditure figures will be more realistic than others'.[6] Moreover, party expenditures generally are greater for Republican candidates than for Democrats (Abramowitz 1988, 25).

Such problems notwithstanding, one could measure campaign intensity in terms of campaign spending ratios. Such an intensity measure could be continuous: the closer the ratio is to 1-to-1, the higher the intensity of the campaign; conversely, the more lopsided the ratio, the lower the intensity. Or it could be divided into just two categories, with races in which an incumbent outspends his opponent (or, in the case of open seats, when one candidate outspends the other) by a 2-to-1 or greater margin classed as low-key races, and races with closer spending ratios considered hard-fought. While the 2-to-1 breakpoint in this dichotomous measure may be somewhat arbitrary, it is a reasonable way to distinguish, *in the absence of other information,* between races in which candidates' resources were roughly equal and races in which one side had an overwhelming resource advantage. It also removes the problems of varying state populations and numbers of media markets, since both candidates are running in the same state.

However, a strict spending-ratio decision rule can run into problems as well, as the following examples illustrate. In Virginia in 1978, millionaire John Warner and Andrew Miller vied for an open seat in Virginia. Miller spent $833,000, or 27 cents per eligible voter, which was far more money per voter than William Scott had spent in defeating incumbent William Spong in 1972, more per voter than challenger Elmo Zumwalt had spent in his hard-fought race against Harry Byrd, Jr., in 1976, and about the same amount per voter that Richard Trible and Richard Davis each spent in their open-seat race in 1982. The ratio rule would score the 1978 race as clearly low-key, because Warner spent three and one half times (nearly $3 million) what Miller spent. But it was actually an extremely hard-fought race, which Warner won by only a small margin. Two other extreme examples come from Wisconsin in 1976 and 1982, when Senator William Proxmire, sure of victory, spent $692 and $0, respectively, in his reelection campaigns. His little-known opponents spent about $62,000 and $120,000 in the two campaigns. A spending-ratio measure would place both Wisconsin races among the hardest of hard-fought when in fact they were actually among the lowest of low-key.

A COMPOSITE MEASURE OF INTENSITY

Because there can be problems with almost any single measure, I employ instead a composite approach to classifying campaigns' intensity. This method takes into account reports on each Senate contest appearing in the *Congressional Quarterly Weekly Report (CQ)* and utilizes campaign spending figures as a supplement. Each of the 304 Senate races in the period 1968–84 will be classified as hard-fought or low-key on the basis of its pre–Election Day description in the biennial special election issue of *CQ*, which appears during October of each election year. On the basis of these descriptions, it is possible to classify about 90 percent of Senate races from 1968 to 1984 as either hard-fought or low-key; in the remaining 10 percent the descriptions in *CQ* either were too brief or insufficiently addressed the question of campaign intensity, and in these cases only, categorization was made solely on the basis of the 2-to-1 candidate spending ratio discussed above.

The *CQ* pre-election rundowns are synopses from the reports of observers monitoring individual Senate campaigns. The reports usually focus on such aspects of a campaign as how much interaction there is between the candidates (through debates or by way of a dialogue through the press or paid ads); what issues, if any, are being debated; the level of apparent public interest in the race; how well organized a challenger is; and how efficiently and effectively the challenger is campaigning. The reports may take into account how much, or how little, news coverage the campaign is getting, how much money the candidates are spending, how well the challenger is doing in the polls, or how widely and frequently the challenger is campaigning around the state.

It should be noted that the 2-to-1 spending-ratio categorization method used as a supplement to the *CQ*-based classification scheme produces categorizations consistent with those of *CQ* in 81 percent of the elections in the period 1972 (the year when reporting expenditures to the Federal Election Commission became mandatory) to 1984. In 19 instances in which the two classification schemes conflicted, the *CQ* summary was given priority. Four of the discrepant cases are among the 12 campaigns whose newspaper coverage is closely analyzed in chapter 4, and close inspection of these campaigns' last 3 months of news coverage confirms that in each instance the *CQ* assessment is accurate. Had the spending-ratio rule been used instead, these races would have been misclassified.

23

In this study the intensity variable is dichotomized, although conceptually, campaign intensity varies along a continuum, and it would certainly be tempting to establish finer gradations. Unlike measures of campaign expenditures or margin of victory, however, summary descriptions such as those available from *CQ* are not readily quantified: an attempt to do so runs a significant risk of producing misclassifications. Moreover, the elements that most directly affect the intensity of a Senate campaign—candidate background, news coverage, paid advertising, and candidate standing in the polls—may build on each other, producing either substantial campaign intensity or none at all. A challenger with initial potential to win might spark the interest of journalists and potential contributors; resultant press coverage and contributions would help produce increases in essential name recognition, reflected in the kind of poll results that attract additional press coverage and contributions. A candidate perceived initially as having no chance to win may receive little attention or funding, which could preclude his mounting a viable challenge. Thus, the intensity of Senate races may be distributed bimodally instead of falling evenly along a continuum. Undoubtedly some campaigns are more "intense" than others within the hard-fought category, and some low-key races are more lifeless than others. The hard-fought/ low-key dichotomy nevertheless serves as a useful tool for investigating how differences in campaign intensity affect the vote decision process, as well as how both campaign-related factors and external factors (such as state party distribution) affect Senate election outcomes.

The classification of each of the Senate elections in the period 1968–84 as either hard-fought or low-key, using *CQ* pre-election campaign descriptions, is arrayed in appendix 1; spending ratio data (from 1972 onward) are used only as a fallback criterion when necessary.[7] As table 2 indicates, 57 percent of Senate races in the period 1968–84 were hard-fought, and 43 percent were low-key. Incumbents running for reelection faced light opposition just as often as they met fierce challenges: 48 percent of the races in which incumbents were running for reelection were hard-fought, and 52 percent were low-key. Eighty-one percent of open-seat races, however, were hard-fought. That only about half of Senate races are hard-fought may come as a surprise to many; as noted in chapter 1, it has often been assumed that Senate races, like presidential elections, almost automatically attract statewide interest and media attention. The fact that the numbers of campaigns that either do or do not attract such attention are approximately equal provides an excellent opportunity for comparisons. A likely key element of the differences between Senate candidates and campaigns is the background and expe-

TABLE 2

Number of Low-key and Hard-fought Senate Races, 1968–1984

Election Year	Type of Race	Races with Incumbent Running	Open-seat Races	Total
1968	Hard-fought	11	9	20
	Low-key	13	1	14
1970	Hard-fought	18	4	22
	Low-key	11	2	13
1972	Hard-fought	12	8	20
	Low-key	13	0	13
1974	Hard-fought	11	6	17
	Low-key	14	3	17
1976	Hard-fought	14	8	22
	Low-key	11	0	11
1978 *	Hard-fought	12	8	20
	Low-key	10	5	15
1980	Hard-fought	13	8	21
	Low-key	12	1	13
1982	Hard-fought	15	3	18
	Low-key	15	0	15
1984	Hard-fought	10	3	13
	Low-key	19	1	20
TOTAL Hard-fought		116 (48%)	57 (81%)	173 (57%)
TOTAL Low-key		118 (52%)	13 (19%)	131 (43%)

* In 1978, in addition to the 33 Class 2 elections there were special elections in Alabama and Minnesota.

rience of Senate challengers, specifically the extent to which the intensity of Senate campaigns relates to the initial prominence of the challenger or of both candidates in an open-seat race.

The Political Experience of Senate Challengers

A Senate challenger's chances of mounting a strong, attention-catching campaign are necessarily affected by how well known he or she is both to the statewide electorate and to political elites such as office-holders, party officials, political fundraisers, and the like. Challengers may already be familiar to voters through having held prominent political office (or being famous for some other reason), or they may be totally unknown in the state. Mezey (1970, 565) suggested that candidates with previous political experience are likely to be "successful over novices presumably because of their organizational contacts and because their previous offices have made them more visible." Ties with political elites within a state and a proven track record should make it much easier to amass the funding necessary to mount a statewide campaign. These assets, as well as an established identity with the state's electorate, may also affect the media's initial perceptions of what sort of campaign is likely to emerge. Referring to the way reporters decide how to cover the earliest stages of presidential primaries, ABC News correspondent Brit Hume ("Campaigning on Cue" 1986) asserted that "coverage tends to go to the candidates who have done the things in the preliminary phases—that is, they have built the organizations, they've raised the money, they've lined up the endorsements—all of the things which give political reporters or those who organize political coverage some reason to believe they have a credible campaign and candidacy."

Like many presidential candidates in the early stages of a campaign, some Senate challengers are almost unknown to most voters in their state, and journalists have to make choices about which of them are worth covering. The mere fact of being a challenger does not automatically confer either recognition or newsworthiness, but some candidates appear to have a head start in both areas, especially if they have previous political experience.

Studies of the political background of congressional candidates have usually focused on the previous experience of incumbents. Matthews (1960, 51–52), looking at the occupations of the 180 senators who held office in the period 1947–57, found that only 9 percent of them had not held political office prior to coming to the Senate, that half had served either as a governor or a representative, and that the average senator "had held about three public offices and had devoted about ten years or approximately half his adult life to officeholding before arriving at the upper chamber."[8] These findings certainly suggest that it takes considerable political experience to win a Senate seat, but these data include only incumbents, who are, after all, *winning* challengers. One must look at *all* challengers to see if previous political background appears to influence the caliber of campaign they are able to achieve.

To do this, I ascertained the highest level of previous political experience of all challengers (and candidates for open seats) from 1968 to 1984. In determining the various levels of experience, consideration was given to two factors: visibility to the statewide electorate and degree of electoral experience. Having held statewide office of any kind was rated higher than any local experience, and within these two levels, having been elected to office was considered higher than having been appointed to office (see table 3).

Apart from incumbents, 366 major-party candidates ran for the Senate in the period 1968–84. The political experience of these challengers

TABLE 3
Highest Level of Past Political Experience of Senate Challengers, 1968–1984

Challenger's Level of Experience	Percentage Running against Incumbents (N=225)	Percentage Running in Open-seat Races (N=141)	Percentage of All Challengers (N=366)
Ex-senator	1	2	1
Governor	6	11	8
Other statewide elective office	10	14	12
Statewide or national nonelective office	2	1	1
Subtotal	19	28	22
U.S. Congressman from state with:			
1–5 districts	7	11	9
6+ districts	13	17	15
Subtotal	20	28	24
State senator	12	9	11
State representative	9	4	7
Mayor	4	7	5
County office	3	4	4
City office	2	2	2
Subtotal	31	26	29
Nonelected party office	3	1	2
Other nonelected political office	4	2	4
Subtotal	7	3	6
No political experience			
Attorney	2	2	2
Other	20	12	17
Subtotal	22	14	19
TOTAL	99%	99%	100%

varied considerably over this period.[9] Experience ranged from little or no previous experience to long stints in the House or as governor. About 20 percent of challengers had been elected (or appointed) to statewide or, in a few cases, federal office. This category includes statewide offices such as governor, lieutenant governor, attorney general, and various state secretary and commissioner posts, as well as cabinet-level or other prominent positions in the federal government. Twenty-five percent of challengers either were currently serving in the House or had been elected to Congress at some time in the past (five had even served previously in the

Senate). Another 18 percent had served in state legislatures, and 11 percent had experience only at the county or city level.

Twenty-five percent of the group had never been elected to any political office; a handful of these, however, had served as party officials at the county or state level. For example, Josiah Spaulding, who challenged Edward Kennedy in 1970, had been chairman of the Massachusetts Republican Committee and was a member of the Republican National Committee. A few others, including Democrat Dick Clark of Iowa, had served as aides to elected officials. These challengers were not unfamiliar with political organization and elections but were essentially invisible to the electorate at the start of their own campaigns.

That leaves 19 percent of Senate challengers from 1968 to 1984 who had held no formal position in politics, either in elective office or in any other official political capacity. Some of this group had run unsuccessfully for office but had gained experience, and perhaps some name recognition, in the process. A few, such as astronauts John Glenn, Harrison Schmitt, and Jack Lousma and basketball star Bill Bradley, had earned recognition in other careers. But most of this group came into their Senate campaigns without previous political experience or ties to political organizations within their states and virtually unknown to their states' voters.

Candidates for open seats had a greater degree of political experience than did candidates challenging incumbents. Fifty-six percent of candidates running for open seats, compared with 39 percent of challengers to incumbents, either had held federal or statewide office or had served in Congress. Jacobson and Kernell (1981) argued that given the advantages of incumbency, running for an open seat is a more justifiable risk than taking on an incumbent. Candidates of any level of political experience would presumably prefer to try for an open seat, but a state's more experienced politicians, with their greater recognition and ties to party and fund sources, often have first chance at the nomination. These data suggest that more experienced candidates are indeed willing to wait for the open seat. Since all congressmen and many statewide officeholders must forfeit their current office to run for Senate, and since losing the election may well mean the end of a career in elective office, an individual who already holds fairly high office will think twice before giving it up to run for an incumbent's Senate seat.

The propensity of "high-level" candidates to wait for the open seat meant that more than 60 percent of challengers to incumbents in the period 1968–84 began their Senate campaigns with electoral experience "below" the statewide or congressional level. About half of this group had served in state, county, or city government, and about half had held no previous political office.

Does challengers' previous political experience affect their chances of *winning* a Senate race? Overall, 20 percent of challengers defeated incumbents in the period 1968–84 (table 4). The proportion of winners in open seats was, of course, 50 percent. By and large, candidates' level of political experience had little relation to whether they actually won the election. Against incumbents, former senators and governors did little better than state legislators and barely outdistanced the least experienced candidates. The success of statewide officeholders resembled that of city and county officials. The most successful at defeating incumbents were candidates who had close ties to a party organization but who had held no elective office. Presumably this group was not nearly as well known to the statewide electorate as governors and ex-senators, yet their victory rate of 38 percent was 25 points higher. The pattern was no clearer in the open-seat races. Here the two groups with least political experience fared less well than the rest, but the differences among the other levels were small and unpatterned. The governor/ex-senator and statewide office groups differed little from those who had served at the city or county level. Perhaps the relatively small number of cases in each category partly explains these findings. A better explanation may be that past political background is less significant to whether a candidate *wins* a Senate race than other factors, most of which come into play after the start of the campaign.

What political background *is* likely to affect is the preliminary evaluations—by candidates themselves, by potential contributors and supporters, and by the media—of whether a viable challenge can be put together, that is, whether the kind of resources can be found that are needed to run a respectable race and get through to the voters (the things candidates need to do if they are ultimately to win). The candidate's ability to put these factors together can make the difference between a hard-fought campaign—in which a great deal of information will be disbursed and in which the opponent is forced to take the candidate seriously—and a low-key, nearly invisible, and therefore ineffective campaign.

In hard-fought races in the period 1968–84, the higher the previous office held by the challenger, the more likely it was that the challenger waged an intensive, competitive campaign (table 4). Candidates with statewide elective experience, congressmen, and mayors of larger cities almost always waged hard-fought campaigns.[10] Over 90 percent of governors and ex-senators, presumably carrying the highest name recogni-

TABLE 4
Percentage of Senate Challengers Who Won, and Who Had Hard-Fought Races, by Highest Level of Past Political Achievement, 1968–1984

Highest Level of Past Political Achievement	Races Won by Challenger						Hard-Fought Challenger Races*			
	Against Incumbent		Open-seat		Total		Against Incumbent		Total	
	%	(N)	%	(N)	%	(N)	%	(N)	%	(N)
Governor, ex-senator	13	(16)	61	(18)	41	(34)	81	(16)	91	(34)
Other statewide or high-level federal office	22	(27)	60	(20)	38	(48)	74	(27)	85	(48)
U.S. congressman from state with:										
1–5 districts	31	(16)	56	(16)	47	(32)	88	(16)	94	(32)
6+ districts	33	(30)	50	(24)	43	(54)	70	(30)	81	(54)
"Big-city" mayor§	17	(6)	57	(7)	31	(13)	83	(6)	85	(13)
State senate	11	(28)	42	(12)	20	(40)	32	(28)	50	(40)
State assembly	5	(21)	50	(6)	15	(27)	24	(21)	33	(27)
County office, small-city mayor, city council	25	(16)	58	(12)	36	(28)	38	(16)	54	(28)
Party office or other nonelected political office	38	(16)	0	(5)	29	(21)	50	(16)	57	(21)
No political office or party position	10	(49)	35	(20)	17	(69)	33	(49)	46	(69)
TOTAL	20	(225)	50	(141)†	31	(366)	52	(225)	63	(366)

* Since nearly all open-seat races during this period were hard-fought, figures for these contests are not presented here.
§ Defined as mayor of any city with population over 500,000, or a state's largest city.
† Two open-seat races had three candidates; in one open-seat race the winner was unopposed.

tion and experience of any challengers at the beginning of a campaign, managed hard-fought races. House members from states small enough that many of the voters were already among their constituents, and where the rest might have heard of them in the news, were more successful than large-state representatives, who are usually little known to the large numbers of people outside their district.[11] But even the latter managed hard-fought campaigns four times out of every five. Challengers with high levels of political experience, then, were very successful in producing hard-fought campaigns.

When challengers' experience was limited to smaller and more local jurisdictions, the proportion of hard-fought campaigns diminished sharply. The exception was large-city mayors, 85 percent of whom ran hard-fought campaigns. Presumably their reputations, by virtue of their newsworthiness as leaders of major cities, had permeated far beyond city limits. State legislators were far less able to manage hard-fought campaigns and were in fact more likely to have low-key Senate races than they were to have hard-fought ones. Against incumbents, two-thirds of state senators and three-fourths of state assemblymen managed only low-key campaigns. Even challengers with at most a county-level political background had a greater proportion of hard-fought campaigns. With the possible exception of those holding leadership positions, state legislators are generally invisible to most of the state's electorate and may be even less visible than other local officials from the standpoint of media coverage. Because hometown papers are likely to cover city (and sometimes county) political events, local and county officials are known to voters in at least one part of the state: their home turf. Spending most of their time at the state capitol, state legislators may not receive even local press exposure.[12]

Half of Senate candidates with no prior experience in elective office but with a background linked to a party organization managed hard-fought races against an incumbent. Only one-third of those without any political experience ran hard-fought campaigns. Indeed, that the last group could reach even 33 percent against incumbents or could be involved overall in hard-fought races 46 percent of the time may seem surprising. Among the "successful" here, however, were many candidates who, while they had no previous political experience, were nevertheless well known in their states. These include astronauts John Glenn, Harrison Schmitt, and Jack Lousma, basketball star Bill Bradley, Florida drugstore magnate Jack Eckerd, famous relatives James Buckley and Nancy Landon Kassebaum, and semanticist and university president S. I. Hayakawa.

Two others, Leo Thorsness and Jeremiah Denton, had received considerable public notice as Vietnam prisoners of war.

These findings suggest that political experience is an important factor not necessarily in winning a Senate race but in being able to wage a strong campaign. Having held statewide or congressional office seems to provide a Senate candidate with either the advance recognition or the organizational ties or status looked for by potential contributors, or some combination of the three, to allow him to put together the ingredients of a hard-fought campaign. This seems especially to be the case in races against incumbents. Candidates with past experience at the statewide or congressional level are likely three times out of four to wage hard-fought campaigns, the kind that depend vitally on the candidate's becoming known to the statewide electorate. By the same token, roughly two-thirds of candidates with lower levels of political experience cannot manage this kind of campaign.

That candidates' previous political experience makes them more likely to mount hard-fought, vigorous campaigns suggests that previous political experience may have its most significant impact as a determinant of how seriously the press initially take a candidate's attempt to put together a serious campaign and indeed of whether the candidate is able to raise enough money to do so. Reporters and their editors may judge the viability of a candidacy on the basis of early polls as well as their impressions of whether the candidate has a chance to win. But early polls are often little more than a measure of name recognition; impressions, which may be based on knowledge of candidates' past performance, may serve as a yardstick of future success, there being little else available on which to judge. Personal characteristics such as drive and determination, intelligence, and ideas are other bases for judging whether someone will be a strong candidate, but editors and reporters have neither the time nor the prolonged access to candidates to assess such factors. Contributors undoubtedly also look at a candidate's standing in the polls, but past political performance could serve to alleviate doubts the potential supporters may have about the candidate's ability to campaign effectively and about the positions he or she is likely to take on issues once in office. Therefore, initial standing in polls, largely determined by recognition and reputation, would be quite an important determinant of whether a race will turn out to be hard-fought or low-key.

As for whether the candidate will win, other factors—party identification distribution in the state, strengths and weaknesses of the incumbent, issues debated during the campaign, popularity of the president, the recent state of the economy—all may come into play. In the course of the campaign, the challenger's name, his views, and some sense of his personal qualities may or may not reach the voters. Until voters are able to identify a challenger as one of two alternatives, they cannot weigh his various characteristics. We are primarily interested, therefore, in studying how candidates gain recognition and how recognition translates into votes. The work of Jacobson (1978, 1980) has clearly identified the importance of campaign expenditures to candidate recognition and is unequivocal in its findings, especially for House elections: "campaign spending helps candidates, most particularly nonincumbents, by bringing them to the attention of voters . . . money buys attention" (1978, 488–89). But Jacobson does not directly address the question of whether the impact of spending comes straight from paid advertisements or through less direct routes.

There is a temptation to assume from findings of this sort that the key to candidate recognition is the amount of money spent—presumably on advertising—in a given campaign. But as I have already noted, expenditure totals themselves do not always reflect the general level of campaign intensity. Goldenberg and Traugott (1984, 59) observed that "money is the grease for the wheels of a successful congressional campaign," but they also noted that "the translation of money into recognition is, of course, indirect. . . . Money buys organized campaign events at which potential voters can meet the candidate in person, and it buys a variety of contact through the media. Some of it takes the form of campaign-produced materials and advertising on TV and radio. Straight news coverage is important as well, and sometimes it can be generated by staging newsworthy events. The norms and practices of news organizations are crucial to candidates' efforts to attain wide visibility and recognition, and close analysis of several Senate campaigns will reveal considerable differences in the ways these campaigns are covered.

3. Political Campaign Coverage and the Public's Sources of News

The amount of information voters have about candidates and the campaign is a central factor in their vote decision process. Therefore, a close look at how the news media cover Senate campaigns should help us to understand how voters decide and why outcomes in Senate elections vary so widely, not only from state to state but within the same state from election to election. Several studies have addressed the increases in candidate use of paid advertising (largely via television) in congressional elections, as well as the significant effects of such advertising on congressional election outcomes (Dawson and Zinser 1971, 1976; Wanat 1974; Jacobson 1975, 1980). Very little research, however, has addressed the effects of news coverage on congressional elections, even though campaign observers have maintained that "free media"—news coverage—has more impact on the vote than does paid advertising.[1] More investigation is needed of free media coverage of congressional campaigns, the differences between newspaper and local television coverage of statewide races, and the extent to which voters turn to each medium for their information about political races.

The evidence suggests that newspapers provide a more complete picture of Senate campaigns and are a better reflection than television news of the actual intensity of a given campaign. There is also evidence that the public obtains as much, if not more, information about Senate campaigns from newspapers as from television news. Accordingly, I will look closely, later in this chapter and in chapter 4, at newspaper coverage of a number of Senate campaigns.

Broadcast versus Print Coverage of Political Campaigns

One might initially assume that television news is the predominant medium in Senate elections in terms of both amount of campaign coverage and voters' attention. This certainly appears to be the case in presidential election contests. Longtime observer of presidential races Theodore White observed in 1986 that "television in modern politics has been as revolutionary as the development of printing in the time of Gutenberg" (in McDowell 1986, 242). Many scholarly studies have confirmed the dominant role of television during presidential election campaigns.[2]

Some have held that television news coverage is also dominant in sub-presidential elections. For example, the manager of Edmund G. Brown, Jr.'s 1974 California gubernatorial campaign was unequivocal on the subject of news coverage in state-level races, defining news as "that which television covers" (in Leary 1977, 20). Political scientist Michael Robinson (1975) argued that one of the many differences between House and Senate campaigns is that while House candidates are "locked out" of local television news coverage, these organizations "regard Senators as important enough to elicit viewer interest" (249). "News coverage," continued Robinson, "will publicize the Senate candidate and, in effect, underwrite the campaign. . . . At the local and state level, the Senate candidate crosses the line between that which makes good copy and that which does not . . . the Senate candidate meets the needs of local TV" (249). Robinson concluded that "Senate candidates get a considerable amount of free news time on TV. In essence, television is frustration for the House candidate but inspiration for the Senate candidate" (251).

These views notwithstanding, there is reason to believe that television coverage of statewide campaigns typically underrepresents the actual intensity of the race, and that in fact newspaper coverage is not only more extensive than television in a given statewide race but indeed a better reflection of the intensity of that campaign.

News coverage of presidential elections is essentially automatic; news judgments are made about how, not whether, to accord coverage, and during the fall information about the presidential candidates virtually fills the airwaves and the headlines of the national news media. During the final months of a presidential campaign, between one-fourth and one-half of the average network evening news program is typically devoted to that campaign, and newspaper coverage by the major dailies is similarly extensive.[3] Because news organizations see continuous coverage of presidential campaigns as mandatory, candidates can often dictate the news. Journalists are placed in the position of needing the candidates "more than vice versa" (Joslyn 1984, 80) and may find themselves "in a daily struggle to find a morsel, an unplanned quote, or a revealing statement" (Swerdlow 1981, 17) about the campaign.[4]

News coverage of subpresidential races, on the other hand, is governed by the priorities and constraints of local news organizations and is weighed against other potential stories for that day's broadcast or edition. National television networks and news magazines devote relatively little time or space to campaigns at the subpresidential level for the obvious reasons that individual state or local races are too numerous and are generally not of sufficient national importance to warrant sustained coverage nationwide.[5] It thus falls to daily newspapers, local television news, and other local media to decide whether individual state-level contests are important enough, or potentially interesting enough, to their particular audiences to warrant the allocation of reporting resources to the coverage of those races. Just being a candidate for election to the Senate or House does not by itself guarantee continuous campaign coverage: as Joslyn (1984, 76) put it, "It is up to candidates to say or do something to attract media coverage." Differing capabilities and goals of television news stations and newspapers produce different decisions about political campaign coverage and, consequently, different amounts of coverage.

News Priorities and Constraints

Newspaper and local television news priorities differ in degree, not in kind. Studies comparing the decisions of television and newspaper editors have found that media personnel select "the same kinds of stories" and emphasize "the same types of facts, despite the wealth of diverse materials available to them" (Clyde and Buckalew 1969), with the exception that "television lags behind print media in the range and depth of issue coverage" (Graber 1980, 178).[6] Indeed, television news editors often refer to that day's newspapers as they determine which stories to use on the air.[7]

If the priorities of metropolitan newspapers and local television news are similar, it is undoubtedly in part because both focus primarily on their own communities. With few exceptions, there are no "statewide

36

media."[8] About 75 percent of a newspaper's available news space is devoted to local news; even large metropolitan newspapers cover primarily local news.[9] Local television news, too, "is firmly grounded in local community happenings and closely parallels local newspaper reporting in its content and focus" (Rubin 1981, 151). In her study of television news, Leary (1977, 36) observed that "local news programs are tethered to the local market. This begets an enormous emphasis on immediacy and localization of news that is closely related to the station's aim of drawing advertising viewers within their signals' reach. Furthermore, there is very little statewide exchange of news between network-linked stations. No television reporter or news editor or station manager suggested that events outside his own market area would justify the cost."

In fact, local television may well be even more local in focus than newspapers. In his study of the press and state government, Wolfson (1985, 137–44) found that most daily newspapers give considerable coverage to the governor and state legislature, while "the only commercial [television] stations to cover legislative news may be the ones located in the capital city." Ed Salzman, longtime observer of California politics, stated that "California's radio and television stations are doing a miserable job of covering state government and politics. . . . With perhaps two or three exceptions, coverage ranges from grossly inadequate to nonexistent" (1977, 123). Newspaper coverage of state politics, he continued, has diminished since the 1950s among most major dailies, largely due to the expense involved in such reporting. "But even the worst of the state's major newspapers," he stated, "does a much better job of informing the public about the political scene than the best radio or television station" (125).[10]

That newspapers are a better source of statewide political news is due in large measure to differences in the ways the two major constraints on news operations—time/space and money—affect the two types of news organizations. For both types of local news media, coverage of events in other parts of the state is discretionary. However, the time constraints of a local television news broadcast are more severe than are a newspaper's space constraints. Ranney (1984, 20) made an observation about national network news that applies to local television news as well when he pointed out that "where newspapers have pages of information, television has only paragraphs. . . . Back at the studio the producers and editors have to decide every day what 1 or 2 percent of the . . . film and videotape their crews have shot they will actually use on that night's newscast. . . . they almost never have an equivalent of the extra news space newspaper editors can commandeer." Indeed, newspapers typically contain many more news stories than do television newscasts. In one week in 1967, reports Robert MacNeil, "the three networks' programs each averaged a few hundred words more than the front pages [alone] of the *New York Times* and the *Washington Post*"; he concluded that "what the television viewer is getting essentially is a headline service" (1968, 40).[11]

In economic terms, it does not make sense, according to Epstein (1973), "for a network to maintain anything more than the minimum camera crews necessary to fill the available news-programming time," because in the view of television executives, the increased costs required to do so do not produce an increase in the viewing audience. Thus, because of the expense of maintaining camera crews and transmitting reports electronically from distant locations, local TV news organizations typically do not send reporters to cover stories occurring away from the local area, particularly when there is deadline pressure. One state capitol reporter's difficulty in covering Richmond, Virginia, for a television station in the nearby Washington, D.C., area was described by Wolfson (1985, 146): "Union camera crews work eight hour days. The trip down and back eats up about six hours, so that only gives you two hours in which to set up, arrange an interview, or sit in on a session." Television has a natural concern with ratings, so that in the limited newsspace it has available, a conscious effort must be made to include a variety of items. Producers of television news "must seek a level of generality in selecting and presenting news far beyond that of newspapers," according to Epstein (1973, 40), and indeed a television news director in San Diego, California, commented with respect to the various California statewide campaigns in 1974: "I haven't seen any candidates for office do or say anything worth putting on the air—not when I have big stories on cab drivers being arrested for transporting illegal aliens, drug busts on local Navy bases, large buildings being burned down in major blazes and many other stories like that, all interesting to people here locally" (in Leary 1977, 47).[12]

Because the various constraints under which news organizations operate affect the print and the broadcast media differently, the inclinations and abilities of these two kinds of organizations to cover statewide elections differ correspondingly, with newspapers far more amenable than local television to covering non-local political campaigns. Neither incumbents nor challengers are likely to be covered at all by a local television news organization unless they make an appearance in the immediate area, since local television's few political reporters are more likely to be assigned either to City Hall or perhaps to the state capital than to a

Senate campaign. On the other hand, newspapers' coverage is not determined by the need for fresh film footage, so they can more readily decide to report on events in remote parts of their state. Press releases, which are of little use to television news without accompanying visuals, can be reproduced by newspapers in full or part, and quite often are.[13] Reporters can be assigned to travel with the candidates, or wire service copy can be utilized. Information can be obtained by telephone without the worry of obtaining film, and print media can more easily make use of "background" reports, which rely less on events and action and more on analysis and review of previously reported facts.

Television and Newspaper Campaign Coverage at the Subpresidential Level: A Comparison

Newspapers' greater flexibility in terms of both space and journalistic resources produced much more newspaper than television news coverage in two statewide campaigns that have been studied in some detail. In their analysis of the 1984 Senate race in Michigan, Goldenberg and Traugott (1985, 11) examined local news coverage in two television markets, and concluded that "relatively little campaign coverage appeared on the local television news. Most of the news about the Senate race came to potential voters through daily newspapers."

Leary's (1977) examination of the 1974 California gubernatorial race also found television news coverage to be considerably less extensive than newspaper coverage. Comparing news coverage of six television and five radio stations with that of four large daily newspapers, Leary found that television provided "only perfunctory coverage" (1) and "generally neglected to give viewers more than superficial glances at the campaign" (3). Noting "a dramatic difference between press and broadcast agencies in the commitment to conveying campaign information," Leary observed that "the largest newspapers in California made significant financial commitments to campaign coverage in an attempt to provide readers with adequate data about the candidates on which to form their decision. Broadcast abandoned political specialists, provided no observable extra time for politics, did no advance planning for coverage of the campaign, and undertook (with . . . two exceptions) little or no travel an no extra expense for coverage. There was a fundamental acceptance among newspapers," Leary concluded, "that politics is important news, and that this election . . . was assumed to be of exceptional interest" (173). By contrast, television news organizations were largely uninterested in statewide politics in general: "Television executives voiced many justifications for their reluctance to cover politics: The personalities were 'dull.' Talk did not suit television. News staffs were too short-handed. Camera crews were too expensive to send with the candidates. There was more photogenic news at hand. The constant complaint of assignment editors was: 'The candidates aren't *doing* anything!' The candidates were talking— and television abhorred talk" (48, emphasis Leary's).

One other pair of studies presents an opportunity to investigate whether newspapers provide more complete coverage of statewide races than do local television news organizations. More than this, the studies provide an opportunity to test which of the two media is a more accurate gauge of the intensity of a campaign. David Ostroff (Ostroff 1980; Ostroff and Sandell 1984) monitored local television news coverage of two statewide Ohio campaigns, the 1978 gubernatorial election and the 1982 Senate election. I compared newspaper coverage of these two races with Ostroff's data.

For both contests, Ostroff monitored television news campaign coverage in Columbus for the five weeks prior to Election Day. I reviewed the *Columbus Dispatch,* the city's largest newspaper, for the same five-week period. In the gubernatorial race in 1978, incumbent Republican James Rhodes faced a stiff challenge from Democratic Lieutenant Governor Richard Celeste. Both candidates waged vigorous campaigns, spending more than $3 million between them in a contest that by October was considered by most polls to be too close to call. One might expect there to have been substantial media attention to such an intensely fought contest during the final month of the campaign, but there was in fact very little television news coverage of this race. The greatest number of television news items about the campaign during the five-week period was 18 (amounting to a total of 8 minutes' coverage) on WCMH. Stations WBNS and WTVN carried 11 and 9 stories, respectively (10 minutes, 15 seconds, on WBNS and 5 minutes, 10 seconds, on WTVN). Through 50 hours (per station) of local television news broadcasts, then, coverage of the state's gubernatorial campaign averaged approximately two and one-half stories per week across the three stations, with each item averaging about 40 seconds in length.

Examination of the *Columbus Dispatch* for the same five-week period revealed quite a different picture.[14] During the five weeks from October 2 to November 7, the *Dispatch* carried 122 news stories relating to the campaign, including 9 editorials and 20 news stories primarily concerned with other campaigns in which the gubernatorial race was mentioned.

For the first half of October, most of these stories were taken from the Associated Press wire service and appeared on inside pages of the paper. By mid-month the paper had assigned its own reporters to follow the campaign, and from October 24 to Election Day, November 7, at least two of their stories were published daily on the front page. In addition, 17 letters to the editor about the race appeared, as well as 18 reports about the results of a straw poll entitled the "Voting Machine Poll." In all, then, the *Columbus Dispatch* published 157 items about the gubernatorial campaign, most of which focused on the views of the two leading candidates and on their attacks on each other. Wherever the two candidates appeared throughout the state, their activities were covered, with Governor Rhodes mentioned in 137 stories, and Lieutenant Governor Celeste in 139. In contrast, Rhodes was mentioned in at most 18 television news items on any one station and was the major focus in at most 10 stories; Celeste was the major focus in at most 8. Moreover, as Ostroff noted, a significant proportion of the total minutes of television coverage by two of the three stations came at the very end of the campaign in the form of one major story on the gubernatorial race. While it is possible that the pressures of competing news events might have caused television news organizations to wait until just before the election to cover their state's gubernatorial race, the data from Ohio provide dramatic, if specific, evidence that a state-level campaign is likely to be more extensively covered in newspapers than by local television news.[15]

The 1982 Senate race in Ohio offers sharp contrast to the 1978 gubernatorial contest. Following the death of Congressman John Ashbrook shortly before the Republican Senate primary, Republicans had selected little-known state senator Paul Pfeifer to face incumbent Democrat Howard Metzenbaum. Pfeifer "was one of the few Republican Senate candidates who could not persuade the national Republican party to give him the maximum legal funding" (Barone and Ujifusa 1983, 908). The Metzenbaum-Pfeifer campaign was a low-key race. The greatest number of news stories about the Senate race by any of Columbus's three local television news organizations was six (totaling 7 minutes, 25 seconds). The other two stations devoted no more than three stories (totaling no more than 3 minutes, 25 seconds) on either the early or the late evening news. Thus, television's news coverage of the 1982 Senate race was even lighter than its coverage of the gubernatorial race in 1978. Differences in the television coverage of the two races were, in absolute terms, rather small, since television coverage of both was so minimal.

The difference in the extent of the *Columbus Dispatch*'s newspaper coverage of these two races was, by contrast, striking. Between October 1 and Election Day, the *Dispatch* devoted 54 stories to the 1982 Senate campaign, including three editorials. It had devoted 68 *more* stories to the gubernatorial race in 1978. The *Dispatch*'s coverage of the 1982 Senate race was, in addition, far briefer than its 1978 coverage had been. Senator Metzenbaum's or challenger Pfeifer's name was mentioned in about five paragraphs per story in 1982, while in 1978 either Governor Rhodes or challenger Celeste was mentioned in an average of approximately 14 paragraphs per campaign story.

Several points emerge from these comparisons of newspaper and television coverage of the two campaigns. First, newspaper accounts of both campaigns were far more comprehensive than television news stories. Second, the difference in intensity of the two campaigns is reflected much more clearly in the relative quantities of *newspaper* coverage each engendered than in the amount of *television* reporting devoted to each. In the *Columbus Dispatch,* the hard-fought 1978 gubernatorial race received substantial coverage, and the low-key 1982 Senate race received very little. On the other hand, television coverage of *both* races was minimal. If the overall news coverage of this particular pair of races is at all typical, it makes sense to assume that it is newspaper coverage of statewide, including Senate, races that more realistically reflects the actual intensity of campaigns.

But how attentive to newspapers are voters when it comes to following Senate campaigns? Some political observers, and some candidates, see television news as the predominant source of voters' information about political campaigns. Austin Ranney (1984) argued that "most Americans consume more political news from television than from newspapers" and that "television newscasts and public affairs programs unquestionably constitute the major source of political reality for most Americans" (16). While this claim was made primarily with reference to presidential elections, Ranney suggested that it applies to statewide races as well.[16] One California professional campaign manager told Leary that "there are three key factors in a political campaign these days . . . No. 1 is television, No. 2 is television, and No. 3 is television. In all our survey work we ask people why they voted the way they did, and it always comes up television. This applies to paid and to free. All free media comes ahead of paid. Free is the news coverage you get. . . . The highest form—well, that's TV" (in Leary 1977, 20). The same claim was made with particular respect to Senate campaigns by Michael Robinson (1975, 249): "Local television meets the [Senate] candidate's needs, the Senate candidate meets the needs of local TV."[17]

Sources of News for the General Public

A great deal of public opinion research has focused on whether people obtain more information from newspapers or from television. John Robinson (1978, 2) argued that the best way to make this determination is to ask people about "their exposure to the various news media on the previous day." Analyzing a University of Michigan Survey Research Center study done in fall 1975 and spring 1976, Robinson found that on a typical day a person is more likely to read a newspaper than to watch a television news program. In 1975 the margin was 14 percentage points; in 1976 it was 19 points. A similar item in Gallup surveys in 1970, 1973, and 1977 asked respondents whether they had read a paper or looked at television news "yesterday." In each case, more people named newspapers than television (in Sterling 1984, 156, 160).

More widely cited, however, is a series of surveys by the Roper organization (Roper 1983) that lead to the opposite conclusion. Since the 1960s the Roper organization has asked a national sample, "Where do you usually get most of your news about what's going on in the world today?" Since 1964, television news has outranked all other media sources, and the gap between TV news and newspapers has gradually widened over the years. In 1980 nearly two-thirds of those polled claimed that television was the source of most of their news, while fewer than half cited newspapers. However, the Roper survey's question wording presented several problems: (1) it refers to news in general, not just political news; (2) it does not distinguish between national and subnational news; and (3) because multiple responses are allowed, it is not possible to determine which medium is the single most relied upon.[18] A number of other studies have distinguished between national and local news and have forced a choice between the two media. Most have reached a common conclusion: that people are more likely to name television news as their primary source of national or international news but newspapers as their principal source of local news.[19] This still leaves open the question of which medium people are most likely to turn to for news about state-level, and particularly Senate, elections.

Beginning in 1971, Roper followed his standard question, quoted above, with a two-part question focusing specifically on information about election campaigns. The first part asked about sources of information about local election campaigns, and the second asked: "What about the candidates running in statewide elections—like U.S. Senator and Governor?" Roper (1983) consistently found that while newspapers are mentioned by a higher proportion of respondents than is television regarding local campaigns, television was chosen over newspapers as the primary source of information about statewide campaigns by a factor of about 5 to 3 (again, multiple responses were allowed). On the other hand, when Clarke and Ruggles (1970, 468) asked Seattle respondents which news medium provided the best coverage of public affairs at different levels of news focus, newspapers were chosen over both television and radio for all levels, and the gap was considerably wider at the state, county, and city levels than at the national and international levels.[20]

What people cite as their major source of information, however, is not necessarily the source from which they actually do obtain most of their information. At comparable levels of education, newspaper readers have been shown to become better informed than television news watchers during the course of a campaign. Thomas Patterson and Robert McClure conducted a panel study during the 1972 presidential campaign and found that people whose predominant means of following the campaign was newspapers learned about the candidates' issue positions as the campaign progressed, but those whose predominant means was television news did not (McClure and Patterson 1974; Patterson and McClure 1976).[21] Patterson (1980) found the same thing in the 1976 election: regular use of newspapers, but not network news, contributed to the accuracy of citizens' perceptions of the candidates' issue positions. These studies controlled for respondents' education, acknowledging that television news audiences tend to be less educated than newspaper readers, but this did not change the findings. As Rebecca Quarles put it, "The fault lies not with the audience, but rather in some aspect of the stimulus." Noting that television has been shown to impart information in presidential debates and special in-depth broadcasts,[22] Quarles (1979, 432) suggested that it is not the medium of television per se but the format and content of news programs in particular that may account for the low level of political knowledge they convey.

Comparing newspaper and local television news coverage of 1974 Senate races in 67 U.S. media markets and using post-election data from the 1974 CPS National Election Study, Clarke and Fredin (1978) found— controlling for education, interest in public affairs, and frequency of exposure to media—that "messages in newspapers confer information beyond what can be expected from general exposure levels. . . . If reasoning about political choice depends at all on the features of an area's media system, those characteristics will be found in the newspapers that circulate there, not in television coverage" (150–51). They concluded that newspapers surpassed television news as "agents of information to help people identify assets and liabilities of important political contenders" (156).

44

There is considerable evidence, then, that newspapers are perceived as a major source of local news and that in fact people learn more about subpresidential campaigns from newspapers than they do from television news. Against this body of evidence is Roper's consistent finding that more people *say* television news is their main source of information about statewide campaigns. There is reason to believe from the findings presented above, however, as well as from what is known about newspaper and television news norms and constraints, that newspapers carry more information about state-level campaigns than television news does and present an amount of information that more closely approximates what campaigns are issuing.

An Analysis of News Coverage in Selected Hard-fought and Low-key Senate Races

People are unlikely to vote for a candidate with whom they are not familiar.[23] The crucial task, therefore, for any candidate for the Senate— or any office—is to become known to voters. One means candidates employ in this effort is to direct their campaign messages at voters through press coverage of political races.

Challengers with established political credentials are more likely to wage hard-fought campaigns. It can be hypothesized, therefore, that news organizations look at the stature, experience, and reputation among political elites of a challenger and combine this impression with information about the candidate's current standing in the polls to assess the general newsworthiness of a given Senate race. But challengers are only one factor influencing press assessments of political races; other factors include the actions and decisions taken by both incumbents and challengers during the campaign, as well as the press's reactions to them.

What kind of newspaper coverage do Senate campaigns receive? Hershey (1984, 166) claimed that senators "receive a lot of media attention, [and] so do their challengers." Salmore and Salmore (1985, 62) reported that the 1982 Wyoming Senate race received "extensive front-page placement in the three newspapers in Casper and Cheyenne" but later asserted that the press have a general "lack of interest" in Senate races (162). There is in fact very little systematic data on this question. One study that addressed this question directly found that "the amount of coverage of the two candidates in a hard-fought race in Michigan was almost identical, with the challenger enjoying a slight edge [over the incumbent]." Monitoring newspaper coverage of the 1984 race between Democratic incumbent Carl Levin and Republican challenger Jack Lousma, Goldenberg and Traugott (1985) examined 29 daily Michigan newspapers for the 150 days between June 15 and Election Day. Over this period the average number of stories per paper about the Senate race ranged from approximately one-half to two-thirds of a story per day between Labor Day and the election. Coverage by four Texas dailies of the 1984 open-seat race between Republican Phil Gramm and Democrat Lloyd Doggett was examined by Hale (1985), who found that between September 1 and Election Day the average number of stories per paper was nearly one per day.

In order to be able to generalize beyond these races, and to explore further the press coverage of different kinds of Senate races, I examined newspaper coverage of a dozen Senate campaigns between 1968 and 1982 for the three months prior to Election Day. Of the races examined, six were chosen from among those classified in chapter 2 as "hard-fought" and six from among those classified as "low-key" (these classifications were made on the basis of descriptions in *Congressional Quarterly Weekly Report* about the general levels of intensity and competition in the campaign). Since this sample is neither large nor random, it was important to avoid selecting a set of specialized, obviously idiosyncratic situations.[24] For this reason, the dozen races to be examined were drawn from both heavily and lightly populated states and from both presidential and midterm election years.[25] The six hard-fought races are from two small states, North and South Dakota, mid-sized Indiana and Wisconsin, and the larger states of Florida and California. The low-key races came from the smaller states of North Dakota and Hawaii, mid-sized Wisconsin and New Jersey, and the large states of Texas and California.

The newspapers chosen for analysis were, whenever possible, those with the largest circulation in the state; when more than one paper was examined, large-circulation papers from other parts of the state were selected. For each candidate, the number of stories in which his or her name appeared between August 1 and the day before Election Day was recorded. Mentions of the candidates were tabulated from all parts of the paper, including editorials but excluding letters to the editor.[26] Paid advertisements, of which there were very few, were also omitted. A distinction was made between stories about the Senate campaign and stories mentioning a candidate in a non-campaign context, since newspapers sometimes cover statements or activities by incumbents, either in Washington or in their home state, without mentioning that there is a campaign in progress. On the assumption that many such statements or activities are made at least in part with an eye toward the upcoming election, such stories were counted as "campaign" mentions. Some stories about incumbents clearly were not related to the upcoming election in any way and were excluded from the count.[27]

Newspaper coverage of the following Senate races was monitored for the last three months before the election (the incumbent's name appears in capital letters unless the race was an open-seat one):

Hard-fought	*Low-key*
South Dakota 1968:	California 1974:
McGovern-Gubbrud	Cranston-Richardson
North Dakota 1974: Young-Guy	Wisconsin 1974: Nelson-Petri
Florida 1980: Hawkins-Gunter	New Jersey 1976:
Indiana 1980: Bayh-Quayle	Williams-Norcross
Wisconsin 1980: Nelson-Kasten	North Dakota 1976: Burdick-Stroup
California 1982: Wilson-Brown	Hawaii 1980: Inouye-Brown
	Texas 1982: Bentsen-Collins

There was very little newspaper coverage of any of the six low-key contests. News coverage of hard-fought races varied, but in all cases it dwarfed that given the low-key races.

In North Dakota in 1974, Republican incumbent Milton Young was challenged by former Governor William Guy. Guy was well known and popular and was considered by the press and by Young himself to be a formidable challenger. Each of the state's four largest daily newspapers devoted extensive coverage to this campaign (see table 5). While there was some variation from paper to paper in the coverage of each candidate, both were mentioned in an average of more than one story per day during the last three months of the campaign. During October and early November, the names of both candidates appeared in approximately two stories per day. Most of these stories were not on the front page but were featured in the same general area of an inside section from day to day. In all of the other hard-fought races examined, newspapers tended to devote a specific part of one section to the Senate race (and, if there was a hotly contested one, the gubernatorial race).

In contrast, the 1976 Senate race in New Jersey between incumbent Harrison Williams and Republican challenger David Norcross received very little coverage. The state's largest newspaper, the *Newark Star-Ledger,* paid scant attention to the campaign itself but did print many stories about Senator Williams's views on current legislation. Norcross, a Trenton attorney with no prior political experience, had been drafted by the state Republican party after half a dozen other potential candi-

TABLE 5
Newspaper Mentions of Incumbent and Challenger in Two Senate Campaigns: North Dakota 1974 and New Jersey 1976

Newspaper	Incumbent							Challenger							Incumbent's Advantage
	August–September		October		All 3 Months			August–September		October		All 3 Months			
	H§	NH	H	NH	H	NH	Total	H	NH	H	NH	H	NH	Total	
							North Dakota 1974								
						Milton Young							William Guy		
Bismarck Tribune	20	37	31	26	51	63 =	114	26	28	46	29	72	57 =	129	− 15
Minot Daily News	22	29	26	31	48	60 =	108	26	21	36	27	62	48 =	110	− 2
Grand Forks Herald	26	47	33	31	59	78 =	137	34	38	50	30	84	68 =	152	− 15
Fargo Forum	23	38	31	27	54	65 =	119	28	32	28	33	56	65 =	121	− 2
MEAN							120							128	− 8
							New Jersey 1976								
						Harrison Williams							David Norcross		
Newark Star Ledger	23	25	20	27	43	52 =	95	9	1	12	16	21	17 =	38	+57
New Brunswick Home-News	5	26	13	22	18	48 =	66	1	7	5	12	6	19 =	25	+41
Trenton Times	4		12	6	16	12 =	28	4	1	7	6	11	7 =	18	+10
New York Times		[6]		[5]			11		[5]		[6]			11	+0
MEAN							50							23	+27

Note: Every page of each newspaper was checked (for the New York Times, index only) from August 1 up to but not including Election Day in November. One point was tallied for each story containing the candidate's name, including editorials.
* Includes days in November before but not including Election Day.
§ H = candidate's name appeared in a headline; NH = candidate's name mentioned in a story but not in a headline.

TABLE 6
Average Number of Newspaper Stories Mentioning Senate Incumbents and
Challengers in Six Low-key and Six Hard-fought Races

Candidate	August–September		October		All 3 Months		
	H*	NH	H	NH	H	NH	Total
Six Low-key Races with Incumbents Running							
Incumbent	7	15	10	17	17	31	48
Challenger	8	10	6	13	14	24	38
MEAN	8	13	8	15	16	28	44
Four Hard-fought Races with Incumbents Running							
Incumbent	22	34	30	41	52	75	127
Challenger	20	28	25	38	45	66	111
MEAN	21	31	28	40	49	59	118
Two Open-seat Hard-fought Races							
California 1982							
Wilson (R)	35	41	33	41	68	82	150
Brown (D)	35	54	37	40	72	94	166
Florida 1980							
Hawkins (R)	14	28	29	32	43	60	103
Gunter (D)	24	26	31	25	55	51	106

*H = candidate's name appeared in a headline; NH = candidate's name mentioned in a story but not in a headline.

dates declined to run (*Newark Star-Ledger*, 31 October 1976). He was virtually ignored by the *Star-Ledger* prior to October and was covered only sparingly during the final weeks of the campaign. Six of the 28 stories mentioning Norcross in October conveyed only the news that he was expected to lose badly. The *Trenton Times*, although it vaguely endorsed both Williams and Norcross, gave almost no coverage to either candidate over the three-month period.

This striking contrast between coverage of hard-fought and low-key races held, without exception, for all of the races examined. For each contest, the average number of stories in which each candidate was mentioned was calculated across all papers monitored. Then these means, one for each race, were themselves combined to yield a mean for the six hard-fought and a mean for the six low-key races (these figures are presented in table 6).

OVERALL COVERAGE OF THE SIX HARD-FOUGHT
CAMPAIGNS

Four of the hard-fought races listed above featured incumbents running
for reelection; both they and their challengers received continual news
coverage in these races. On average, incumbents were mentioned in 127
stories between August and Election Day, and challengers in 111. This
amounts to nearly 1.5 stories per day. Only occasionally did a story focus
on one candidate without referring to the other; most of the time stories
about the Senate campaign provided substantive information about both
candidates. As for the likelihood of reaching potential voters, it is undoubtedly preferable for any candidate to be featured in a headline rather
than be mentioned only in the body of a story. As Ranney (1984, 12)
observed, "Most Americans simply make no effort to read every day all
the stories, editorials, columns, and features on politics that their newspapers print. They typically glance at the headlines and perhaps a lead
paragraph or two." In each of the six hard-fought campaigns, headline
coverage was sporadic in August, picked up after Labor Day, and became
continual during the final weeks of the race. In the earlier period there
was, on average, a headline story once every third day. In October and
early November, both incumbents and challengers were featured in at
least one headline story just about every day. During the final month, it
was not unusual to find a pair of stories daily, side by side. The proportion of headline mentions to non-headline mentions was similar for both
the incumbent and the challenger in the August–September period and
during the final month. In both periods each candidate appeared in the
headline of just less than half of all the stories in which he was mentioned.[28] The heaviest news coverage occurred in the open-seat race in
California in 1982. There, the names of both Governor Brown and San
Diego Mayor Wilson appeared in over 150 stories each over the three
months analyzed and in a headline just about every day during the last
five weeks.

News stories about hard-fought campaigns fell into three general
areas of focus. Some featured the candidates more or less equally; some
focused on one candidate almost exclusively; and some featured one candidate primarily, with some discussion of the other candidate as well. The
first category included stories announcing or reporting on debates and
joint meetings, comparing receipt and expenditure of campaign funds, and
reporting on poll results. Often, such stories featured the names of both
candidates in one headline and gave nearly equal space to each. The stories oriented toward only one candidate included coverage of statements

by an incumbent about proposed or pending legislation (these tended to appear in August and September, before Congress had adjourned), reports of specific events or appearances, and in-depth background pieces. The last two types of stories focused as often on the challenger as on the incumbent.

Most frequent were stories on candidate policy positions and attacks on opponents. In the four cases involving incumbents, the challengers continually criticized some aspect of the senator's record or called into question his capability. In all six cases (and least in the Young-Guy contest), the candidates entered into a continuous dialogue, alternately answering the opponent's charges and countering with new criticisms. Newspaper reports focused heavily on this contentious aspect of the campaign, often making one day's story a continuation of the previous day's.[29] When candidates agreed on an issue, that issue received short, and often one-time-only, coverage. When they disagreed, not only did newspaper stories tend to be longer and to go into more detail but the candidates' own need to rebut often led to a continuous airing of the issue over a span of days or weeks. Controversy, it seems, was newsworthy; agreement generally was not. When the challenger found a way to attack the incumbent, and especially when the incumbent responded, numerous headline stories were often the result. While each individual story tended to focus more on the candidate making the most recent statement, the opponent's position or previous statements were usually included as well.

Overall, then, newspapers covering the six hard-fought races gave substantive and evenly distributed coverage to both candidates, and this coverage was steady and frequent for at least the month prior to Election Day, qualities that were also evident in the *Columbus Dispatch*'s coverage of the 1978 Ohio gubernatorial race and that are generally characteristic, as well, of press coverage of presidential elections.[30]

OVERALL COVERAGE OF THE SIX LOW-KEY CAMPAIGNS

Daily newspaper coverage was substantially lighter in the six low-key Senate campaigns than in the hard-fought races. During August and September, few headlines containing either the incumbent's or the challenger's name appeared in coverage of any of the low-key races. On average, the incumbent's name appeared in a headline only seven times during this two-month period, and the challenger's name eight times—in other words, barely once a week. The number of appearances rose only slightly during the final five weeks, presumably the period during which prospective voters are most attuned to the campaign.[31] The average number of headline mentions of the incumbent after October 1 for the six low-key races was ten, while the average for the challenger was six—approximately twice versus once a week. The candidates were mentioned slightly more often in stories whose headline did not include their names, but even adding these mentions increases the total only a little. Over the three months before the election, then, the name of the challenger in these six races was mentioned in an average of just 38 stories, or about once every three days.

It is important to note the possibility that light news coverage of certain Senate races could be related more to a particular newspaper's priorities than to the nature of a given campaign: perhaps some newspapers do not generally concentrate on politics. Examination of the same newspapers for one hard-fought and one low-key race in three states—California, Wisconsin, and North Dakota—produced ample evidence to contradict this notion. The heavy coverage of the 1982 California Senate race by both the *Los Angeles Times* and the *San Francisco Chronicle* suggested that their light coverage of the 1974 campaign was not due to any general policy on the part of those newspapers to give short shrift to statewide political campaigns. In medium-sized Wisconsin and the small state of North Dakota, the same newspapers covered some campaigns heavily and others lightly.

More perspective on this point is gained by comparing a given newspaper's Senate campaign coverage with its treatment of other ongoing political campaigns. For example, the *Dallas Morning News* covered the Bentsen-Collins Senate race in 1982 rather lightly, while its coverage of the gubernatorial race that same year was extensive. Governor Clements's name appeared in 65 headlines between August 1 and Election Day, and challenger Mark White's in 37; while Bentsen's appeared in only 23 headlines, and Collins's in 19. Similarly, although the *Honolulu Star Bulletin* barely covered the Inouye-Brown race, it did cover other races in 1980 heavily. Between September 1 and Election Day in front-page stories alone the *Star Bulletin* featured 13 stories about the Honolulu mayor's race and 9 about the city prosecutor's race, yet not a single story about the Senate contest appeared on the front page throughout the entire fall. Clearly the light coverage of these campaigns was not a function of the general news coverage policies of the newspapers selected.

What is the substance of the coverage in hard-fought and low-key Senate races? Observers of presidential campaigns have noted that television networks' job "is to analyze and criticize what the candidates' words really mean" (Robinson and Sheehan 1983, 233). As Salmore and Salmore (1985, 157) put it, "Network television reporting of presidential campaigns is analytic, thematic, and critical." McClure (1983, 140) characterized presidential coverage as follows: "What the candidate does and says, what he emphasizes, the media deemphasizes. The audience gets little exposure to the 'real' campaign trail—to the main live events of the day." These characterizations of the content of presidential news coverage do not appear to hold for the 12 Senate races examined here. In the hard-fought races, most stories detailed what the candidates did and said, with little interpretation, analysis, or further commentary. Because presidential campaign coverage in general is so much greater than Senate campaign coverage, coverage of candidates' statements and stances about issues and policy is probably greater, in *absolute* terms, in presidential elections. But it appears that at least in hard-fought Senate elections, news coverage tends to focus as much on issues and candidates as on hoopla and other horse race aspects.[32]

In the low-key campaigns, the amount of issue coverage varied somewhat over the six campaigns examined. In the Hawaii race, for example, it was almost impossible for a reader of the *Honolulu Star Bulletin,* even looking painstakingly, to discover how the candidates stood on any issues. Thirteen headlines mentioned Inouye in the *Star Bulletin* over the last three months of the campaign, while challenger Brown's name appeared in just three headlines, and none of the three articles contained any information about Brown's issue positions. The headlines in the *Honolulu Star Bulletin* during the Inouye-Brown campaign that mentioned either Inouye's or Brown's name are shown in table 7.

Brown's views were discussed in three of the other (non-headline) stories, but it was difficult to obtain from them even a sketchy view of his political ideology. One of these pieces identified Brown as a "self-proclaimed liberal," an environmentalist, and in favor of wage and price controls and the Equal Rights Amendment (29 October 1980, D-1). But another noted his support for conservative economist Milton Friedman's plan to eliminate the graduated income tax system in favor of an across-the-board 23 percent tax rate with no possibility of deductions (5 September 1980, D-2). Most of the stories featuring Senator Inouye's name in a headline focused on the incumbent's chances of winning, his ties to the party, his campaign contributions and endorsements, and his attention to constituents. Most of the non-headline coverage of Inouye consisted mainly of the endorsement announcements of various interest groups (all of which endorsed him). Essentially, then, press accounts of issue differences in this race were negligible.

In other low-key races, coverage of the candidates' views varied by paper. For example, while the *Los Angeles Times* devoted little day-to-day coverage to either candidate, it featured H. L. Richardson in a num-

TABLE 7
Headlines in a Low-key Race: Inouye versus Brown, Hawaii 1980

Headlines Mentioning Senator Inouye		Headlines Mentioning Challenger Brown	
Date	*Headline*	*Date*	*Headline*
August 6	Inouye Urges Hefty Tax on Gasoline		
September 5	GOP Candidates Assail Inouye and Carter		
7	Inouye to Hawaiians: It's Time for Unity		
14	Inouye, Carter Staffs Join Forces		
		September 16	Brown Fund-Raiser
18	Keeping a Low Profile Paying Off for Inouye	18	Weissman Says Brown's Tale Is Incorrect
19	Inouye, Heftel and Akaka Expected to Breeze Through in Congress Races		
22	Inouye Says He's Content with Senate Role		
27	Hits Inouye Vote		
27	Carter OKs Inouye Act		
October 14	Inouye Cites Perils in Iran-Iraq Fighting		
		October 20	Brown Fund Event
23	Inouye Backs Spencer		
November 2	Inouye: Discovering "Mole" a Victory for U.S. Espionage		
2	Re-elect Inouye, Heftel, Akaka		

ber of in-depth pieces, and one could get from these some feel for his candidacy, including his views on many issues. But the *San Francisco Chronicle* ran no such backgrounders, and even the most attentive reader could gain little information there. Many mentions of the challengers in the low-key races contained no more information than the fact that they were running, and in some cases that they were likely to lose.

Senate Coverage Compared with House Coverage

Even the hardest-fought Senate races do not receive the level of constant media attention afforded presidential contests. How does the degree of Senate campaign coverage compare with House campaign coverage? Looking at five midwestern House races in 1970, Manheim (1974) found that "roughly twice as much coverage is devoted to the congressional campaign in rural areas as in more urbanized areas," and he concluded that "rural newspapers play a much more central role in the development of congressional level campaign settings than do those in urbanized areas" (653). Manheim examined 26 dailies in the five districts over the twelve weeks prior to Election Day and found coverage to range from an average of 15 stories in one urban Illinois district to an average of 95 stories in the northernmost district of Wisconsin. In the last 10 days of the campaign, coverage ranged from an average of only 5 stories (1 every other day) in the papers of Illinois's Thirteenth Congressional District to an average of 19 stories (nearly 2 a day) per paper in Iowa's Second District.

In 1978 the Center for Political Studies augmented its National Election Survey by having a clipping service monitor news stories, editorials, opinion columns, advertisements, and letters pertaining to congressional campaigns from the two largest daily newspapers in each of the 108 districts in the national sample. Analysis of these data by Clarke and Evans (1983) revealed that the mean number of House campaign stories over this 42-day campaign period was 8.9 articles per day, or about 1 article every 5 days,[33] and that in "thirteen of these districts . . . major daily newspapers failed to carry any pre-election coverage" (38n). Discovering that the NES data excluded "roughly two-thirds of the campaign articles and advertisements," Goldenberg and Traugott (1984) looked at all news items in 33 dailies covering 46 districts for "every other week during the last six weeks of the [1978] campaign" (133 n. 15). They found that "on average there were 6 news stories and 12 articles of all types" per paper for the three weeks examined, with extremely wide variation from paper to paper (124). "Not surprisingly," the authors noted, campaign coverage "increases with the vitality and competitiveness of the race" (126), yet these findings reflected "hardly an overwhelming quantity of attention" (124).

Orman (1985) monitored local media coverage of his own race for a House seat in Connecticut in 1984. In what even Orman conceded was a safe-seat race for his seven-term incumbent opponent, two area newspapers ran 50 and 35 campaign stories, respectively, between July 1 and Election Day (averages of 1 story every 2.6 and 3.7 days), while apart from televising one debate each, the three television stations in the area essentially did not cover this contest. The most news coverage provided by any of the stations appears to have comprised fewer than five or six items over the entire campaign (758).

Comparing the coverage of the 1978 House campaigns they had examined with the coverage of the 1984 Senate race they studied (that of Michigan incumbent Carl Levin against challenger Jack Lousma), Goldenberg and Traugott (1984) found that "as expected, news coverage of the Michigan Senate race was heavier than coverage of an average House race." Specifically, they found that coverage of this race (which I classify as hard-fought in appendix 1) was "50% greater for the Senate race [than for the average 1978 House race] in the last few weeks before Election day" (126).

My examination of the 12 races described above permits further comparison of news coverage of House and Senate campaigns in two ways. While monitoring the coverage of the two North Dakota Senate races (1974 and 1976) in the 12-state sample, I also kept track for each year of the number of stories during August, September, and October on North Dakota's at-large House race in both the *Grand Forks Herald* and the *Fargo Forum*. The overall coverage of North Dakota's hard-fought Senate race in 1974 was considerably greater than that of the House campaign, with the difference coming primarily in news coverage of the challengers in these races. House incumbent Mark Andrews was covered somewhat less, overall, than Senate incumbent Milton Young, though the two were the subjects of roughly equal numbers of headlines overall (113 for Young, 109 for Andrews). The name of Senate challenger Guy, on the other hand, appeared in nearly three times as many headlines in the *Grand Forks Herald* as did House challenger Dorgan's (84 to 32), and in both papers the difference in overall coverage of the two challengers was considerable.

In striking contrast, the low-key 1976 Senate race in North Dakota actually received less coverage than that year's House race. Neither Senator Quentin Burdick nor his challenger, Robert Stroup, was featured in as many articles as was Congressman Andrews (120 on Burdick, 92 on Stroup, and 153 on Andrews). Coverage of House challenger Lloyd Omdahl was equivalent to that of Senate challenger Stroup in the *Forum* and greater in the *Herald*. Such levels of news coverage for a House race are clearly considerably higher than the average for House races found in Goldenberg and Traugott's study of 1978 House races; perhaps this was due to the fact that North Dakota has only one House seat, and its members of the two houses of Congress represent identical constituencies. A second, more general comparison can be made between Goldenberg and Traugott's average house news coverage figures and the average amount of coverage of the six hard-fought and the six low-key Senate races examined here. There was an average of about 1.5 stories per day for the six hard-fought races in which an incumbent sought reelection, and even greater coverage for the two hard-fought open-seat contests. This is significantly greater coverage than the average of 3–4 articles per week that Goldenberg and Traugott found for the House campaigns. On the other hand, the level of coverage of low-key Senate races was essentially the same as that of the average House race in 1978.

It would appear from these findings that Senate campaigns per se are not necessarily more likely to be covered by the press. Contrary to Fenno's (1982, 10) observation that the media are "much more interested in U.S. senators as a class of politicians than in U.S. representatives," these data suggest that Senate campaigns are not necessarily viewed as *inherently* more newsworthy. Instead, it seems that the nature of particular campaigns to some extent determines the volume of their news coverage, and in the case of low-key Senate races that volume would appear to be very close to that of most House races.

4. A Closer Look at Four Senate Campaigns

During the last three months of a hard-fought race a newspaper reader can encounter the names of the Senate candidates in more than 100 stories. If a challenger's name has been headlined 50 times over this period, there is a good chance that his or her name will have become familiar to most voters by election day, even to those inclined only to skim headlines. On the other hand, coverage of low-key Senate races affords neither the incumbent nor the challenger much attention, making it difficult for the challenger to become known to the electorate. What accounts for this great difference in levels of news coverage? Producing an average of more than one story per day, it is likely that reporters covering hard-fought races probably are covering most of the candidates' campaign activities, overlooking very few of the events candidates designed for press consumption. In low-key races, however, it is more difficult to identify the link between what candidates are doing and what journalists and their editors report in the newspaper. Was coverage determined by the activities and statements—or lack thereof—of the candidates themselves, or did reporters and editors decide, independently of what the candidates did or said, that certain campaigns were simply not newsworthy enough to warrant serious coverage?

In considering these questions, we will look closely at two low-key and two hard-fought races drawn from the twelve reviewed in chapter 3. In order to reduce the influence of spurious, or extraneous, factors, the four races are taken from two states, Wisconsin and California. One hard-fought and one low-key race from each of the two states is examined, minimizing the possibility that differences in news coverage are more a function of the habits and styles of particular news organizations than of the activities and decisions made by the Senate campaigns themselves. I focus specifically on the extent to which news coverage of a Senate race may depend on the behavior and activities of the candidates and on whether candidates can by their actions promote or subvert the conditions that make a "good" story for journalists. I also look at the extent to which news coverage depends on the initial judgments of editors and reporters about the closeness of the race or the viability of a challenger's candidacy.

Petri versus Nelson in Wisconsin, 1974: A Low-key Campaign

In 1974 in Wisconsin, two-term Democratic Senator Gaylord Nelson ran for reelection, facing freshman Republican state senator Thomas Petri. None of the state's strongest Republicans had been willing to challenge Nelson, and the state Republican party endorsed Petri in May 1974. Petri's only opposition for the Republican nomination came in the September 10 primary, where, by a 5-to-1 margin, he defeated a production scheduler from General Motors who "could not afford the time away from his job and family" to mount a campaign (*Milwaukee Journal*, 27 August 1974). Senator Nelson ran unopposed in the Democratic primary.

Political observers in Wisconsin expected Petri to lose to Nelson, and indeed he did, by a 61 percent to 38 percent margin. It was very much a low-key contest. The *Milwaukee Journal,* with the largest circulation in the state, barely covered the campaign. Between August 1 and November 4 the *Journal* ran a total of 18 headlines containing Nelson's name and 12 containing Petri's (see appendix 2). Overall, 36 stories mentioned Petri, 18 of them in October, when voters were presumably most likely to be tuned into the campaign. Four stories featured the Republican's name in a headline, and 10 more gave no more information about him than the fact that he was running.

Why did this campaign attract so little coverage? The *Milwaukee Journal* described Petri as "a man virtually unknown outside his district challenging an incumbent whose campaign buttons just say 'Gaylord'— everybody knows Gaylord Who" (20 October 1974, 13).[1] Having served just two years as state senator from Fond du Lac, Petri had no hope of defeating Nelson, a popular senator, without first acquiring widespread

59

name recognition throughout the state. Petri began the fall campaign knowing that he would have very little financial support either from the national Republican party or from the state party; during August the state party had refused his request that it double its ten-thousand-dollar contribution to his campaign, citing already large debts. President Nixon's recent Watergate troubles had severely damaged the standing of the Republican party in many parts of the country, and many Republican candidates, including some in Wisconsin, hoped that Nixon's resignation would improve their chances in November. But as the *Milwaukee Journal* noted, "Predictions of an improved Republican situation were made in the context of a remarkable weakness and penury for the party that controlled Wisconsin government only a few years ago." Petri "likened his party to the Packers at their low ebb: down but building" and proceeded with his campaign under the assumption that he would receive only minimal financial support from the GOP (11 August 1974, 12).

The political atmosphere in which Petri launched his campaign, then, was not one favoring Republican challengers in Wisconsin. In addition, the Republican party chose to emphasize this political problem rather than downplay it. The Wisconsin press may have "forgotten" Petri while he was walking the state in part because he had never been seen as a possible winner in the first place. Not only was his likely defeat evidenced by his low standing in the polls, it was acknowledged even by Petri's own supporters. Republicans were as likely to consider Nelson's reelection a certainty as were Democrats (7 October 1974, 1), not only in conversations with reporters but in public speeches as well. The *Milwaukee Journal* reported on October 6: "Republicans have had nice things to say about State Sen. Thomas Petri . . . but not much to say for his chances of winning. In introducing him at a recent GOP dinner in Fond du Lac, State Sen. Walter Hollander of Rosendale said: 'If he doesn't win this time—and nobody expects him to win this time—he'll win next time' " (6 October 1974, 4). Nelson's supporters did not overlook the opportunity to reinforce this perception. Minnesota Senator Walter Mondale, campaigning for Wisconsin Democrats, quipped, "I hear we might just squeak Gaylord Nelson past his opponent. I hear Gaylord doesn't even know the name of his opponent yet" (7 October 1974, pt. 2, 1).

Against this backdrop, Petri searched for a way to drum up voter interest and media coverage, and he decided to campaign by walking the state. This strategy had successfully introduced Lawton Chiles to the Florida electorate in 1970, and since then it had been regarded by a number of other statewide candidates around the country as an inexpensive way to garner media coverage. One Wisconsin reporter complimented

Petri's choice of strategy: "The walk is an endless media gimmick. It gives the press in every town something tangible to photograph and write about, and gives every little radio station an interesting guest for the open line show. It's also cheap and it's probably the only kind of sustained campaign Petri could have run" (20 October 1974, 13). Petri crisscrossed Wisconsin from July through Election Day, logging about thirteen hundred miles. By his own calculation, he traveled at about three miles per hour, "with breaks at factory gates and baseball games" (6 August 1974, 3). As he traveled, he released a series of position papers outlining his views on improving the economy and reducing government bureaucracy.

For all of his efforts, though, Petri was not getting through to the electorate. Why not? Walking the state, as the reporter suggested, can be useful if it engenders media coverage. But there is nothing about such a campaign strategy that compels reporters to respond to it on a continuous basis. While Petri may have received the kind of attention he hoped for when he first entered a new town or city (the *Milwaukee Journal* covered his arrival in Milwaukee on August 6), there is no guarantee that such coverage will continue, either while the candidate is in town or after he moves on. This means that he must either rely on one press exposure per town to last until Election Day or make repeated swings through the area. If the Milwaukee coverage is indicative of the kind Petri received in other parts of the state, the walking method, with no supplementary tactics, produces very little coverage in any given paper over the course of the campaign. When the candidate is gone, he is in effect forgotten by the press.[2]

Petri's walk-the-state strategy represented a positive decision in favor of a tactic designed to obtain press coverage. But two other factors hindered this effort: first, that Petri's political views were not substantially different from Nelson's; and second, that Petri refused to engage in political attacks on his opponent. Considered a moderate-to-conservative and "regarded even by Democrats as a rational and practical man" (20 October, 13), Petri campaigned against tax breaks for big business and suggested that the national defense budget could be cut. As one reporter put it, "The campaign he's mounted is . . . the campaign of an updated La Follette progressive." This did not endear Petri to conservatives in the Republican party, and he acknowledged that such a strained relationship was "not a nifty way to raise money" (ibid.). Evaluating why Nelson would be a shoo-in for reelection, Donald Pfarrer, of the *Journal*, pointed to Nelson's remarkable reputation and accomplishments. But before getting to these, he led off by saying: "The systematic examination and criticism of his stewardship that might have emerged from the present campaign has not

61

materialized. Instead, his opponent . . . has advanced a program that could have been inspired by Nelson himself" (31 October 1974, 1). Another reporter wrote that "little has been said about issues because Nelson and Petri do not disagree strongly" (3 November 1974, 18).

There is every indication that Petri was a serious, thoughtful candidate with a well-developed set of proposals, but no sign that he engaged in much dialogue with Nelson, whom he refused to confront with political attacks. Press motivation to follow a campaign closely may be considerably reduced if early polls show that a challenger has little chance of winning, and journalists are even less inclined to follow a challenger if he does not even generate any of the kind of controversy that constitutes "news." One reporter, in an article entitled "Petri: A Tenacious Candidate for Senate," wrote: "He looks like a pushover. . . . But the tenacity of this rather eccentric young man suggests otherwise—suggests that even if he loses in November as everybody confidently predicts he will, there will be other Novembers and improving chances for Thomas Evert Petri" (20 October 1974, pt. 2, 1). In an editorial endorsing Nelson, the *Milwaukee Journal* described Petri as "an honorable fellow with considerable promise" (27 October 1974). After the election, another reporter remarked of Petri: "He campaigned for more than four months and his forthrightness, intelligence and amiability were everywhere acclaimed" (6 November 1974, 19).

Nevertheless, Petri's disinclination to confront Nelson on the issues left little that was unusual or controversial for the press to write about, despite their high regard for him as a candidate. Part of the reason Petri never achieved such dialogue with Nelson was that Nelson basically ignored him. But that situation, too, was partly of Petri's own making. Early on, Petri let it be known that his campaign would not be aimed at Nelson: "I have no interest in going around throwing mud at people or trying to talk down the other guy" (27 August 1974, 7). While this position may have gained Petri the respect of reporters—"Petri is a gentleman who thinks a constructive and affirmative campaign is the best kind" (31 October 1974, 1)—it may also have diminished the amount of news coverage of his campaign, coverage he needed in order to gain the public recognition necessary to be a real contender.

To what extent, then, did the Petri-Nelson campaign reach the voters of Wisconsin? In all, Petri's name appeared in headlines in the *Milwaukee Journal* 12 times, while Nelson's appeared in 10 headlines. By contrast, the campaign for governor received considerably more press coverage than the Senate race, with incumbent Governor Lucey's name appearing in headlines 58 times between August 1 and November 4 (though not always because of the gubernatorial campaign). The name of his opponent, Dyke, appeared in 27 headlines, always in a campaign context, and in at least as many additional stories.

Due to a lack of funds, Petri's campaign ran very little paid advertising; not surprisingly, this combined with the lack of press coverage to guarantee that his initial obscurity would endure throughout the campaign. In a mid-October survey, 385 Wisconsin adults were asked to name the candidates for governor, senator, and attorney general. Nearly six in ten were able to identify incumbent Governor Patrick Lucey as a candidate, while about 22 percent could name his Republican challenger. On the other hand, only 25 percent of all respondents could offer the name of Gaylord Nelson as a senatorial candidate (another 14 percent guessed Proxmire, Wisconsin's other incumbent senator), and just 6 percent could come up with Petri's name. Of course, one need only recognize (rather than recall) a candidate's name to associate what has been said about him in the press with one's own decision on how to vote, and it is likely that *recognition* rates for Nelson were much higher.[3] While there was very little press coverage of his 1974 reelection campaign, Nelson's past press had been, in one reporter's view, "just short of goggle-eyed: Over the years the Wisconsin press has offered its readers an image of a man whose affability, wit and charm will knock Republicans on the head at the polls . . . the coverage has been a press secretary's dream" (31 October 1974, 4). Petri, on the other hand, had no past political experience outside Fond du Lac, and it would be surprising if very many Wisconsinites would have either recalled or recognized his name at the time of the survey. Voters are far less likely to vote for a Senate candidate with whom they are unfamiliar (see chapter 5). They might vote for a little-known challenger in order to cast a vote against the incumbent, or they might vote solely on the basis of party label. But in the 1974 Senate race in Wisconsin, where the Democratic incumbent was popular and the party of the challenger was not, the invisibility factor ensured that Petri's loss would be a big one; Nelson's reelection margin was 26 percentage points.

Cranston versus Richardson in California, 1974: A Low-key Campaign

In California in 1974, Democratic Senator Alan Cranston ran for a second term against Republican state senator H. L. Richardson. Watergate had placed the Republican party on the defensive in California as in Wisconsin, and the state's strongest Republicans chose to pass up a challenge to Cranston, who was popular and displayed no apparent exploitable weaknesses. Outgoing Governor Ronald Reagan, former Lieutenant Governor Robert Finch, educator and semanticist S. I. Hayakawa, and a number of congressmen, including Barry Goldwater, Jr., had been mentioned as possible opponents, but all declined to run. A poll commissioned by Cranston in August 1973 showed the senator leading Governor Reagan by 14 percentage points with only five percent undecided. "In other words," offered the *Los Angeles Times,* "it would have been an uphill struggle for Reagan" (21 October 1974, pt. 2, 1).

Richardson, an unabashed archconservative from a Los Angeles suburb, defeated former Reagan aide Earl Brian in a quiet primary. Neither Republican enjoyed statewide name recognition, and Richardson began his general election campaign as a clear underdog, while incumbent Cranston was considered the probable winner from the start. In late August 1974 the California Poll showed Cranston leading by 23 points (a lead that would grow to 35 points in October). Neither the press nor political leaders from either party gave Richardson any chance. Cranston was so confident of reelection that he announced in early September that he would spend less than half the amount of money he had spent in his previous race and that he would not begin campaigning until mid-October.

Richardson had neither the personal nor the party funding necessary to mount a television campaign in which he could spend two or three months introducing himself and his views to Californians in waves of prime-time spots. With this option ruled out, his only hope of winning, aside from mistakes the Cranston camp might make, was to generate enough media coverage throughout California to be considered by the voters as an alternative to Cranston. Richardson did run a fairly energetic campaign, but he never received abundant press coverage. Part of the reason for this may have been that reporters did not cover the campaign as thoroughly as they could have, but part of the reason also lies in Richardson's consistent failure to make the best of the circumstances under which he was operating.

Richardson seemed actually to resist press coverage by staying away from people who were more newsworthy, by virtue of their position or status, than he was. Close association with prominent Republicans such as Governor Reagan or President Ford might have gained coverage for Richardson through coverage of them, and it might have given him access to resources—both funds and manpower—at their disposal. Richardson's avoidance stemmed from his longstanding poor relationship with others in the Republican party: his extreme conservatism had never appealed to moderates in the party; moreover, instead of trying to get along, Richardson had stridently criticized California Republicans over the years, including conservatives whose views did not coincide with his own. And his attacks on colleagues had not been exclusively verbal; in 1973 Richardson actually punched a liberal state senator in the mouth "for calling him an ass" (*San Francisco Chronicle*, 22 March 1985). He was unwilling to compromise his ideological views, and his poor relationship with other Republicans meant that initial support for his candidacy among party leaders and their supporters was very weak. As the campaign got under way, Richardson exacerbated the situation instead of attempting to mend fences. He did receive brief campaign visits from three conservative but not particularly well-known U.S. senators during September and October, but those in the best position to help him gain recognition—Governor Reagan and President Ford—kept their distance.

It was not that Governor Reagan was too busy to campaign; he campaigned actively for Republican gubernatorial candidate Houston Flournoy and various congressional and state candidates throughout the fall. But Richardson was not Reagan's favorite Republican. He had refused to vote for any of Reagan's state budgets (*San Francisco Chronicle*, 26 September 1974), had "provided the crucial vote to overturn Reagan's veto of a bill for the first time" (*Los Angeles Times*, 4 September 1974), and had consistently disagreed with Reagan on law-and-order issues. Said the *Los Angeles Times*, "It's no secret . . . that up to now there has been little love lost between the two men. Before he announced his Senate candidacy last year Richardson . . . strongly criticized the governor, saying many California Republicans were tired of him and that he had not done a very good job of either reducing crime or keeping down government expenditures" (31 October 1974, 22). Reagan, in turn, was irked by Richardson's challenge and defeat of Earl Brian, the Governor's "personal choice" for the Senate nomination in June (ibid., 20 September 1974).

When asked whether he would seek Reagan's support during the campaign, Richardson replied that he would not, because he was "campaigning on federal issues, not state issues" (ibid., 21 September 1974). In fact, Reagan had been campaigning around the country in support of other congressional candidates and had been speaking at length about "federal issues." Many of Reagan's biggest financial supporters shared his cool attitude toward Richardson. Some, such as Justin Dart, actually contributed to Cranston's campaign. The *Los Angeles Times* reported that Richardson "has no financial backing from the usual Republican sources. His money . . . is coming from tiny contributors" (3 November 1974, pt. 8, 1). Richardson's conspicuous absence from dinners and other campaign functions that were attended by Governor Reagan, Lieutenant Governor Flournoy, and other Republican candidates was noted in the press (e.g., *San Francisco Chronicle,* 26 September 1974). This dissociation continued until late October, when Cranston hinted that Reagan might actually favor him over Richardson: "I see no evidence that he would prefer Richardson . . . and he has done nothing to discourage some of his closest associates from openly supporting me or quietly helping in one way or another" (*Los Angeles Times,* 29 October 1974, pt. 2, 1). Reagan responded just before the election by filming a campaign spot for Richardson. More than a week before, Richardson had "reached the point in which he is willing to abandon some of the rigid independence he has maintained thus far" and had publicly declared, "I'm going to ask Gov. Reagan to help me" (ibid., 21 October 1974, 8). Cranston's remark finally forced Reagan to declare his outright support for Richardson, but as the *Times* pointed out, "the fact is that Tuesday night's reception . . . and the making of the television commercial are the first things that Reagan has done for Richardson in the course of the Senate campaign" (31 October 1974, 22).

Richardson also criticized President Ford. Before he pardoned Richard Nixon on September 9, Ford enjoyed high public support and was a positive media attraction for Republican candidates. Seeing this, gubernatorial candidate Flournoy asked Ford to come to California later in the fall to campaign for him, and Ford accepted. Richardson, however, had already given the new president reason to exclude him from his list of endorsements by calling Ford's choice of Nelson Rockefeller to be vice president "lousy" and saying it amounted to "throwing a Rockefeller wrench into the Republican Party machinery in California" (*Los Angeles Times,* 21 August 1974, 32). Richardson's remark that he would not appear on the same platform with the likes of Rockefeller was offered as a partial reason why former San Francisco Mayor George Christopher and eleven other Bay Area Republicans finally endorsed Cranston (*San Francisco Chronicle,* 4 October 1974, 9); nevertheless, Richardson continued to refer to Ford's "lousy" selection and to say that he disliked Rockefeller not only politically but personally. When he learned that Ford was coming to California to campaign, Richardson said, "I don't intend to impose on his time . . . nor do I intend to ask him" (*Los Angeles Times,* 21 September 1974, 23). In October, Richardson openly criticized Ford's proposals for the economy as "inflationary." And lauding Reagan after the governor agreed to help him in late October, Richardson added "that he felt the country would be 'a lot better off' if Reagan were President instead of Gerald Ford" (ibid., 31 October 1974, 22). When Ford visited California in the week before the election, an occasion that received full television and newspaper coverage, he campaigned for Flournoy but not for Richardson.

It is evident from various accounts in the *Los Angeles Times* that Richardson ran an energetic campaign—that he was serious about wanting to win, wasted little time engaging in non-campaign activities, and spent considerable time campaigning throughout the state. Although the *Times* did not start reporting regularly on the campaign until mid-October, there were references to Richardson's "long" campaign, to his practice early in the campaign of "talking about one controversial issue after another in a bewildering rush," and to his being a "heavy" campaigner (25 and 14 October 1974). Richardson spent the summer writing campaign pamphlets, or "tracts," as he called them, which were mailed to interest-group members most likely to share his conservative views. By early October he claimed that three million pamphlets had been distributed in California and estimated that six million would go out by Election Day (*Los Angeles Times*, 8 October 1974, 2). A reporter who had occasionally covered the Richardson campaign in September declared in October: "There are signs that Richardson, through sheer hard work and a likeable personality, may get more votes than first expected" (ibid.). Richardson's light press coverage cannot, therefore, be explained by a lack of effort on the part of the candidate; he was out there campaigning throughout the fall.

But there is also evidence that for all of its energy, Richardson's campaign was inefficiently run. With so little financing to start with, Richardson had to spend valuable time away from the hustings in order to raise money. Instead of using the rest of the time he had available to attract press coverage, he at times seemed unconcerned with such calculations. In fact, much of his coverage in August and September focused on how "strange" (a term used more than once) his way of campaigning seemed. At times, he seemed not only unconcerned with press coverage but uninterested in using the standard press-the-flesh techniques to gain recognition among the voters and perhaps a few minutes on the local television news as well. Richardson made appearances before very small gatherings and before groups of voters who were already committed to him, when it would have been more efficient to target larger audiences of undecided voters. For example, in mid-October Richardson arrived at the

San Diego campus of the University of California. When he saw that he would be addressing students outdoors, during the lunch hour, he left. Asked why, Richardson responded, "I will talk to people who come to hear me but I have too much respect for the office I'm running for to bark at people like a common carnival barker. I won't stand at a booth at some damned county fair either . . . and I won't ride in parades" (ibid., 14 October 1974, 18). In early September Richardson chartered a plane and flew 260 miles from Sacramento to Bakersfield to address a labor group. When his speech was delayed, he refused to wait and flew 240 miles back to Oakland; from there he drove another 20 miles to address a small group of the "already converted" (ibid., 20 September 1974, 3).

Scheduling gaffes in Richardson's campaign were in part attributed to his attempt to "run everything in his own campaign, down to the tiniest details." He lacked assistants, which apparently hurt. In September the *Los Angeles Times* reported that "thus far, one of the hallmarks of the Richardson campaign is the absence of a visible political structure, at least in the usual sense" (20 September 1974, 26). This was evident, for example, when Richardson responded to an interested caller from a San Francisco talk show that the only way to get additional information about the Richardson campaign was to contact his state senate office in southern California; he had no Bay Area organization (ibid.).

Even when Richardson did court the press, he sometimes failed to give first priority to his candidacy. "In Red Bluff . . . the candidate was interviewed at the local newspaper for half an hour, talking so little about the Senate race that one of those interviewing him came running after his party when he left to ask what office he was seeking" (ibid., 11 August 1974, 21). In October, Richardson was scheduled to appear in a four-day "camper caravan" designed in part to attract votes from owners of mobile homes but presumably intended to attract media attention as well. However, when the audience at the first stop was very small, Richardson reacted, not by playing instead to reporters, but "by indignantly walking out on his first speaking engagement" (ibid., 16 October 1974, pt. 2, 3).

There are bound to be scheduling coordination problems in any campaign. But these examples suggest that Richardson was especially inept at courting the kind of press attention needed to increase a candidate's favorable recognition. One reason for this was undoubtedly the lack of funds to support a campaign staff capable of maximizing his name recognition in a large state with many media centers. Another reason, however, was Richardson's strong, extremist views. In fact, it is possible that

Richardson received more of his press coverage for continually espousing extreme positions than he did for being the Republican Senate candidate.

On August 11, Richardson was interviewed by a small paper in northern California about his position on the proposed $80 million Tehama-Colusa canal, a project that some said would increase the annual value of local crops 30 to 40 times. Richardson, who favored cutting domestic programs to balance the budget, did not waffle on the issue: he flatly stated his opposition to the appropriation of any money for the canal, and he repeated this view on a local radio show, admitting that he "was losing votes" by taking such a stand (ibid., 11 August 1974, 3). In October, under the headline "Richardson Saying What He Thinks Even If It Costs Votes," the *Los Angeles Times* reported that when a conservative San Joaquin rancher asked Richardson what he would do to keep ranchers from being ruined by labor unions (for which Richardson had no liking), Richardson replied, "I'm not going to do anything. . . . It's none of my damned business." This sort of response was typical, assured the reporter:

> He tells farm audiences . . . that the government must end all of its supports and subsidies to agriculture. He tells business people their support of government regulation and subsidy is responsible for many of their present woes. He tells working men and women that minimum wage laws are causing unemployment and that welfare programs for the unemployed is the first area in which government must cut costs. . . . He tells Republicans their party is "dying," it has "no heart . . . no soul" and he would support a third party if the right one would come along. (21 October 1974, 8)

Although the *Los Angeles Times* covered Richardson's campaign more heavily than did the *San Francisco Chronicle,* up until the last few weeks of the campaign only a few of the stories in either paper consisted of typical campaign reporting about where the candidate went and what his views were. The amount of such mainstream campaign news appearing in the two papers was similar in quantity, but the *Times* printed numerous articles focusing on the unusual, surprising, or even comical aspects of what Richardson was doing and saying. Although the *Times* typically runs more "backgrounder" stories than the *Chronicle* does, one can speculate that if Richardson's campaign had not been seen as somewhat eccentric, the total number of articles appearing about his campaign would have been much smaller. In terms of the goals of Richardson's election campaign, it is difficult to know whether no coverage at all might have been preferable to the negative publicity he garnered.

Nelson versus Kasten in Wisconsin, 1980: A Hard-fought Campaign

In 1980, six years after he coasted to victory over Thomas Petri, Wisconsin Senator Gaylord Nelson narrowly lost his Senate seat to former U.S. Congressman Robert Kasten. Press coverage of this campaign started out much like that of 1974. Senator Nelson spent most of the summer in Washington, and until after the September 9 primary had determined his Republican opponent, the only attention the *Milwaukee Journal* paid to Nelson was to report on a few of his legislative activities and to wonder whether he might have a tougher fight this year than in the past. His name was also mentioned occasionally in the few reports the *Journal* devoted to the Republican Senate primary.

One might expect that a September primary would help a Senate challenger's quest for statewide visibility by inviting press coverage that might not otherwise be forthcoming. However, for Kasten (as for Petri in 1974 and Hawaii's Cooper Brown in 1980) the fall primary produced almost no news coverage. The lifeless character of the Republican primary campaign (Nelson was unopposed in the Democratic primary) was described in late August by the *Journal* reporter assigned to cover the 1980 Senate race:

> The four Republicans fighting for the honor of challenging Sen. Gaylord Nelson this fall are shadowboxing their way to the September 9 primary. Nobody knows when he lands a blow, nobody howls when he's hit and nobody really knows how tough Nelson will be in the main event. The campaign has generated little interest and less controversy. . . . [One candidate's assistant] charged early this summer that one of his boss' rivals had made racist statements. The charge was far-fetched and got scarcely a yawn from the Wisconsin press. After that the campaign resumed its clean but dull identity, lapsing into a summer somnolence from which it has yet to emerge. With 16 days to go the candidates don't seem to have made much of a dent in the consciousness of the voters. (*Milwaukee Journal*, 24 August 1980, 1)[4]

Kasten won his party's primary by just eight percentage points, but not because he had any advantage in media coverage. As a matter of fact, reported the *Journal*, the outcome was unclear to the end because of the race's virtual invisibility: "The campaign had attracted so little attention, and contained so many imponderables, that few observers of the political landscape were making predictions" (10 September 1980, 1).

Senate campaign coverage picked up a bit during September, as Kasten began to blast Nelson's record as too liberal. Except on weekends,

Nelson remained in Washington during September, and either he chose not to respond to Kasten's charges or reporters chose not to write about any responses he may have given. At the beginning of October Congress adjourned until after the elections, which freed Nelson to return home to campaign. At the same time, Kasten released a poll showing himself running even with Nelson. News coverage of the Senate campaign increased dramatically at this point.

Kasten's poll results were a surprise, at least to reporters of the *Milwaukee Journal* (3 October 1980, pt. 2, 3). An earlier poll, conducted by the *Journal* in March, had shown Nelson leading Kasten by 40 percentage points, and stories on the Senate race in August and September had portrayed Nelson as seeming safe. Kasten may have been unaware that Nelson might be vulnerable, or perhaps Kasten had known this but the *Journal* had simply not devoted much coverage to Kasten's campaign efforts.

Once back in Wisconsin, Senator Nelson went on the attack immediately. He began courting the business community—touting his influence as chairman of the Senate Small Business Committee—in an attempt to "undercut . . . potential Republican opposition by winning friends in a traditional Republican constituency" (4 November 1980, 20). He began a sustained attack on former Congressman Kasten's attendance record in the House, an issue derived from Kasten's having missed half the House roll calls in 1978 while campaigning in Wisconsin for the gubernatorial nomination. Nelson also attacked as deliberately deceitful Kasten's earlier charges that Nelson had favored the construction of a new Senate office building, proclaiming that both he and Senator Proxmire had voted against its funding.

Nelson's suddenly active campaign may have been a direct response to the results of Kasten's poll. Some observers had expected that Nelson would do little campaigning for several more weeks. The state Republican party chairman, commenting in September on the difficulty Kasten would have igniting a campaign against an incumbent who was content to stay out of sight, had said, "Nelson is going to lie in the weeds until about the middle of October. Then there is going to be an explosion. You won't be able to turn around without bumping into Nelson" (14 September 1980, 18). If the Republican chairman's observation was correct, it appears that Nelson decided to move up the start of his campaign by two weeks.

The two candidates debated three times. Kasten continued to brand the incumbent as a free-spending liberal who had lost touch with the needs of the people of Wisconsin. Instead of ignoring Kasten and confining himself to reminding voters of his accomplishments as a three-term senator, Nelson returned the fire. In addition to claiming that Kasten "took full salary for half service" in the House in 1978, Nelson attacked Kasten's opposition to aid for railroads and to the SALT treaty and called him indifferent to the needs of the poor and unemployed. Kasten accused Nelson of "slinging mud" by distorting his House attendance record and took out an ad reprinting a *Milwaukee Sentinel* article that had questioned Nelson's attempts to portray Kasten as chronically absent from the House when during three of his four years in Congress Kasten's attendance record was better than Nelson's. In late October, Kasten accused Nelson of "abusing his administrative budget to finance his campaign" by spending taxpayers' money to get reelected (27 October 1980, 1). Nelson's supporters denied the charges, and the state Democratic party chairman called them "reprehensible campaign tactics" (29 October 1980, pt. 2, 1).

With each candidate questioning the personal integrity of his opponent, campaign news coverage played up the confrontational tone. For example, in an article entitled "Nelson, Kasten fling barbs in talk to business people," the *Journal*'s lead was that the candidates "had another blistering confrontation Wednesday morning. . . . The two men mixed personal invective with a sharp discussion of the issues" (8 October 1980, pt. 2, 1). Other headlines featured charges of unfair campaigning, "dirty play," and taking the "low road." Such charges and counter-charges were traded throughout October.

Both candidates also gained some press attention by displaying the support of other prominent party leaders. Nelson appeared with Vice President Mondale, President Carter, Mondale again, AFL-CIO chief Lane Kirkland, Mondale again, and then President Carter again. Kasten was endorsed in visits from presidential candidate Reagan, former President Ford, and Senator Howard Baker and received active support from Governor Dreyfus, the man who had defeated him for the gubernatorial nomination in 1978. Several of these appearances produced both headlines and photographs in the *Journal*.

Over the course of the campaign, then, coverage by the *Milwaukee Journal* of the 1980 Senate race between Nelson and Kasten was considerably heavier than its coverage of the Nelson-Petri race in 1974. Between August 1 and Election Day in 1980, Senator Nelson's name appeared in 40 headlines and 102 stories overall. Challenger Kasten was mentioned in 33 headlines and in a total of 68 stories. In 1974, in contrast, the senator's name appeared in 10 headlines and just 37 stories overall, and challenger Petri was mentioned in 12 headlines and 36 stories overall (see appendix 2).

Brown versus Wilson in California, 1982: A Hard-fought Campaign

In early 1982 California Republican Senator S. I. Hayakawa, facing a strong field of primary challengers, decided not to run for reelection. San Diego Mayor Pete Wilson won a tough primary in June and faced Governor Edmund G. Brown, Jr., in the general election. Brown, who was ending two terms as governor, defeated two little-known and poorly financed opponents, as well as writer Gore Vidal, in the Democratic primary but won with only 51 percent of the vote.

Having been governor for eight years, Brown was much better known than Wilson, but he was also disliked by a fairly large portion of the electorate: from October 1981 on, the proportion rating him "poor" or "very poor" outweighed the proportion rating him "excellent" or "good" by an average of 15 percentage points (41 percent to 26 percent). Wilson therefore concentrated his campaign on Brown himself—his actions as governor, his judgment, and his character. Brown, on the other hand, because of his high negative rating, needed to steer the spotlight away from himself. To do so, his advisers argued, he needed to frame the campaign around policy issues and to go on the offensive by attacking Wilson's issue positions.

Each of the candidates set new California spending records, with Brown spending over $7 million and Wilson nearly $5.4 million (both figures are nearly $5 million more than had been spent by California Senate candidates of their respective parties in the past). Beginning immediately after the primary, the two candidates waged a largely negative campaign, and one that engendered much statewide and national media coverage. Throughout what one *Los Angeles Times* reporter called a "long and mudthrowing contest" (31 October 1982), there were almost daily accounts of one candidate attacking the other. Wilson called Brown's tactics "calculated character assassination," and Brown accused Wilson of waging "a smear a day" campaign (*San Francisco Chronicle*, 31 October 1982, A-12).

In 1974 neither the *Los Angeles Times* nor the *San Francisco Chronicle* had paid much attention to the Senate race between Cranston and Richardson early in the campaign. Even in August and September combined, nine headline mentions was the most either of those candidates

73

had received from either paper. In marked contrast, both newspapers covered the 1982 Brown-Wilson race steadily from the June primary onward, and each carried an average of more than two articles per day during September and October that focused on one or both candidates. (In both the *Times* and the *Chronicle,* both Brown and Wilson received more coverage in August and September of 1982 than either Cranston or Richardson had received during the entire period between August 1 and Election Day in 1974.) Brown and Wilson continually attacked each other on both policy-oriented and personal-level issues. Wilson accused Brown of constantly "flip-flopping" on issues as the political winds changed, criticized Brown's association with leftist activist Tom Hayden (which included appointing him to a state commission), and questioned the propriety of a number of contributions to Brown's campaign, such as one for eight thousand dollars from the family of a judge around the time Brown had appointed him to the bench. He also unleashed a barrage of attacks on Brown's character, accusing the governor of using "scare tactics," telling deliberate lies, and generally behaving reprehensibly in his campaign.

Brown characterized Wilson as uninformed and inexperienced (calling him a "shoot-from-the-hip" candidate) and charged that many of Wilson's votes as a member of the San Diego city council had been influenced by campaign contributions. He also accused Wilson of having used an improper "tax dodge" to avoid paying federal income tax in 1980 and of having lived rent-free for over a year in a condominium provided by wealthy supporters.

The candidates also spent considerable time attacking each other's positions on issues of public policy, and received considerable news coverage for doing so. Brown, presumably in line with a strategy to take the focus off of his own rather unfavorable image, attacked Wilson as a champion of "Reaganomics" and as an opponent of a nuclear freeze. In both cases, Brown was able to keep the issues in the campaign limelight by focusing on the economic recession and high unemployment and by continually portraying Republican Wilson as guilty by association with Reagan's economic policies. He attempted to characterize Wilson's opposition to the California nuclear freeze ballot initiative as support for nuclear weapons development and the arms race. Wilson, who opposed the initiative's specific content but not the notion of arms control (he said he wanted actual reductions rather than a freeze in place), attacked Brown as deliberately misrepresenting his position.

Brown and Wilson argued the issue of Social Security reform, and Wilson spent a great deal of time attacking Brown as weak on law and order. Of the twelve campaigns examined, this campaign featured the greatest variety of issues debated and the most rancorous attacks by candidates on each other—and the most voluminous newspaper coverage.[5]

Variations in News Coverage of Senate Campaigns

Clearly, the quantity of news coverage of Senate campaigns can vary tremendously. This variation may be attributable entirely to press decisions about what to print or entirely to candidate actions. It may be that even though a challenger is campaigning efficiently and aggressively, his campaign receives scant coverage because political editors decide early on that the race is not particularly newsworthy. Or it may be that members of the press approach all races with essentially the same intention to report whatever happens and that some candidates simply are less active than others. The former interpretation places responsibility for light campaign coverage directly on the press and suggests that an editor might deliberately ignore a campaign regardless of how serious or energetic the efforts of the challenger may be. According to this view, a low-key campaign ensues in large part because reporters have already decided that the race is not going to generate much news.[6]

At the other extreme is the possibility that the amount of news coverage of a race is governed by decisions made not by the press but by the candidates—that reporters write about whatever candidates are doing or saying and that low-key races occur whenever candidates, particularly challengers, fail to generate news events. According to this view, a challenger who cannot afford campaign travel, who is inept, or who perhaps is not entirely serious about his or her candidacy attracts little media attention because he makes few campaign appearances or statements. These possibilities define two ends of a continuum; falling somewhere between them is the notion that the press decide in advance neither to ignore a race nor to cover a candidate's every move but instead look for campaigns that contain elements and events that might be controversial or otherwise merit news coverage. If nothing happens to justify their attention, regardless of how hard the challenger is trying to attract it, editors and reporters will turn their attention elsewhere.

The four case studies above suggest that each of these explanations applies in certain situations. A Senate race with candidates of *solid political background* that shows promise of developing into a *horse race* receives more press attention from the start. The degree to which a campaign provokes *conflict or controversy* influences whether reporters are assigned to a race and how much space their stories are given, and *can-*

didate behavior can have an effect on the amount of coverage received. One of the most common elements to appear in definitions of news is that it involves noteworthy people. In Gans's (1979, 10) study of who makes news, senators and congressmen ranked soon after the president and presidential candidates as being among "the most newsworthy people." Fenno (1982, 10) had no trouble identifying the more newsworthy of the two types of congressman in the campaigns he traveled with: "I cannot recall an instance in which a reporter accompanied us for a day during a House campaign, but reporters are frequent daily companions in senatorial campaigns." Fenno attributed reporters' greater interest in Senate campaigns to a generally greater interest in senators as a "class of politicians" and to a greater interest in the Senate as a legislative body. He concluded that incumbent senators are often newsworthy even when they do not draw attention to themselves. According to Tidmarch and Karp (1981), "Senators *and their challengers* are seen as anything ranging from slightly to vastly more deserving of coverage than the House candidates as a lot. . . . Reporters and editors tend to view the words and deeds of Senators *and aspiring Senators* as more newsworthy" (emphasis added).

The notion that some candidates are covered more readily than others, not because of the events and activities of their campaigns, but on the basis of a preconceived perception of their newsworthiness, may also account for why some Senate challengers are covered more than others. In his study of reporters and public officials, Dunn (1969, 25–26) found that "the 'bigger' the name, the more newsworthy are the events with which the name is associated." As Vermeer (1982, 18) put it, newsworthy people are those who have done something worth reporting in the past and are, in consequence, likely to be newsworthy in the future. In some cases the current or recent occupation of one individual may gain him more news attention than another. We have already observed that the national media consider the president to be automatically newsworthy, no matter what he does. A governor may well enjoy the same status with the media in his own state.[7] One governor claimed to have been "the focal point of attention almost every day" on the 14 television stations and in the 150 newspapers in his state. Jerry Brown not only was governor of the largest state but had, through his interests in Buddhism, rock star Linda Ronstadt, and space research, achieved a sort of celebrity status as well. It seems reasonable to assume that Brown's Senate campaign would have attracted a fair measure of media coverage even if he and San Diego Mayor Wilson had not engaged in a mudslinging contest. We saw in chapter 2 that virtually all governors and former senators, plus most congressmen (especially those whose constituencies encompassed large proportions of the state) and big city mayors, manage to wage hard-fought campaigns. It is possible that quite apart from any benefit these candidates derived from their experience in the areas of political fund-raising or the staging of campaign media events, their initial status in the hierarchy of inherently newsworthy figures led reporters to pay more attention to the campaigns of Brown and Wilson than they would have given to the campaigns of less notable figures.[8]

Of the challengers in the case studies above, neither Pétri nor Richardson had any initial status with the press; they were virtually invisible figures at the time they ran for Senate. However, among the 12 races examined, there were several in which the small amount of press coverage of the race cannot be accounted for simply by this "initial status" explanation. James Collins's Texas race in 1982, for example, received almost no news coverage, despite the fact that he was a congressman. True, he was only one of 24 Texas congressmen and therefore would have had less chance than a representative from a smaller state (such as Kasten) to acquire an identity with members of the press around his state, but even the *Dallas Morning News* ignored his campaign, and he was one of Dallas's representatives in the House. On the other hand, Pete Wilson, though he was the mayor of California's second largest city, was not well known statewide, yet his Senate campaign was the subject of extensive news coverage. These examples suggest that prior credentials alone do not explain the extent of news coverage a campaign receives.

The "horse race" element of campaign coverage is widely acknowledged by journalists.[9] Commenting on how news organizations decide which presidential primary candidates to cover, ABC News correspondent Brit Hume ("Campaigning on Cue" 1986) observed, "There's no question that the horse race analogy affects all of the coverage, or almost all of the coverage. The issues coverage is secondary." In Hume's view, what matters "to people in the street is who's going to win and who's ahead." If a key concern in campaign news coverage is the "horse race," it should not be surprising that Senate races in which challengers are perceived to have a good chance of winning receive more press attention than races whose results are a foregone conclusion. In many races it is clear that the nominee is in the race because other, more viable candidates have chosen not to run; stronger candidates may have decided that the incumbent is too formidable, or they may feel that the time is not right for their party and so stay out of the race. If editors and reporters are aware that a challenger is his party's token candidate, they may conclude early on that he has no chance of winning, and their conviction may be confirmed by early polls. Despite any inherent importance of the

U.S. Senate or of the process by which senators are elected, in cases where there is no "horse race" editors may feel that the campaign will be of no interest to their audience.

In 1974 in Wisconsin, one-term state senator Petri was essentially unknown outside his own state senate district, had very little political experience, and had few ties to the Republican party in the state. He was unable to obtain more than a small amount of funding from his party or from other potential contributors in Wisconsin. In fact, some of his Republican colleagues publicly stated that nobody expected him to win. This lack of support and early poll results were undoubtedly noted by editors deciding how to allocate resources to cover the 1974 Senate campaign. Essentially, foregone conclusions do not make good copy, no matter how intelligent or energetic the challenger proves to be. As Hershey (1984, 22) put it, "The media focus on likely winners; a candidate who is reported to be trailing will rapidly lose the spotlight." But the spotlight in a one-sided race does not necessarily remain on the "likely winner" either. At least in Senate elections, it appears that tight races, not likely winners, attract press attention. Press coverage of the six low-key races explored earlier suggests that the media focus less on the "likely winners" in Senate races for a compelling reason: senators who are already front-runners do not engage in active campaigning if they can possibly avoid it.

These considerations may in fact have influenced the decision of editors at the *Milwaukee Journal* and the *San Francisco Chronicle* not to assign reporters to follow Petri or Richardson full-time around their states. Yet it is not always the case that the overriding importance of an event's content determines whether it will receive any news coverage. In 1968, for example, former South Dakota Governor Archie Gubbrud joined other state Republican candidates in riding a campaign train through part of the state for a week during August. The *Sioux Falls Argus Leader* ran seven articles about this event. Little of what Gubbrud actually said was reported; the news stories, which were quite brief, focused mainly on such topics as who was on board, where the train stopped, and its next destination. The *Milwaukee Journal* could presumably have accorded the same level of coverage to Petri's walking tour of Wisconsin. But Gubbrud's tour was considered newsworthy in his state, while Petri's was not in his. Richardson's efforts in California received equally negligible coverage from the *San Francisco Chronicle*. Consequently, although both Petri and Richardson put in long hours throughout their campaigns, and although neither lacked for positions on issues, neither campaign received much news coverage. Even in races where the challenger is politically experienced and well known statewide and where the outcome is expected to be close, there is no guarantee that a reporter will be assigned to cover the campaign regularly. Kayden reported that in Indiana Senator Birch Bayh's 1974 campaign against Indianapolis Mayor Richard Lugar, "no newspaper reporters were assigned to cover the campaign on a regular basis, though the more important papers in the state would send reporters to travel with the candidate for varying periods of time" (1978, 125).

There are indications in other races as well that reporters and editors may make deliberate decisions to deemphasize coverage of certain Senate races. We saw that in Hawaii in 1980, challenger Cooper Brown received almost no news coverage in the state's largest newspaper. Equipped with very little money and almost no name recognition, Brown also attempted to attract media coverage by walking around the state. In what was, ironically, one of the only mentions of Brown's campaign in the *Honolulu Star Bulletin*, a member of his campaign committee protested in a letter to the editor:

> Brown . . . set out on June 30 to walk from Waialua Sugar Mill on the North Shore to Kailua. . . . His week-long walk . . . was done without the use of gimmicks. It therefore was not deemed "newsworthy" by the local television stations. The following weekend, Brown walked and talked to the residents of Molokai. Again, he did it without gimmicks and again, his efforts were considered not worthy of news coverage despite the fact that a video tape crew covered his activities there. (9 August 1980, A-9)

Evidently, not only were the news media well aware of Brown's appearance but a television crew had been sent to record it. But the event was reported neither on television nor in the newspaper. In Idaho in 1984, another practically invisible challenger, Democrat Pete Busch, was running a very poorly financed campaign against incumbent James McClure. In an article focusing on the hopelessness of Busch's effort, reporter Aaron Epstein noted that "the local paper and TV were invited to his appearances. But they didn't show up" (*Portland Oregonian*, 22 October 1984, B-2). In both cases, the candidates *were* campaigning, and the news media *were* aware of their itineraries in advance, but the events were not reported.

The Kasten-Nelson race in 1980 also demonstrates press interest in the "horse race" aspects of a Senate campaign. Neither the Republicans' September 9 primary nor Kasten's campaign during the rest of September received much media coverage. But as soon as Kasten's poll appeared showing him tied with Nelson, Kasten's campaign began to be covered.

It is true that at this same point Senator Nelson began campaigning in earnest (undoubtedly in response to the Kasten poll), and this alone would have generated some increase in coverage. But it would not adequately explain the emergence of stories in the *Milwaukee Journal* that did not focus directly on Nelson.[10] Articles on Kasten's campaign, such as those entitled "Kasten fights chill, Nelson" (5 October 1980, 3) and "Kasten campaigns in traditional ways" (18 October 1980, 11), began to appear. It seems that when the incumbent was perceived to be a likely victor, the press had little interest in covering Kasten's actions. When it became evident that the race might be a close one after all, the Senate campaign became newsworthy.

The emergence of widespread polling in Senate elections has undoubtedly had an increasing impact on the decisions editors make about how to cover Senate races. John Chancellor, of NBC News ("Campaigning on Cue" 1986), observed that a presidential primary candidate's standing in the polls strongly affects news reporter's decisions about whether to cover him. Robinson and Sheehan (1983, 83), referring to the 1980 presidential race, wrote: "Obviously for both media [CBS network news and the UPI wire service] the single most important criterion for granting newsspace, before the caucus and primary voting began, was standing in the polls." Goldenberg and Traugott (1985, 7) suggested that in the 1984 Senate race in Michigan, "had the polls indicated a closer contest, news coverage might have been even heavier." Nowadays, nearly all Senate candidates commission polls, and information about how well a challenger is doing is made available to news organizations either by the candidates themselves or through the news organizations' commissioning their own polls. It is therefore easier for editors to make informed initial decisions about whether to concentrate on a Senate race (e.g., reassign reporters away from their regular beats). Moreover, the release of poll results itself often constitutes a news event. In the hard-fought Brown-Wilson race, between August 1 and Election Day eight news stories in the *San Francisco Chronicle* and five in the *Los Angeles Times* focused primarily on the results of recent polls. In low-key races, on the other hand, it is rare to find stories about poll results. The *Milwaukee Journal* published no polls during the Petri-Nelson race in 1974. Nor was there any mention of the Williams-Norcross Senate race in *Newark Star-Ledger* reports on their Eagleton Poll or the Grambling Poll in late September 1976.

While editors may decide early in a campaign that without a horse race it will not be worth covering, they doubtless consider as well whether the candidates are providing that ingredient so essential to the news: *controversy*. As many journalism texts put it, controversy is a basic and necessary element of news.[11] According to Epstein (1973, 4), Reuven Frank, when he was executive editor of NBC Evening News, told his staff that "every news story should, without any sacrifice of probity or responsibility, display the attributes of fiction, of drama. It should have structure and conflict, problem and denouement, rising action and falling action." Joslyn (1984, 77) put it this way:

> It is up to candidates to say or do something to attract free media coverage. On one level, this means timing campaign appearances to accommodate media production schedules; providing media representatives with typewriters, telephone lines, and press releases; and arranging the travel and accommodations of traveling journalists. . . . *On another level, however, it means providing stories* that can be simplified and condensed, *that contain drama or conflict,* that present something novel or unexpected, and that lend themselves to stories about the likely outcome of the campaign. (Emphasis added)

In low-key races, light press coverage may stem from a lack of controversy, or conflict, between the opponents. In most low-key races there is little reason for conflict, because incumbents try not to respond to challengers' attacks. A common strategy of incumbents facing weak or little-known challengers is to refuse to debate them, figuring that debates will produce media coverage, which could help increase the challenger's name recognition. In California in 1974, gubernatorial nominee Jerry Brown "started the campaign with a huge lead in the polls, and he schemed to stay ahead by making his contest with Republican Houston Flournoy as dull as possible" (Leary 1977, 1). Said Brown's campaign manager: "It was our feeling that the less coverage the better. . . . The duller the race the better. We wanted this dull, dull campaign" (ibid., 33). This strategy can backfire if the refusal to debate becomes a campaign issue itself and thus draws news coverage. Some incumbents, therefore, agree to debate but establish ground rules—such as forbidding direct exchanges—that make it difficult for the challenger to place the incumbent on the defensive.

Reasonably certain that they would win comfortably, neither Nelson (in 1974) nor Cranston did much campaigning, and both ignored their opponents whenever possible. According to Patterson (1980, 22), "An incumbent who ignores his challenger altogether and indeed spends little time campaigning gives the press little incentive to cover a race." With one side refusing to talk, it is difficult for the other side to establish a dialogue; if there is no dialogue, there is little news to report other than what the challenger is saying. And unless he is very clever, the challenger in this position is likely to exhaust his supply of "out-of-the-ordinary" things to say fairly quickly. This is not to say that incumbents can avoid campaigning altogether; according to Senator Daniel Inouye, there is an optimum balance. As he observed about his race in 1980: "One might look at this race and conclude, 'Well, he doesn't have to do anything.' But I've been in this business long enough to know that if I didn't do anything there would be a natural reaction from some people . . . that I would be taking things for granted. . . . On the other hand, if I spent a lot of money and made myself highly visible, there would be an . . . opposite reaction that I am trying to do too much" (*Honolulu Star Bulletin*, 21 September 1980, A-2). In fact, Inouye stayed in Washington that year until just before Election Day.

That there is little dialogue between opponents does not preclude the challenger's attacking the incumbent in the hope of generating some controversy of interest to the press. According to Joslyn (1984, 108), "To a journalist, observable conflict is one of the handiest ways of presenting either a real or a contrived drama. Using conflict may simply mean reporting the charges and countercharges/responses made by the newsmakers." Petri reduced his chances for coverage by deliberately not attacking his incumbent opponent on issues. This may have earned him the admiration of members of the Wisconsin press, but it did little to enhance the likelihood that they would cover his campaign. With the controversy angle removed from the press's grasp, Petri proceeded to remove still another chance for attracting coverage: the possibility that reporters might point out differences between the candidates even if the candidates themselves refused to do so. Instead of putting forth a set of clear alternatives to Nelson (other than suggesting himself as "new leadership"), Petri actually emphasized that he and Nelson shared many of the same issue positions.

Richardson, by contrast, did attack Cranston on issues. But he also attacked his own party and its candidates. His attacks on Cranston generally were all alike and drew no response from the incumbent. The few reporters assigned to his campaign likely grew tired of repeating the same story. Early in the Richardson campaign the *San Francisco Chronicle*, which later covered the Brown-Wilson race quite heavily, stopped repeating Richardson's unanswered attacks on Cranston and the "liberal mentality." We know from the *Los Angeles Times*'s more continuous coverage that Richardson continued to make such attacks, but even the *Times* began to concentrate more on the eccentricities of Richardson's campaign than on reiterating his issue positions.

These events speak to the general point that Patterson (1980, 30) made about presidential campaigns, namely, that "once a candidate makes known his position on an issue, further statements concerning that issue decline in news value." Hershey (1984, 23) contended that repetition of "a small number of themes quickly becomes old news, because news, to reporters and editors, is what's different, what's out of the ordinary." What is "out of the ordinary," however, is not always what a challenger would like the press to cover, and candidates' attempts to generate favorable coverage can backfire. In 1982 Congressman James Collins challenged Texas Senator Lloyd Bentsen. Collins tried to carry on a lively campaign by attacking the incumbent as a liberal. Collins's campaign was very lightly covered even in his own district's *Dallas Morning News* (see appendix 2). Collins did spend considerable time and energy pushing a "Liberal Lloyd" campaign; the *Morning News* wrote on September 6 (8-A): "James Collins is crisscrossing the state and using the airwaves to bombard listeners with a broken-record refrain—Lloyd Bentsen is a liberal . . . a liberal . . . a liberal . . . a liberal." But as the tone of this report indicates, this message was not considered worthy of sustained news coverage. Another reporter pointed out (ibid., 15 August 1982, 3-G) that the "liberal" accusation against Bentsen was not even very accurate, and coverage of this aspect of Collins's campaign was quite sparse. However, it was considered newsworthy indeed when Collins released a private poll showing a fellow Republican, Governor Bill Clements, trailing in his race for reelection against challenger Mark White. That Collins would voluntarily make public information detrimental to a candidate of his own party was seen by some as simply an error in judgment, but others viewed it as a calculated effort to lend credibility to the poll's other finding—that Collins was pulling close to Bentsen in the Senate race. While the Collins-Bentsen part of the poll was reported on just once, on August 13, the Collins "faux pas" and Clements's angry reaction were mentioned prominently in *Morning News* articles and commentaries on August 18, 25, and 30 and September 6, 11, and 24.

In striking contrast to the absence of conflict in the low-key races, both the Nelson-Kasten and the Brown-Wilson race were loaded with debate between and attacks by both candidates and their followers. In Wisconsin, instead of ignoring Kasten's accusations and attacks on his records, incumbent Nelson responded in kind. Charges reported one day were followed by countercharges reported the next day. The two debated several times. The ongoing controversy made reporters' work easy. They did not have to look for a new angle to the same old story—Kasten attacks Nelson—because Nelson was attacking Kasten as well.

A similar level of controversy characterized the open-seat race in California in 1982. Table 8 distinguishes between headlines involving conflict

TABLE 8
Conflict-oriented versus Other Types of News Stories in Two Newspapers:
1982 Senate Race between Jerry Brown and Pete Wilson, August 1–November 1

	Los Angeles Times	San Francisco Chronicle
Conflict-oriented headlines		
Direct head-to-head	30	21
Candidate vs. other than opponent	17	18
News of debates (without attacks)	2	5
Focus on poll results	5	8
Fund-raising edge	6	5
	62 (62%)	57 (57%)
Reports on issue positions	17	11
Reports of candidate activities, events	3	8
Backgrounder pieces, candidate "profiles"	4	5
Endorsements	5	2
	29 (29%)	26 (26%)
Editorials, opinion columns, articles in which the headline gave little indication of the content	7	19
TOTAL HEADLINE STORIES	98	102

and those reporting on events or candidates' issue positions where no antagonism was evident.

It turns out that 62 percent of the *Los Angeles Times's* stories and 57 percent of the *San Francisco Chronicle*'s focused on some sort of conflict between the Brown and Wilson camps or between one of the candidates and a third party (e.g., between Wilson and other Republicans over whether federal judges should be elected, or between Brown and Democratic gubernatorial candidate Tom Bradley, who continually tried to distance himself from Brown's record as governor). Only 29 percent and 26 percent, respectively, of the two papers' stories were straight reports of events or candidates' issue positions. Of course, we cannot know whether the papers would have maintained this high level of overall coverage if conflict had not permeated this campaign. Perhaps any governor or other well-known candidate running for higher office would be covered just as extensively. But given press norms, the likelihood that conflict between the candidates is what generates "news" about a race must be considered a primary reason for extensive coverage of a campaign.

In discussing press norms with respect to conflict and controversy, we have suggested that *candidates' own actions and decisions* can also affect the level of coverage their campaigns receive. A candidate's ability to engage in a dialogue seems strongly to influence campaign coverage. Throughout the course of a campaign, candidates and their staffs must also make decisions about how and when to make local appearances, publicize issue positions, and otherwise conduct themselves. As Hershey stated, "Campaigners soon learn that to get much-needed media exposure, they must generate the kind of activities that reporters and editors define as newsworthy. If the prevailing definition of 'news' among media people refers to a timely and discrete event that is controversial or dramatic in tone, then candidates who want media coverage must supply these qualities" (1984, 21).

There are many accounts of how candidates and their staffs—in presidential and subpresidential campaigns alike—have tried to manipulate news coverage by creating "media events."[12] Journalists acknowledge that such attempts are made, and some have tried to resist these efforts. But other news organizations are just as glad to encounter "media events," since they usually provide easy stories.

Petri chose a method of campaigning against Nelson that would have required editors to assign someone to travel with him if he were to be covered continuously. The editors of Wisconsin's largest newspaper made the decision not to expend a reporter in this way, largely because they judged that Petri would lose badly and because they did not feel that a walking campaign was interesting enough to merit their constant attention. Perhaps Petri could not afford to travel widely around a state as expansive as Wisconsin, but removing himself for long stretches of time from the vicinity of the news organizations in the state's largest media markets did not help him gain visibility. Richardson, too, often seemed uninterested in cultivating news coverage. He preferred to meet with small groups of people, some of whom were already his supporters. On several occasions, even when the press were on the scene, Richardson seemed more inclined to avoid them than to seek them out.

When challengers who are not automatic subjects for news coverage themselves are able to find ways of associating with more prominent party leaders, they can attract considerable coverage to their campaigns. David Rosenbloom (1973, 40) reported that George Bush's 1970 Senate campaign in Texas, in addition to being "well-supplied with money and professional campaign management," was "blessed with an almost continuous airlift of Cabinet members, Republican Congressional leaders, the Vice President and even the President himself." This "traveling road show was very heavily covered by television news, nationally almost every night and locally wherever the high-level officials stopped."[13] In California, as we have seen, Richardson refused throughout most of the campaign to associate himself with either Governor Reagan or President Ford, who were themselves the subjects of a good deal of media coverage during the 1974 campaign: Governor Reagan because he was expected to run for president in 1976, President Ford because the president is always covered. Richardson's approach contrasted sharply with that of Kasten in 1980, who met with nationally prominent Republicans whenever they were in his state and set aside his differences with Wisconsin's popular Republican governor to make appearances with him also. All of these meetings afforded Kasten newspaper coverage he would not otherwise have received (and, whenever the presidential candidates were in town, probably television news coverage as well).

What we have seen of challengers' political backgrounds and of press coverage of Senate campaigns leads to the suggestion of the following dynamic. Certain challengers to Senate incumbents have an established political track record and have, through holding previous office, become recognized by at least some voters in their state. Their names might not be household words, but they are not entirely invisible either. These challengers, usually governors, congressmen, big-city mayors, or former holders of these offices, have by virtue of their political background established ties with contributors and party elites. Such ties, plus their already established statewide name recognition, make them viable candidates for senator in the eyes of the press. Incumbents, pressured by a challenge, have to decide whether to respond to their challengers' criticisms and attacks. The media, already inclined to cover the activities of these challengers, are even more inclined to cover an ongoing dialogue, where they can report charges, reactions, and countercharges.

On the other hand, challengers without the political background to give them name recognition are likely to receive little initial press attention, since they lack ties to party elites and may be poorly funded and show badly in the polls; many such challengers were nominated only after potentially stronger candidates declined to run. Unless challengers can overcome these deficiencies, a lack of news coverage of their campaigns will aid neither their empty campaign coffers nor their standing in the polls, and there will be no incentive for further press attention. In essence, press coverage may further polarize "strong" and "weak" candidates by giving more name recognition to candidates who already have some and by ignoring candidates who are initially unknown, thereby making it difficult for them to gain even a little recognition.

One implication of this dynamic is that the amount of press coverage different Senate campaigns receive is not only a function of the activities of the candidates and of the initial impressions of political reporters and editors. There is evidence that low-key races feature fewer events, and are less "busy," than hard-fought campaigns, but one point that has emerged from the preceding case studies is that lightly covered campaigns are not simply the result of low-energy challengers' spending little time on the campaign trail. The Richardson campaign may have made a number of foolish mistakes and may even have wasted its resources, but Richardson was out there day after day trying to get his views across to a statewide audience, as was Petri in Wisconsin. In Minnesota in 1976 Republican Gerald Brekke took on the formidable, even hopeless, task of challenging Hubert Humphrey. Instead of running an easygoing campaign, reported the *Grand Forks Herald*, Brekke did everything he could with almost no funding, spending long days on the road "traveling around the state alone in his farm pickup. . . . At first, he slept in a sleeping bag in the pickup, but now he stays with relatives wherever he can" (13 October 1976). Energy and daily campaign activity were not the missing ingredients in Brekke's effort to win election, nor in Cooper Brown's in Hawaii or Pete Busch's in Idaho. What was lacking was the translation of all this activity into press coverage.

Of course, part of the reason for these uneventful races is lack of money. If candidates are running on a shoestring, they cannot hope to stage as many "media events," cannot fly to as many places—in short, cannot make as much "news"—as candidates with substantial financial and staff resources can. Another reason some of the low-key races are as "inactive" as they are, and therefore provide fewer events worthy of news coverage, is that the candidates may be inept in their pursuit of such coverage. And a candidate who does not seriously see himself winning the election in the first place may not particularly care about attracting news coverage of his campaign. The information produced in Senate campaigns has varied effects on the public at whom it is directed; there are corresponding effects on the vote decision process when news coverage provides voters with information about one, both, or neither of the candidates in a Senate campaign.[14]

5. The Effect of Campaign Intensity on the Vote Decision

The amount of information disseminated by the news media varies considerably across Senate races, and the volume of news about the candidates in hard-fought races is considerably greater, on average, than in low-key races. This diversity of news coverage affects individuals' vote decisions in Senate elections by causing variations in the amount of contact voters have with Senate candidates through the news media, the level of information they have about Senate candidates, and the ways that information affects their decisions on whether to vote for their party's candidate or to defect.

Voter Attention to Senate Campaign News Coverage

In order to assess the effects on voters of the information directed at them through the news media during a campaign, we need to know not only how attentive the electorate are to Senate elections but whether their attentiveness is affected by the intensity of the Senate race. As part of this assessment, the extent to which voters come into contact with senators and Senate challengers must be measured as well. The 1978 Center for Political Studies National Election Study's biennial November survey asked respondents the following question:

> There are many ways in which U.S. Senators have contact with the people from their states. On this page are some of these ways. Think of [name of incumbent]. Have you come into contact with or learned any-

thing about [him/her] through any of these ways: —met him personally? —attended a meeting or gathering where he spoke? —talked to a member of his staff or someone in his office? —received something in the mail from him? —read about him in a newspaper or magazine? —heard him on the radio? —saw him on TV?

The survey goes on to ask, "How about [name of challenger] who also ran for the U.S. Senate in the last election. Have you come into contact with or learned anything about him/her through any of these ways?" It should be noted that these questions do not refer specifically to the current campaign. Where incumbents are concerned, respondents might be thinking of the present campaign, of the senator's last few years in office, or even of his entire career as they frame their answers. This ambiguity of referent occurs in part because the three media-related questions are preceded by questions referring to contacts made either by the member or by his staff, through the mail or in person. This line of questioning is as likely to bring to the respondent's mind *casework* and other longer-term associations as it is to suggest only campaign-related contacts. Responses about challengers, on the other hand, are much more likely to refer specifically to the current campaign, since in many cases the campaign represents the only contact the respondent has ever had with that candidate.[1]

The proportion of respondents who had heard about hard-fought and low-key Senate races on television, on the radio, or through reading newspapers or magazines in 1978 is shown in table 9. The responses indicate clear differences in people's attention to hard-fought and low-key Senate races. In hard-fought Senate campaigns, two-thirds of respondents claimed to have seen both the incumbent and the challenger on television (the question makes no distinction between advertising and news coverage), and half said they had read about both candidates in newspapers or magazines. The proportion is much lower for radio, doubtless reflecting this medium's relatively sparse news coverage. This contrasts strikingly with the attention given to the candidates in low-key Senate campaigns. Only one-fourth of respondents said they had seen both candidates on television or had read about both candidates in the newspaper, and only one in ten had heard about both candidates on the radio. The vast majority of the rest either reported that they had heard of neither candidate or recalled noticing the incumbent only. It is perhaps not surprising that people would have heard only of the incumbent in a low-key race, since incumbents spend considerable time both during campaigns and during the course of their tenure in office attempting to establish a positive image with their constituents. Some incumbents cam-

TABLE 9

Electorate's Attention to Various Media in Hard-fought and Low-key Senate Campaigns, Incumbents Running, 1978 (in percent)

Respondent has come into contact with:	Newspapers or Magazines		Radio		Television	
	Hard-fought (N=606)	Low-key (N=203)	Hard-fought (N=606)	Low-key (N=203)	Hard-fought (N=606)	Low-key (N=203)
Both incumbent and challenger	52	24	31	11	68	25
Incumbent only	11	26	11	21	8	34
Challenger only	4	4	4	2	4	1
Neither candidate	33	47	54	66	20	41
TOTAL*	100%	100%	100%	100%	100%	101%

Source: 1978 CPS/NES survey.
* Percentage totals may exceed 100% due to rounding.

paign vigorously for reelection even against only token opposition (an extreme case was Russell Long, who spent nearly $500,000 in 1974 even though he was unopposed). But most telling is the fact that in the low-key races 52 percent did not recall reading anything *even about the incumbent,* and 42 percent said they had not seen even the incumbent on television.

This difference in voter attention levels between hard-fought and low-key Senate races is consistent with my findings about news coverage of Senate campaigns. In hard-fought races the media devote considerable news coverage to both the incumbent and the challenger, and most people report having seen both candidates as a result. In low-key races, on the other hand, press coverage tends to be minimal, even though challengers may campaign diligently and may on rare occasions even outspend the incumbents. News coverage of low-key campaigns is generally so light, in fact, that a portion of the respondents in the CPS/NES survey who indicated some recollection of incumbent contact were likely referring to contact with the incumbent as an officeholder rather than as a campaigner. But regardless of how incumbents have managed to communicate—whether during their time in office or in previous campaigns—the CPS/NES data underscore the point that when news coverage of a campaign is extremely light, it is unlikely that the *challenger* will become very well known to much of the electorate. Goldenberg and Traugott's work on the 1984 Michigan Senate campaign corroborates the point that an individual's information about a pair of candidates depends largely on the amount of media coverage the campaign received: "The amount of information available to readers with roughly equivalent reading habits varies considerably depending on the content of their newspapers. . . . Overall, the heavier the coverage of the Senate race in a person's newspaper, the more likely was that person to be able to recognize and rate the candidates" (1985, 8).

THE VISIBILITY OF SENATE CHALLENGERS

Political scientists have assumed that "few incumbent presidents, governors or senators face challengers who fail to become known by the electorate" (Luttbeg 1983, 412), that "publicity comes automatically to a statewide challenger" (Mann and Wolfinger 1980, 622), and that Senate races "provide a choice between two candidates known and in contact with the voters" (Hinckley 1981, 50). This conventional wisdom is not borne out by our findings. We know that 43 percent of Senate races from 1968 through 1984 (and fully half of those races in which incumbents were running) were low-key affairs; with low-key Senate races typically garnering very little news coverage, Senate challengers in such races are by no means well known to the electorate. As far as personal contacts are concerned, only a minute proportion of respondents to the 1978 CPS/ NES question cited above—on contacts with candidates—reported any personal contact with a challenger; more than two-thirds claimed never to have received any mail from the challenger. For challengers, then, means of "contact" seem to be limited almost exclusively to media sources. There is good reason, then, to question the widely held belief that all Senate challengers are or ever become extremely well-known and to take a closer look at the generalizations made about Senate challengers.

The 1978 CPS/NES Survey and Senate Elections Research

In addition to the survey question examined above, the 1978 CPS/NES survey contained a battery of questions tapping respondents' perceptions of congressional candidates. These items, which tested whether respondents could recognize and evaluate House and Senate candidates, led to the first systematic studies comparing voting in House and Senate elections. Prior to the 1978 survey, the CPS/NES, as well as most other national polls, had asked respondents to *recall* the names of the candidates. But tapping voters' recall ability is not the relevant test if one's goal is to see how many citizens cast votes having knowledge of the candidates. The relevant test is whether, when they enter the voting booth, voters *recognize* a candidate's name printed on the ballot.

One of the most widely reported findings to come out of studies based on the 1978 CPS/NES survey was that House members are a great deal more familiar to voters than their challengers, while Senate challengers are nearly as well known as Senate incumbents.[2] The extent of these House-Senate differences is displayed in table 10, which indicates for both House and Senate elections the percentage of voters able to recognize incumbents, challengers, and candidates for open seats.

There was a 41-point difference between voters' ability to recognize and rate Senate challengers and their ability to recognize and rate House challengers, which is indeed striking. Citing this difference in her work on congressional elections, Hinckley (1981) theorized that voters use very different decision rules in House and Senate elections. In House races, she suggested, the challenger is virtually unknown to most voters, and thus the vote decision fits a "general-choice" model, in which the vote is based on party identification, perception of party positions, or habit (choosing the incumbent because he was chosen before). In Senate elections, she suggested, both candidates are well known, and the voting decision fits a "specific-choice" model, in which "the voters know a choice must be made and can use specific information for a decision" (33). In essence, she concluded, because both candidates are known to them, voters compare the specific attributes of Senate candidates before deciding between them.

Similar differences between House and Senate elections were noted by Ragsdale (1981, 213): "Voters' final decisions [in Senate elections] rest on a choice they can make between two alternatives," whereas "for many House voters the decision has already been made—by default, in the absence of challenger information." Hinckley (1981, 134) summed up the House-Senate distinction this way: "In congressional races, information varies with the office contested and the kind of candidate. Senate candidates are visible enough to be recognized and to be cited for their contact with voters. People have had 'some contact with' or 'learned something about' the two competing candidates. In many House races, in contrast, voters know one but not the other of the competitors: incumbents are known and the challengers are not."

But this generalization, to the extent that it refers to Senate challengers, is in fact overdrawn. The widely cited point that Senate challengers are as well known as the incumbents they run against seriously overestimates the actual proportion of Senate challengers who manage to become known to the voters. As a matter of fact, the dynamics of many Senate

TABLE 10
Voter Familiarity with House and Senate Candidates, 1978

Candidate	Percentage of Voters Able to		Percentage of Voters Having Some Contact with Candidate
	Recognize Candidate	*Recognize and Rate Candidate*	
Incumbent			
Senate	99	95	97
House	97	92	94
DIFFERENCE	2	3	3
Challenger			
Senate	93	85	85
House	63	44	46
DIFFERENCE	30	41	39
Open seat			
Senate	95	88	93
House	92	74	77
DIFFERENCE	3	14	16

Sources: The data on recognized candidates are adapted from Mann and Wolfinger 1980, 623, table 4; the remaining data are adapted from Hinckley 1980a, 644, table 1.

elections are more similar to those of House elections. Had it been possible for the 1978 CPS/NES survey to sample voters from all Senate elections that year, this similarity would have been more evident, and the generalizations about Senate elections cited above would probably not have been as readily formulated or accepted. What, then, are the particular biases of the 1978 CPS/NES survey that detract from its usefulness in the study of Senate elections?

PROBLEMS WITH THE 1978 CPS/NES SAMPLE

A national sample can be an ideal tool for studying voters' responses in presidential and House elections, but it is not as well suited to studying Senate elections.[3] Because only two-thirds of states elect senators in any election year, the respondents from states holding Senate elections are a substantially reduced subset of the national sample. Moreover, the size of the reduction varies considerably across the three classes of Senate seats and is a particular problem in years with Class 2 elections, as shown below:

Proportion of the U.S. Population in Each Senate Class (1980 Census)

Class 1 seats (1970, 1976, 1982) 75%

Class 2 seats (1972, 1978, 1984) 52%

Class 3 seats (1974, 1980, 1986) 72%

The relatively small proportion of people in Class 2 election states is due to the coincidence that only one of the nation's five largest states holds a Senate election in this set of years. The other four largest states elect their senators in Class 1 and Class 3 years, so that in 1974, 1976, 1980, and 1982 about three-fourths of the respondents in a random national sample come from states having Senate elections. In years such as 1978 and 1984, however, only 52 percent of the respondents come from states holding Senate elections. This underrepresentation of respondents from states holding Senate elections in the Class 2 years is compounded by the fact that in midterm election years turnout is usually less than 40 percent of eligible voters (in 1978 it was 35 percent). Thus, a random sample of two thousand respondents in a Class 2 election year in which there is no presidential election would include fewer than five hundred people voting in a Senate election. Even the simplest tabular analysis of such data would yield very sparsely populated cells, presenting problems for statistical analysis. Indeed this was the case for the 1978 CPS/NES survey, which contained 583 respondents who voted in a November Senate election; it is a problem acknowledged by many of those who have analyzed Senate elections using this data set.

There is another significant bias inherent in the 1978 CPS/NES survey, indeed in any national random survey, related to the proportions of respondents from large and small states. In any given year, each Senate election is as important as any other; in many respects, the meaningful unit of study is the *state*. Students of Senate elections should be as interested in the voting decisions leading to the election of Alaska's senators as they are in those leading to the election of California's, and the ideal sample would draw an equal number of respondents from each of these states. But any random sample based on the national population inescapably yields a disproportionately high percentage of respondents from large states and correspondingly few from small states. This is a critical problem for all three classes of Senate seats (see table 11); it is most pronounced in Class 1 years, when there are Senate races in 10 of the nation's 11 most populated states and in 5 of its 6 least populated, resulting in 62 percent of the sample coming from the largest quartile of states and only 3 percent from smallest quartile.

The population of the single largest state in Class 1 (California) is eight times that of the five smallest states *combined*. In any national random sample drawn in a Class 1 election year, the eight largest states will provide over 20 times as many respondents as the eight smallest states. The area sampling method used in most national surveys can compound

TABLE II
Percentage Distribution of State Populations by Senate Class

State Quartiles, Grouped by Population	Class 1 (N = 33)	Class 2 (N = 33)	Class 3 (N = 34)
Top	62%	55%	59%
Second	26	27	23
Third	9	13	14
Bottom	3	5	4
TOTAL	100%	100%	100%

Source: Derived from 1980 census: U.S. Department of Commerce, Bureau of the Census, Current Population Report Series, Series P-25, May 1984.

Note: The percentage in the second quartile and the one in the Class 3 third quartile apply to nine states; all others to eight. For example, 62 percent of the population of Class 1 states reside in the eight most populous states of the Class.

this problem: in 1976 the CPS/NES sample included not a single respondent from any of the eight least populated states.

Clearly, then, analysis of Senate voters based on national surveys is largely an analysis of voters from large states, and any generalizations based on such analysis hold only insofar as voters in the other states behave similarly. This assumption was particularly evident in analyses of the 1978 CPS/NES survey with respect to the above-mentioned data on recognition and rating of Senate challengers. We know that in 1978 there were 20 hard-fought and 15 low-key races; of the races involving incumbents, 12 were hard-fought and 10 were low-key. In fact, the hard-fought races in 1978 occurred mainly in heavily populated states, while most of the low-key races occurred in smaller states.[4] And it is clear that voters in smaller states are undersampled in national surveys in relation to their participation in Senate elections; in 1978 the CPS/NES sample included no voters at all from five small "Senate" states but 73 voters from Michigan, 55 from Texas, and 50 from Illinois, who together constituted 43 percent of the entire sample of voters in Senate states where incumbents were running. These two facts—that most low-key contests occurred in small states and that the 1978 CPS/NES survey undersampled respondents from small states—lead to a very important point: voters from states with low-key Senate races were greatly underrepresented in the 1978 CPS/NES survey. With 80 percent of the voters in that year coming from states that had hard-fought elections, analyses of Senate elections based on such data are basically investigations of 1978's hard-fought elections. The effects of the skewed 1978 CPS/NES sample are apparent in table 12.

For most of the smaller states, there are so few respondents that the percentages should be interpreted as rough estimates only. Four of the nine states that had low-key races were not sampled at all (three of them—Alaska, Rhode Island, and Idaho—were among the year's most markedly low-key races). The mean media contact rate for challengers in the remaining five low-key states was 54 percent. The overall mean contact rate for challengers in 1978 was 81 percent (see table 10).[5] But these data overlook the substantial differences between hard-fought and low-key Senate races, and because the 1978 CPS/NES sample contains mostly voters from hard-fought races, the 81 percent figure is too high. By the same token, the overall figure in table 10 for how well voters were able to recognize and rate Senate challengers in 1978 is also undoubtedly too high. Granted, most of the challengers in hard-fought races *were* recognized by nearly all voters; this is perhaps not surprising given that across hard-fought races 88 percent of voters reported some kind of contact with these candidates. However in the low-key races the mean challenger recognition score was only 60 percent. Had the voters from the states of Alaska, Rhode Island, and Idaho been sampled—states where there were low-key races—overall familiarity ratings of the challengers would probably have been quite low, perhaps closer to the scores for the races in Georgia and Kentucky (38 percent and 31 percent) than to the low-key mean of 60 percent. The outcomes of the races in Alaska, Rhode Island, and Idaho were characterized as foregone conclusions by both *Congressional Quarterly* and the *Almanac of American Politics,* and the incumbent in each race won by a huge margin. If these missing low-key states could be included, the already low mean score for low-key races might well drop even farther, perhaps even falling below the mean recognition rate for House challengers reported in table 10.[6]

The findings in table 12 support the notion that voters' familiarity with Senate challengers is closely related to the amount of media coverage the challengers received during the campaign. However, these findings also seriously undermine the widely held view, cited by Sinclair (1983, 120) in her review of various aspects of congressional research, that based on the 1978 CPS/NES survey, "we now know that . . . House challengers are little known while Senate challengers are recognized almost as frequently as incumbents." In fact, as we have seen, data from the 1978 CPS/NES survey present a misleading picture of candidate visibility in Senate elections. While it is true that a substantial number of Senate

TABLE 12

Incumbent's Margin of Victory and Challengers' Media Contact with Voters and Recognition Rates in Hard-fought and Low-key Senate Elections, 1978

	Incumbent's Margin of Victory	Challenger's Media Contact with Voter*		Challenger's Recognition Rate§	
State		(%)	(N)	(%)	(N)
		Hard-fought Races			
Tennessee	+16	76	(33)	83	(29)
South Carolina	+12	100	(9)	100	(9)
Illinois	+8	92	(52)	94	(50)
Texas	+0	93	(57)	86	(55)
West Virginia	+0	88	(8)	100	(8)
New Hampshire	-2	—	NS	—	NS
Iowa	-4	82	(11)	100	(11)
Massachusetts	-10	85	(33)	97	(32)
Michigan	-16	91	(78)	92	(73)
Minnesota	-16	96	(22)	95	(19)
Colorado	-18	84	(25)	88	(25)
Maine	-23	73	(15)	100	(15)
MEAN	-4.4	88	(343)	92	(326)
		Low-key Races†			
Georgia	+67	33	(21)	38	(21)
Alaska	+52	—	NS	—	NS
Rhode Island	+50	—	NS	—	NS
Idaho	+36	—	NS	—	NS
Kentucky	+24	38	(16)	31	(13)
Oregon	+24	41	(17)	73	(15)
Delaware	+18	100	(12)	90	(10)
North Carolina	+9	68	(25)	74	(23)
New Mexico	+6	—	NS	—	NS
MEAN	+31.8	54	(91)	60	(82)

Source: Media contact and recognition rates are from the 1978 CPS/NES Survey.

Note: NS = no respondents were sampled from this state.

* Percentage figures represent the percentage of respondents who saw the Senate challenger on television, heard him or her on the radio, or read about him or her in newspapers or magazines.

§ Percentage figures represent the percentage of respondents who could recognize *and* rate the Senate challenger on a feeling thermometer.

† The Louisiana race was another low-key race, but Senator Johnston won the open primary with enough of a margin that under Louisiana rules he did not have to face a challenger in November.

races do pit well-recognized candidates against one another, there are many races in which the challenger never becomes well known.

An Examination of State-level Data on Senate Elections

Using state-level data removes the problem of small Senate samples inherent in national surveys and solves the problem of overrepresentation of large states at the expense of small states. Each state-level sample is representative of the state it covers and provides enough respondents for fairly detailed analysis. Interpretation of state-level surveys can be somewhat difficult due mainly to a lack of coordination among pollsters: important variables are sometimes unavailable, item wordings can differ from survey to survey, and some surveys are conducted closer to the time of the election than others. These variations must be kept in mind in making comparisons across states, and sometimes even across elections within the same state.

The data examined here were drawn from 47 Senate elections in 28 states covering the period 1964 to 1984.[7] Most of the surveys were conducted prior to Election Day, usually in mid or late October. The data comprise a reasonable cross section of elections: some are from presidential elections, and some are from off years; the states included are large and small, urban and rural, and they are not clustered in any one section of the country. Most races included incumbents, but some involved open seats as well. Appendix 3 lists the sources of the data. The state-level data are invaluable in addressing whether patterns of voter defection in Senate elections vary according to the intensity of a Senate campaign, as well as the extent to which voters' recognition of Senate candidates varies in hard-fought versus low-key races and thus influences the defection rates.

DEFECTIONS AND THE ADVANTAGE OF INCUMBENCY

In the first major study of voting behavior in congressional elections, Stokes and Miller (1962) established that a large proportion of voters in the 1958 elections were actually unfamiliar with the candidates.[8] They found that voters' choices in these elections were not based on knowledge of candidates' issue positions; rather, they were based—for lack of other cues—on voters' own party identification. The principal exceptions were voters who were able to recall the name of one, but not both, of the candidates; these voters tended to vote for the candidate they knew, who was usually the incumbent. Research on more recent elections has found that incumbency has become an increasingly effective advantage in attracting votes from the other party, leading Cover (1977, 535–36) to remark that for voters of the party whose candidate is not in office, "partisan identification is now a meaningless voting cue . . . in congressional elections."[9]

The 1978 CPS/NES data suggest that senators do not benefit from incumbency nearly as much as do House members. Research using these data has shown that most incumbent senators are able neither to attract the massive defections from the other party that prompted Cover's comment nor to hold onto votes from their own party (Abramowitz 1980, table 1). An investigation of the available state-level data yields different findings: in some races, defections from both parties are fairly evenly divided; in others, defections to one party greatly outweigh defections to the other, and not always in favor of the incumbent.[10] In the 1976 contest in New Jersey between longtime incumbent Democrat Harrison Williams and Republican David Norcross, the defection rate to the challenger was only 2 percent. In the same year in New Mexico, one-third of the Democrats deserted incumbent Joseph Montoya for his Republican opponent. In North Dakota in 1974, Democrats stayed with the challenger, former Governor William Guy, with only 10 percent voting for veteran Republican Senator Milton Young. However, over half of the Democrats defected to Republican incumbents in Wyoming in 1972 and in New Mexico in 1978.

At first glance, then, analysis of state-level data does not seem to reveal a specific defection pattern. However, when data from hard-fought and low-key elections are examined separately, a clear pattern emerges. As can be seen in table 13 defections in hard-fought races were moderately high, both to and away from the incumbent; the incumbent had a mean advantage of five percentage points.

In low-key races, the results are strikingly different. Defections *away from* the incumbent's party were low, as in most House races. Defections *to* the incumbent's party varied but on average were rather high. The mean advantage to the incumbent in low-key races was 24 percentage points, with the two highest cases being Wyoming in 1972 and Nebraska in 1982: in Wyoming, 53 percent of Democrats favored Cliff Hansen, whereas only 5 percent of Republicans planned to defect to challenger Mike Vinich; in Nebraska, 47 percent of Republicans favored incumbent Zorinsky, while only 3 percent of Democrats chose his Republican challenger. What causes these large differences between the defection rates in hard-fought and low-key Senate races? To what extent are they related to variations in the levels of voters' awareness of the two candidates?

TABLE 13
Defection Rate in 47 Senate Races, 1968–1984

State	Month/Year	Candidates*	Defection		Incumbent's Advantage
			From Incumbent Party to Challenger	From Challenger Party to Incumbent	
Incumbent running		*Hard-fought Races*			
Pennsylvania	11/68§	Schweiker-Clark	18%	22%	+4
South Dakota	11/68§	McGovern-Gubbrud	7	35	+28
California	10/70	Tunney-Murphy	16	18	+2
Iowa	10/72	Clark-Miller	18	22	+4
Texas	9/72	Tower-Sanders	12	38	+26
Colorado	10/74	Hart-Dominick	18	12	−6
North Dakota	11/74	Young-Guy	9	10	+1
California	10/76	Hayakawa-Tunney	27	18	−9
Maryland	10/76	Sarbanes-Beall	18	20	+2
New Mexico	10/76	Schmitt-Montoya	35	19	−16
New York	11/76§	Moynihan-Buckley	18	21	+3
Wyoming	10/76	Wallop-McGee	17	18	+1
Massachusetts	10/78	Tsongas-Brooke	28	38	+10
Michigan	9/78	Levin-Griffin	11	16	+5
Colorado	10/80	Hart-Buchanan	24	18	−6
Georgia	10/80	Mattingly-Talmadge	37	19	−18
Indiana	10/80	Quayle-Bayh	18	15	−3
Missouri	10/80	Eagleton-McNary	23	33	+10
Mississippi	9/82	Stennis-Barbour	15	35	+20
Missouri	9/82	Danforth-Woods	20	33	+13
Tennessee	9/82	Sasser-Beard	15	24	+9
Utah	9/82	Hatch-Wilson	10	11	+1
West Virginia	10/82	Byrd-Benedict	11	32	+21
Illinois	10/84	Simon-Percy	8	20	+12
Iowa	11/84	Harkin-Jepsen	15	5	−10
North Carolina	10/84	Helms-Hunt	15	33	+18
		MEAN DIFFERENCE			+5

	Date	Candidates			Difference
Open seats					
California	10/68	Cranston(D)-Rafferty(R)	25	20	−5
Florida	11/68§	Gurney(R)-Collins(D)	36	35	−1
Iowa	10/68	Hughes(D)-Stanley(R)	20	14	−6
Ohio	11/68§	Saxbe(R)-Gilligan(D)	25	8	−17
New Jersey	10/78	Bradley(D)-Bell(R)	23	13	−10
Florida	10/80	Hawkins(R)-Gunter(D)	33	18	−15
Massachusetts	10/84	Kerry(D)-Shamie(R)	24	13	−11
West Virginia	10/84	Rockefeller(D)-Raese(R)	23	25	+2
MEAN DIFFERENCE					−8
MEAN DIFFERENCE, HARD-FOUGHT RACES					+2

Low-key Races

	Date	Candidates			Difference
Incumbent running					
Wisconsin	11/64§	*Proxmire*-Renk	15%	20%	+5
Illinois	11/68§	*Dirksen*-Clark	8	23	+15
North Carolina	11/68§	*Ervin*-Sommers	9	14	+5
Wyoming	10/72	*Hansen*-Vinich	5	53	+48
California	10/74	*Cranston*-Richardson	8	32	+24
New Jersey	10/76	*Williams*-Norcross	2	30	+28
North Dakota	11/76	*Burdick*-Stroup	6	20	+14
New Mexico	10/78	*Domenici*-Anaya	12	51	+39
California	10/80	*Cranston*-Gann	13	31	+18
Nebraska	10/82	*Zorinski*-Keck	3	47	+44
MEAN DIFFERENCE					+24
Open seats					
Alabama	11/68§	Allen(D)-Hooper(R)	6	36	+30
Wyoming	10/78	Simpson(R)-Whitaker(D)	5	19	+14
North Dakota	10/80	Andrews(R)-Johanneson(D)	6	42	+36
MEAN DIFFERENCE					+27
MEAN DIFFERENCE, LOW-KEY RACES					+25

Sources: See appendix 3.

* The name of the winning candidate precedes that of the loser, and the incumbent's name is in italics. If the seat was open, figures refer to the party of the previous incumbent.

§ Post-election survey.

VOTER AWARENESS OF SENATE CANDIDATES

One of the dominant conclusions produced in analyses of the 1978 CPS/ NES survey was that Senate challengers (unlike House challengers) manage to become almost as well known to voters as do incumbents. Different findings emerge, however, from an analysis of state-level data. Sixteen state-level data sets allow an examination of the degree of voters' awareness of both candidates (see table 14). In these instances, respondents were asked to recognize, or recognize and rate, both candidates. (The exact wording of all awareness items is given in appendix 4.)

Nine of the races examined were hard-fought. In four of them, incumbents were defeated, and in a fifth, the incumbent won by less than a percentage point. Three were open-seat contests by virtue of the incumbent's having been defeated in the primary. These nine races, and the awareness figures for both candidates, are listed in table 14. The other seven races were relatively low-key. In the six seats with incumbents running, the challenger was unable to attract media coverage or to raise an amount even close to the incumbent's campaign fund. In Wyoming in 1972 and in Maryland in 1982, challengers Mike Vinich and Lawrence Hogan were outspent by ratios of 16 to 1 and 17 to 1, respectively. In New Jersey in 1976, challenger David Norcross was outspent by over 8 to 1, was written off early by the newspapers as a sure loser, and, as we saw in chapter 3, received almost no news coverage. In 1980, California incumbent Alan Cranston was one of a half-dozen liberal Democrats targeted for defeat by conservative political action committees. But Cranston had accumulated a large war chest, and his opponent, Paul Gann, was never able to get a campaign off the ground. There was almost no coverage of Gann's campaign, and early out-of-state contributions quickly dried up. One low-key race involved an open seat, due to the retirement of incumbent Clifford Hansen in Wyoming. His party's nominee, the son of former Senator Milward Simpson, was expected to win by a large margin (and did) over an underfinanced perennial challenger.

Much of the variation in awareness from line to line in table 14 is very likely due to differences in question wording between surveys. In the most demanding instance, recall of the candidates was required, while in other polls the less difficult criterion of name recognition was used. The important comparisons in table 14 are between different columns in the same line, which are produced by the same measure of familiarity.[11] The table indicates that challengers in hard-fought campaigns are nearly as familiar to the public as the incumbents they face. The widest gap in this group, 14 points, occurred between Massachusetts Senator Edward Brooke and

Fifth District Congressman Paul Tsongas. Awareness rates in two of the three hard-fought open-seat races in table 14 were also about equal; in the third, the name of basketball star Bill Bradley was somewhat more familiar to voters than that of the Republican who had defeated Clifford Case in the primary.

In the low-key races, however, incumbents (or the stronger candidates in open-seat races) are much more familiar to the public than the candidates they face. In one of the most low-key races in the period studied, the recognition gap between Wyoming Senator Hansen and challenger Mike Vinich was 50 points. In California in 1980, Paul Gann trailed Cranston in recognition by 15 points. He may have been aided by his role two years before in the celebrated Jarvis-Gann tax-cutting initiative, Proposition 13; nevertheless, he was unable to attract much media coverage during his senatorial campaign.

Table 14 also demonstrates that in hard-fought races, the challenger, while generally a little less known than the incumbent, tends to surmount this slight disadvantage among his own party's identifiers.[12] In Wyoming in 1976, Gale McGee's advantage over Malcolm Wallop was 10 points. Among Republicans, however, Wallop was as well known as McGee. This is important, since an awareness advantage theoretically is prerequisite to eliciting defections from voters who identify with the other party. Lacking other information, and normally inclined to remain loyal, these partisans are likely to be induced to defect when they become aware, and presumably not negatively so,[13] of the other party's candidate but not of their own party's candidate.

In sum, the levels of voter awareness of challengers do vary according to whether the race was a hard-fought or a low-key one. If a Senate challenger is little known statewide, achieving a hard-fought campaign that receives heavy news coverage seems to bring him to parity with the incumbent in voter recognition. However, in a low-key race, with little news coverage, Senate challengers suffer the same curse of invisibility that plagues so many House challengers.

Effects of Awareness Levels on Defection

We have seen that levels of awareness of Senate challengers can vary greatly and that in low-key races, where voter recognition of the challenger is likely to be low, incumbents tend to attract large numbers of defections from the other party, while challengers attract very few defections. In hard-fought contests, where both candidates are likely to become widely known, defections tend to balance out. We know from

TABLE 14
Awareness of Senate Incumbents and Challengers, by Identifiers with Each Party

Race	Poll Date	Percentage Aware of Incumbent among:			Percentage Aware of Challenger among:			
		Incumbent Partisans	Challenger Partisans	All Respondents	Incumbent Partisans	Challenger Partisans	All Respondents	Incumbent's Advantage
Incumbent running					Hard-fought			
North Dakota	9/74	98%	94%	94%	91%	98%	94%	0
California	9/76	85	87	84	80	87	81	+4
Wyoming	10/76	92	89	89	72	87	79	+10
Massachusetts	10/78	92	92	93	69	83	79	+14
Indiana	10/80	100	99	99	87	94	91	+8
Minnesota	9/82	—	—	85	—	—	78	+7
MEAN DIFFERENCE								+7
Open seat								
California	10/68	83	71	75	69	76	72	+3
Florida	10/78	98	99	96	98	99	97	−1
New Jersey	10/78	84	71	77	87	86	87	−10
MEAN DIFFERENCE								−3
TOTAL MEAN DIFFERENCE, HARD-FOUGHT RACES								+3

				Low-key				
Incumbent running								
Wyoming	10/72	80%	77%	73%	22%	31%	23%	+50
New Jersey	10/76	28	27	35	12	6	14	+21
California	10/80	94	95	92	78	83	78	+15
Maryland	10/82	—	—	88	—	—	55	+33
Alabama	10/84	—	—	82	—	—	68	+14
New Jersey	10/84	—	—	94	—	—	48	+46
MEAN DIFFERENCE, INCUMBENTS ONLY								+25
Open seat								
Wyoming	10/78	74	60	65	60	54	54	+11
TOTAL MEAN DIFFERENCE, LOW-KEY RACES								+27

Note: All figures represent the percentage of respondents able to recognize and rate candidates, except figures for New Jersey 1978 and 1984, Florida 1980, Indiana 1980, California 1980, and Maryland 1982, which represent recognition only, and New Jersey 1976, which is the percentage able to recall the candidates' names. See appendix 3 for poll sources and appendix 4 for exact question wordings. For open seats, figures refer to the party of the previous incumbent.

TABLE 15
Defection by Awareness Levels of Incumbent and Challenger Partisans

Race	Incumbent Partisans Aware of:				Challenger Partisans Aware of:			
	Both	Incumbent Only	Challenger Only	Neither	Both	Incumbent Only	Challenger Only	Neither
Hard-fought Races								
Incumbent running								
North Dakota (9/74)	13 (251)	0 (18)	— (2)	— (3)	7 (300)	— (4)	0 (18)	— (5)
California (9/76)	29 (251)	0 (17)	— (2)	24 (37)	24 (128)	— (6)	— (6)	9 (11)
Wyoming (10/76)	20 (258)	7 (76)	— (1)	11 (28)	18 (365)	27 (22)	0 (12)	21 (34)
Massachusetts (10/78)	28 (78)	27 (61)	— (4)	27 (74)	33 (185)	44 (135)	9 (11)	38 (209)
Open seat								
California (10/68)	29 (283)	6 (71)	92 (12)	14 (50)	16 (395)	90 (31)	5 (64)	22 (88)

					Low-key Races			
New Jersey (10/78)	22 (238)	22 (18)	54 (24)	14 (22)	15 (295)	25 (12)	3 (79)	7 (42)
Florida (10/80)	34 (1,100)	7 (27)	31 (29)	13 (15)	18 (595)	— (7)	4 (23)	— (6)
Incumbent running								
Wyoming (10/72)	8 (64)	3 (193)	— (6)	4 (60)	31 (72)	66 (132)	8 (12)	56 (52)
New Jersey (10/76)	0 (20)	0 (30)	— (2)	3 (128)	— (5)	42 (33)	— (3)	28 (101)
California (10/80)	13 (366)	1 (86)	— (8)	5 (19)	29 (316)	51 (49)	— (5)	14 (14)
Open seat								
Wyoming (10/78)	7 (276)	0 (72)	— (6)	2 (103)	27 (186)	34 (47)	8 (26)	3 (119)

Note: All figures represent the percentage of respondents able to recognize and rate candidates, except figures for New Jersey 1978, Florida 1980, and California 1980, which represent recognition only, and New Jersey 1976 and Massachusetts 1978, which represent the percentage able to recall the candidate's name. For open seats, dashes indicate that the number of cases is insufficient to provide for an entry in the cell.

studies of House elections that the extent of voters' familiarity with both, one, or neither of the candidates can have a considerable effect on the vote. Ferejohn (1977) showed that in House elections from 1958 through 1970, defection rates were consistently fairly low when voters knew both or neither of the candidates; when only one candidate was known, there was virtually no defection from voters of his own party and, after 1966, a substantial defection rate among voters of the other party. Nelson (1978–79, table 6) found the same pattern,[14] and she also found that in every election between 1968 and 1974 over half of out-party identifiers who were aware only of the incumbent defected. Data from state-level surveys suggest that the same dynamic is at work in Senate elections.[15] The data in table 15 demonstrate that people familiar with both, or neither, of the candidates tended to remain loyal to their party's candidate. But people aware of only *one* of the candidates were very likely to vote for that candidate. These data therefore support the notion that people who are familiar with only one candidate are most likely to forgo party loyalty in favor of candidate familiarity.

This pattern turns up in both hard-fought and low-key Senate contests. What is different about the two kinds of elections is the distribution of voters across awareness categories. The effectiveness of the challenger's campaign in a hard-fought race results in most voters' getting to know both candidates. Those voters who are familiar only with incumbents are still likely to defect to them (provided of course that they are not perceived negatively), but such voters are not numerous enough to give incumbents an advantage.[16] In low-key elections, on the other hand, a sizable proportion of the voters are familiar only with the incumbent. Their voting patterns consequently have a significant impact: challenger partisans defect to the incumbent in large numbers, while virtually all incumbent partisans remain loyal. But since scarcely any voters in low-key races recognize only the challengers, there can be no compensating defections toward them.[17] This sizable advantage to incumbents, produced by voters' awareness only of them, is augmented by another pattern in low-key races: a tendency for voters familiar with both candidates or with neither candidate also to favor the incumbent.[18]

The amount of information disseminated during a campaign can affect more than just candidate recognition rates and voter defections. For while simple candidate familiarity is a powerful incentive for the vote choice, voters often bring other priorities to bear as they decide between two Senate candidates. In selecting political representatives, they may seek candidates whose ideological stances or issue positions they find acceptable. And to the extent that a voter wishes to consider either of the candidates' ideology or issue positions by comparing the candidates with each other or by comparing their views with his own, he or she needs the kind of information that campaigns are intended to provide. But if the campaign generates little or no information about one or both of the candidates, such as in a low-key race, the average voter will have a hard time evaluating the candidates' issue positions or ideological postures. On the other hand, in a hard-fought campaign, sufficient information may be generated for many voters to be able to choose a candidate on the basis of ideology or individual issues instead of falling back on party identification or incumbency as decision criteria.

6. Ideology, Issue Voting, and Senate Campaign Intensity

In a discussion of the 1986 midterm elections, CBS news correspondent Lesley Stahl asked print journalists Don Oberdorfer and Albert
Hunt how important the state of the economy would be to Democrats'
efforts to reclaim control of the Senate ("Face the Nation," 20 July 1986).
When Hunt replied that he did not see the economy as a major factor,
Stahl asked Oberdorfer whether the determining factor for voters would
instead be the president's position on sanctions on South Africa or some
other foreign policy issue. Oberdorfer responded that he had learned as
a political reporter that foreign policy matters have little impact on
voters' choices in congressional elections. Stahl pressed her point: if the
economy is not a factor, would not voters have to decide on the basis of
foreign policy? Oberdorfer reminded her that local issues, too, often have
an impact on voting in House and Senate elections.

The reporters' exchange reflects the commonly held belief that people
decide to vote for or against particular congressional candidates on the
basis of public policy stances and that policy issues strongly affect Senate
election outcomes in particular. Perhaps not only because this view seems
to be reasonable but because it conforms to an idealized conception of
how citizens ought to make voting decisions, it is popular among the
news media, elected officials, candidates and campaign organizations,
and other observers of American electoral politics.

Early voting studies based on survey research found that in fact very
few voters appeared to cast votes on the basis of issues or ideology in

110

either presidential or congressional elections during the 1950s.[1] The idea that policy issues do have a substantial impact at the presidential level has gained ground since the 1960s, as has the assumption that voters cast their votes on the basis of policy considerations whenever possible at the subpresidential level as well. Wright and Berkman (1986, 570), for example, recently wrote:

> We assume that most of what voters want to accomplish in senatorial voting can be summarized by three objectives. First, voters would like to elect the "best" representative, in the sense of one who is an effective policy maker, who shows the capacity for leadership, accomplishes things for the state and generally has the personal characteristics and qualifications the voter associates with being a good senator. Second, citizens are assumed to want policy representation, in the sense of having a senator who votes and works on issues in ways that are generally consistent with the voter's own preferences on the issues of the day. Third, congressional elections provide the opportunity to register sentiment about the president, his performance in office, and his handling of the economy.

Implicit in Lesley Stahl's question during the 1986 campaign, and explicit in her colleagues' answers, are these same assumptions that people cast their votes either on the basis of issues in a state campaign or in response to national economic conditions or presidential performance.

Voters' decisions in Senate elections may depend either on a comparison of two candidates' positions on one or more specific issues (issue voting) or on their evaluations of a Senate candidate's general political views and comparison with their own (ideology voting). But how do variations in Senate campaign intensity affect the likelihood that people's vote choices are influenced by either issue voting or ideology voting, and what is the *relative* degree of issue voting resulting from hard-fought as opposed to low-key campaigns?

"Issue Voting" and "Ideology Voting"

There are important distinctions to be drawn between voting that is based on assessment of candidates' positions on various issues and voting that is based on the general ideological perspective of the candidates. Clearly, one need not be familiar with a candidate's specific issue positions to be aware of his general philosophical stance. The casual observer may know, for example, that a candidate or elected official is a conservative without being aware of his particular economic, social, or foreign policy positions. Such a voter could decide to vote for or against

111

that candidate solely on the basis of this limited information. On the other hand, a voter might know no more about a candidate or his general ideological philosophy than his stance on one particular issue. Even if a voter were very familiar with the candidate's general philosophy, he might choose to focus instead on the candidate's stance on a single issue. Decisions about whom to vote for, therefore, may be made on the basis of the general ideology of a candidate or entirely on the basis of one or more of the candidate's specific issue positions. Yet an essential prerequisite for either issue voting or ideology voting is that voters have an awareness of the general ideology and/or specific policy positions of the candidates and that they themselves have a set of ideological (or specific issue) commitments against which to evaluate the candidates' positions.

Studies of House elections have found little relation between ideology and the vote, since voters are seen to have too little information about the candidates to be able to compare them on ideological grounds.[2] Less research is available on the role of ideology in Senate elections. Jones (1981, 103) concluded that ideological considerations were "important contributions" to the defeats of four liberal senators in 1980. Using national-level survey data, Abramowitz (1980, 1981) and Wright and Berkman (1986) found a relationship between ideology and the vote for the 1978 and 1982 elections, respectively. Comparing the impact of ideology in the vote decision in House and Senate elections in 1978, Abramowitz (1980, 638) found that "while ideological proximity to the incumbent had little impact on candidate choice in House elections, it had a substantial impact on candidate choice in Senate elections among two groups of voters: independents and supporters of the challenger's party. The ability of Senate incumbents to draw support from independents and voters of the opposing party depended largely on their ideological position."[3]

The variations we have observed in the levels of information dissemination among hard-fought and low-key Senate contests might lead us to expect issue voting or ideology voting to occur, if at all, more in hard-fought Senate races than in low-key races. In hard-fought elections most voters have information on both candidates and are thus better equipped to choose between them. In low-key races incumbents are usually the only candidates recognized by most voters, while challengers are not. In low-key races, then, ideology- or issue-based voting could only take the form of a referendum on the known candidate (unless the voter simply assumed that an unfamiliar candidate's political philosophy was the same as his own).

Ideology Voting in Senate Elections

If the vote decision process includes consideration of a candidate's political ideology, what is the relationship between a voter's general political philosophy and the likelihood that he will defect to the other party's Senate candidate? Are conservatives in the Democratic party and liberals in the Republican party more likely than their fellow partisans at the other end of the ideological spectrum to defect to the other party's candidate? To assess the extent to which this may happen in Senate elections, it is necessary first to measure voters' political philosophies. There are at least two ways to do this. One is to ask voters directly whether they consider themselves to be liberal, moderate, or conservative. However, many voters do not think of themselves as liberal or conservative and may even be unaware of the meaning of these terms. Fifty-seven percent of the 1980 CPS National Election Study's survey respondents, for example, were found by Luttbeg and Gant (1985) to be unable either to explain the terms or to give definitions of them. A measure based on asking voters to describe themselves as either liberal or conservative, therefore, risks misclassifying those who guess at the question and would lose entirely the many respondents who answer "Don't know."

The other way to assess voters' political philosophies is to obtain their views on a battery of issues and align them along a scale, placing those voters giving consistently "liberal" responses at one end, those with consistently "conservative" responses at the other, and those with centrist or mixed responses in between. For purposes of the analysis to follow, I have used the second approach—creating a liberal-conservative index comprising items each having a liberal and a conservative response option—to examine the relationship between voters' political ideology and the extent to which they defect from their party identification. Data from the CPS/NES surveys of 1972, 1974, and 1976 were pooled to form the basis for the ideology index, since for each year these surveys contained items tapping attitudes on the rights of women, minorities, and those accused of crimes, the appropriateness of protest and civil disobedience, the role of government in aiding the poor or unemployed, and the preferred allocation of taxes. When available, items with liberal and conservative options regarding the legalization of marijuana, Vietnam policy, and perception of big business were also included. For each year, the respondents were grouped into one of five ideological classifications ranging from strongly liberal to strongly conservative.[4]

Pooling the data from three successive CPS/NES surveys provides a reasonably representative group of Senate election respondents for analysis, minimizing the problems inherent in using the results of any single NES sample in an analysis of Senate elections (see chapter 5). The pooling of NES data assures that there are respondents from all states and that ample respondents are available from states that had both hard-fought and low-key races. There were a total of 59 hard-fought and 41 low-key campaigns during the elections of 1972, 1974, and 1976. After removing the nonvoters and the pure independents, for whom it is impossible to examine defection patterns, there were 2,233 respondents in the pooled sample, 57 percent from states with hard-fought races and 43 percent from states with low-key races.[5]

Voters were divided into five ideological groups of equal size. The top fifth are called liberals; the next fifth, moderate liberals; and the middle fifth, moderates. Moderate conservatives and conservatives round out the five categories. The defection patterns in races of Democrats and of Republicans in each of the five categories are shown in table 16.

The relationship between ideology and defection is not particularly strong among either type of partisan identifier. Liberal Republicans were slightly more likely to defect to Democratic Senate candidates than were conservative Republicans, but on the Democratic side liberals actually defected at a higher rate than did conservatives. At first glance, then, these data suggest that a voter's own ideological perspective has little impact on his vote for senator.

Returning, however, to the distinction between hard-fought and low-key Senate races, we have seen that in hard-fought campaigns most voters tend to become equally familiar with both candidates, while in low-key contests, where news coverage is light, most voters remain much more familiar with the incumbent than with the challenger. (Although question wording differed from survey to survey, state-level data have shown that incumbent recognition rates are typically in the 80–90 percent range in both hard-fought and low-key races.) In a hard-fought race, therefore, a high level of information dissemination enables voters to evaluate and then choose between the two candidates on the basis of their philosophies. In low-key elections, where most voters have little basis on which to evaluate challengers, the only way for them to vote on the basis of ideology is to vote up or down on the general philosophy of the incumbent (or the better-known candidate in the case of a low-key open-seat race). Many voters may not actually be reminded of an incumbent's political philosophy, even if they have grown "familiar" with him during his time in office, until campaign debate brings it out. In a low-key campaign where, for example, an incumbent keeps a low profile and engages

114

TABLE 16

Defection in U.S. Senate Elections, by Political Ideology, 1972–1974–1976
Pooled National Sample

Respondents	Democrats Defecting*		Republicans Defecting*	
	%	(N)	%	(N)
Liberals	32	(369)	28	(74)
Moderate liberals	21	(282)	24	(156)
Moderates	25	(206)	25	(226)
Moderate conservatives	25	(211)	24	(255)
Conservatives	28	(200)	17	(254)

Sources: CPS/NES surveys, 1972, 1974, 1976.
* Partisan independents are included with strong and weak identifiers of each party.

in little political dialogue with his opponent, an incumbent's ideology may not necessarily be brought into focus, and voting up or down on an incumbent's ideology in a low-key election may be quite unlikely. A voter's own political ideology has a much greater chance of affecting his vote choice in a hard-fought election than in a low-key election.

Democrats' and Republicans' defection rates within the five categories of ideology are compared in table 17, this time distinguishing voters in hard-fought Senate races from voters in low-key races. Low-key elections are further separated into contests in which the Democratic incumbent faced a weak challenge and contests in which the Republican incumbent had the upper hand;[6] as the cell sizes in table 17 indicate, low-key Republican races were rare in the period 1972–76. With respect to low-key races, table 17 generates the same pattern we saw when looking at state-level data in the chapter 5: defections toward the incumbent greatly outweigh defections toward the challenger. The relationship between ideology and defection *away from* the incumbent is fairly flat. Only five percentage points separated the rates at which the most liberal and the most conservative Democrats defected away from Democratic incumbents. (Liberal Republicans were 22 points more likely than conservative Republicans to defect from Republican incumbents in low-key races, but it should be noted that the cell sizes for low-key Republican races are very small.) Defections *toward* incumbent Senators in low-key races, while high among both Democrats and Republican identifiers, also had little to do with voters' ideology. In "low-key Democratic" races, conservative Republican identifiers, who should have the least philosophical reason to vote for a Democrat, defected at a greater rate than moderately liberal Republicans (37 percent to 26 percent) and at essentially the same rate as the remaining three ideology groups. In "low-key Republican"

115

TABLE 17

Defection in Low-key Democratic, Low-key Republican, and Hard-fought
Elections, by Political Ideology, 1972–1974–1976 Pooled National Sample

Respondents	Democrats Defecting		Republicans Defecting	
	%	(N)	%	(N)
Low-key Democratic elections				
Liberals	5	(131)	41	(17)
Moderate liberals	13	(93)	26	(34)
Moderates	6	(63)	38	(60)
Moderate conservatives	10	(82)	41	(75)
Conservatives	10	(90)	37	(92)
Low-key Republican elections				
Liberals	79	(34)	27	(11)
Moderate liberals	58	(19)	13	(24)
Moderates	64	(22)	19	(26)
Moderate conservatives	80	(10)	8	(26)
Conservatives	63	(8)	5	(20)
Hard-fought elections				
Liberals	13	(196)	24	(45)
Moderate liberals	22	(164)	25	(91)
Moderates	27	(119)	21	(138)
Moderate conservatives	32	(114)	19	(145)
Conservatives	40	(102)	6	(136)

Sources: CPS/NES surveys, 1972, 1974, and 1976.

Note: Low-key Democratic elections were those in which the Democratic candidate faced a low-key campaign against Republican opposition; low-key Republican elections were those in which the Republican candidate faced a low-key campaign against Democratic opposition. Partisan independents are included with strong and weak identifiers of each party.

races, the liberal Democrats had nearly the highest defection rate toward the Republican incumbent (79 percent) rather than the lowest as might have been expected.

Whether flat or choppy, these patterns for the low-key races suggest that voters' ideological perspectives had little effect on the voting in these races. Largely unaware of the issue positions of the candidates and thus unable to compare them, voters in low-key races generally do not bring their own ideologies into play. In some cases, such as when well-known conservative Barry Goldwater faced Democrat Jonathan Marshall in 1974, unfamiliarity with the challenger may pose no obstacle, since voters may be reacting to the ideological stance of the incumbent. But in other cases a challenger's inability to reach the voters with his campaign seems to preclude any involvement of ideology in the vote choice. Perhaps this is because the messages that do get through—those of the incumbent—are aimed at moderating any preexisting ideological reputation the incumbent may have.[7] Or perhaps most voters are simply unfamiliar even with the incumbent's ideological position. Whatever the explanation, the data for the period 1972–76 show very little relationship between ideology and the vote in low-key Senate elections.

By contrast, table 17 displays a rather strong relationship between voters' ideological views and their defection in hard-fought races. Among Democratic identifiers, the defection pattern is monotonic across the five categories of ideology, and fairly steep. Conservative Democrats were 27 percentage points more likely than liberal Democrats to defect to the Republican candidate. Among Republican identifiers, the difference between the extremes was similar; conservative Republicans rarely defected to the Democratic candidate—the figure for the three-election period was 6 percent—while liberal Republicans defected at a 24 percent rate. The defection rates for the three middle ideological groups were 25 percent, 21 percent, and 19 percent, leaving the relationship between ideology and defection among Republicans rather less uniform than among Democratic identifiers. The evidence does allow the suggestion, however, that when campaign messages from both candidates reach the electorate, more voters accumulate enough information to distinguish between the general ideologies of the candidates: when the other party's candidate seems more ideologically compatible, some voters defect.

Implicit in the discussion so far is the assumption that a Democratic candidate for the U.S. Senate is more liberal than a Republican candidate. It is not surprising to find, in the hard-fought races, that many conservative Democrats preferred Republican candidates over the Democrats and that many liberal Republicans preferred Democratic candidates. If two candidates were essentially similar in their views, however, there would be much less reason to expect defections on the basis of voters' ideology. To test properly the impact of ideology on the vote, a distinction should be made between elections in which the candidates' ideological perspectives differ substantially and those in which they are very similar.

To make this determination for all races in the period 1968–84, a three-category measure was constructed based on an average of Americans for Democratic Action (ADA), Committee on Political Education (COPE), and Americans for Constitutional Action (ACA) ratings for all candidates for which these were available (incumbent senators, and those challengers who had served in the House). For challengers for

117

whom there were no ratings by these interest groups, *Congressional Quarterly Weekly Report,* the *Almanac of American Politics,* the *American Political Report,* and other available sources were searched for ideological descriptions.[8]

It turns out that from 1968 through 1984 most Senate races did involve two ideologically distinct candidates.[9] In about 40 percent of contests a liberal faced a conservative. In another 42 percent of races a moderate faced either a liberal or a conservative. In all but three of these instances the Democrat was more liberal than the Republican.[10] In 82 percent of the 212 Senate races in this period, then, the assumption on which the foregoing analysis is based is justified. In 18 percent of the 47 races over this period, however, the general philosophies of both candidates were very similar. Half these pairings involved conservatives; most of them were in southern or border states. In 14 races both candidates were liberals (most of these in the Northeast), and in 10 cases both were moderates. This is not to say that in 47 races the candidates were ideologically *identical,* only that it would not be surprising if most voters in these races were unable to ascertain enough difference between the candidates to use ideology as a voting criterion.

In table 18, hard-fought races between candidates of similar ideology have been removed. In the races where there was a real philosophical difference between the opponents, the defection pattern found in table 17 is sharpened. Among Democratic identifiers 9 percent of the most liberal quintile defected to the Republican, whereas 43 percent of the most conservative quintile did so. Among Republicans the pattern was similar: 35 percent of the liberals but only 3 percent of the conservatives defected to the Democrat. Ideology appears not to have played a role in contests between candidates of similar ideology; for Democratic and Republican identifiers alike, the defection rates of the most liberal and most conservative voters were more alike than those of the moderates.

These findings support the proposition that when there are discernible differences, voters do consider candidates' philosophical positions in making their decisions in Senate elections. And the findings underscore the importance of the role of political information in the vote decision process. In races in which a candidate cannot get his message across, the resulting low-key campaign leaves the bulk of the electorate unable to distinguish between the general philosophies of the candidates and therefore unable to bring their own ideological preferences to bear in their decision. In races in which a challenger can generate information about both himself and his opponent, voters can, and sometimes do, choose on the basis of political ideology if they can discern ideological differences.

118

TABLE 18
Defection in Hard-fought Races between Ideologically Distinct Senate
Candidates, by Political Ideology, 1972–1974–1976 Pooled National Sample

Respondents	Democrats Defecting		Republicans Defecting	
	%	(N)	%	(N)
Liberals	9	(153)	35	(23)
Moderate liberals	18	(115)	19	(73)
Moderates	26	(89)	15	(99)
Moderate conservatives	32	(78)	21	(102)
Conservatives	43	(63)	3	(103)

Sources: CPS/NES surveys, 1972, 1974, and 1976.
Note: Partisan independents are included with strong and weak identifiers of each party.

This line of reasoning should apply as well to both House and presidential elections. As discussed in chapter 3, in most House elections an incumbent faces an unfamiliar challenger who cannot generate the kind of media attention it takes to reach the electorate. Because House incumbents generally can get their messages to more voters than their challengers can, incumbents can augment their considerable name-recognition advantage by publicizing popular issue positions. But an incumbent is not likely to try to make a name for himself at either end of the ideological spectrum unless he believes that most of his constituency is also located at that end.[11] We should expect, then, that in the typical House election voters' ideology would play the same negligible role that we saw in low-key Senate elections. Unable to rate the candidates ideologically, and usually unclear about the ideological inclinations of the incumbent, voters would not tend to use ideology in making their vote decisions.

Table 19 confirms that the relationship between ideology (measured the same way that it was for the Senate) and defection in House elections in 1972, 1974, and 1976 was in general a weak one. In 1972 and 1976 there was some tendency for conservative Democrats to defect to Republican candidates; the spread between the most liberal and most conservative Democratic voters was 12 points in 1972 and 17 points in 1976. The relationship between ideology and defection among Democrats in 1974 and among Republicans in all three years was very weak. In 1974, 9 percent of moderate Democrats defected to the Republican House candidate (a figure resembling that of liberal Democrats). However, the defection figure for moderate liberals, 20 percent, even surpassed that of conservative Democrats. In 1976, conservative Republicans defected far less than other Republican identifiers, but there was no difference in the

TABLE 19
Defection in House Elections, by Political Ideology, 1972, 1974, and 1976

| | 1972 | | | | 1974 | | | | 1976 | | | |
| | Democrats Defecting | | Republicans Defecting | | Democrats Defecting | | Republicans Defecting | | Democrats Defecting | | Republicans Defecting | |
Respondents	%	(N)	%	(N)	%	(N)	%	(N)	%	(N)	%	(N)
Liberal	9	(184)	38	(66)	12	(153)	22	(18)	10	(188)	29	(40)
Slightly liberal	16	(134)	20	(110)	20	(96)	32	(57)	19	(150)	26	(78)
Moderate	15	(121)	22	(136)	9	(86)	16	(79)	17	(116)	27	(114)
Slightly conservative	20	(123)	15	(117)	14	(117)	24	(87)	25	(100)	27	(142)
Conservative	21	(98)	22	(121)	18	(79)	41	(118)	27	(115)	15	(162)

Sources: CPS/NES surveys, 1972, 1974, and 1976.
Note: Partisan independents are included with strong and weak identifiers of each party.

TABLE 20
Defection in Presidential Elections, by Political Ideology, 1972 and 1976

| | 1972 | | | | 1976 | | | |
| | Democrats to Nixon | | Republicans to McGovern | | Democrats to Ford | | Republicans to Carter | |
Respondents	%	(N)	%	(N)	%	(N)	%	(N)
Liberal	10	(234)	28	(80)	12	(219)	17	(45)
Slightly liberal	37	(163)	9	(127)	15	(188)	26	(92)
Moderate	49	(142)	9	(159)	20	(145)	17	(136)
Slightly conservative	59	(84)	2	(133)	25	(120)	16	(162)
Conservative	77	(92)	3	(140)	33	(131)	4	(183)

Sources: CPS/NES surveys, 1972 and 1976.
Note: Partisan independents are included with strong and weak identifiers of each party.

defection rates of the other four groups of Republicans. In 1974, however, 41 percent of the conservative Republicans defected, a figure outdistancing those for the other four groups by an equally great margin. The frequency of a random or exceedingly weak relationship between ideology and defection in House races suggests that voters generally do not have sufficient information about House candidates to make decisions based on ideological preferences.

At the other extreme are presidential elections. Here, both candidates are covered continually and in great depth by the news media, and information on the ideological differences between the candidates is likely to reach the bulk of the electorate. The relationship between the voter's ideology and presidential defection in 1972 and 1976 is shown in table 20. In 1972 most voters were aware that George McGovern was considerably more liberal than Richard Nixon (Miller et al. 1976, 760), and this ideological difference yielded even greater ideological voting than we saw in the case of hard-fought Senate elections between ideologically distinct candidates (table 18). Democratic liberals defected to Nixon at a 10 percent rate, as compared with the conservative Democrats' defection rate of 77 percent. In 1976, ideological differences between candidates Ford and Carter were less pronounced, and the defection patterns in table 20 for 1976 are also less pronounced than those for 1972, although they are nevertheless clearly evident.

According to our analysis, when Senate races are hard-fought, that is, when voters have information about the campaign and the candidates, ideological voting is much more likely to occur than it is in low-key races, when information about both candidates' ideologies may not have reached most voters. This same dynamic can be applied to most House

121

races; the difference between these two types of elections is in the number of hard-fought races occurring in the aggregate. Jacobson (1983, 119) was correct when he said that "competitive challenges also make it possible for more voters to make ideology and policy decision distinctions between House candidates," but it may have been an overgeneralization when he continued that they thus produce contests "that are more like Senate elections, in which policy issues and ideology usually play a larger role." Senate elections should not be considered a generic set of elections in which ideology voting "play[s] a larger role," since nearly half of them are low-key races in which ideology has little apparent effect on choice of candidates. Rather, when Senate races (or, it is possible to speculate, House races) are hard-fought, and enough information reaches the voters to make ideology voting possible, it appears that ideology voting can occur.

Issue Voting: An Overview

It is often claimed that individual issues have a significant impact on the vote. Observing that "every American election is, in a certain sense, decided on the basis of issues," Fenton and Austern (1976, 103) concluded that "the winner in a campaign is that candidate who, through skillful use of election propaganda and sometimes the mistakes of his opponents, fastens on one or two issues that can be helpful to him, and beats his opponents to death with them." Thus quite apart from the possibility that voters relate their own general political outlook to those of the candidates, they may decide whom to vote for by considering which candidate is closer to their own views on particular issues. Obtaining evidence to test this notion, however, is a difficult task. Several conditions must be met before it can be asserted that issue voting has occurred. First, an issue must be salient enough to voters to justify the assumption that it could have been the basis for the vote choice. Second, the voter must be aware of the candidates' positions on that issue. If it can be concluded that the voter's concern about a particular issue was sufficient for him to evaluate both candidates' positions on it and then vote for the candidate whose position was closer to his own, only then can it be asserted that issue voting has occurred.

If issue voting occurs at any level, it is most likely to be in presidential elections, since of all campaigns, voters are most likely to pay attention to, and therefore receive information from, presidential campaigns. Even if neither candidate has held national public office before, presidential candidates and their views make news starting a year or more before an election. While voters' main focus is not always on candidates' issue positions,[12] by Election Day they have had an opportunity to learn how the candidates stand on numerous issues.

Early studies, such as Campbell et al.'s *The American Voter* and *Elections and the Political Order*, found that for the most part, issues took a back seat to such factors as party loyalty and candidate attributes. By the 1968 election, issues were found to play more of a role. Converse et al. (1969) found, for example, that people voting for George Wallace did so largely because of their views on various policy questions. Investigating the 1972 election, Miller and Miller (1975) wrote that the "civil rights movement, the war in Vietnam, riots in the cities, crime in the streets," and other issues had produced "an increase in 'issue-voting' which emphasized intra-party polarization on various non-economic issues" (393).[13] With a "transformed" electorate now concerned with "questions of public policy," they wrote, issues took on increased importance as "determinants of the vote decision: Ideology and issue-voting provide an exceptionally powerful explanation of the 1972 campaign when compared with other explanations such as the social characteristics of voters, the events of the campaign, the candidates, political alienation, voters' cultural orientations or their partisan identification" (394).

In assessing the extent of issue voting at the subpresidential level, a primary consideration is the level of availability of political information. As we have seen, the availability of such information in Senate elections is less intensive and more sporadic, because local newspapers and television news organizations cover state and local elections much less extensively than the national media cover presidential elections. Consequently, the amount of political information voters are likely to have on the policy positions of congressional candidates is not as great. At least as far as most House elections are concerned, findings are fairly consistent on this point: generally, voters do not have enough information about the candidates to be able to choose between them on the basis of their specific issue stances.[14]

There has been speculation that issue voting might play a more important role in Senate campaigns than in most House campaigns. As Hershey (1984, 166, 168) put it, "News coverage of a Senator's actions puts more emphasis on national policy issues; thus Senators' stands on controversial issues are likely to be better known and to be a factor in their public images. . . . Senate campaigns, it has been suggested, usually revolve more around issues than House campaigns do." According to Kuklinski and West (1981, 438), "discussions of salient problems and solutions to them are an integral part of most Senate campaigns." A number of case studies of Senate elections specifically addressing the possibility of issue voting suggest that certain issues have been powerful influences on the outcomes of particular races, although none of them has included analysis of data on voter preferences. Richard Nixon's 1950 Senate race in California against Helen Gahagan Douglas was described as "an outstanding example of a campaign which had been successfully reduced to a single issue [anti-communism]" (Anderson 1970). An analysis of the 1970 race in Maryland between incumbent Joseph Tydings and Republican challenger J. Glenn Beall described Tydings's support of gun control (displeasing conservatives), his floor managing of a bill authorizing "no knock" searches and wiretapping in the District of Columbia (displeasing blacks and liberals), and a *Life* magazine story accusing Tydings of conflict of interest concerning a business deal. About this race Bibby and Davidson (1973, 50) concluded, "Tydings was whipsawed by a combination of these issues, each of which affected a segment of the population deeply enough to persuade it to oppose the incumbent."

The issue of freedom to choose to have an abortion has been cited as substantially influencing voters in a number of Senate elections. Iowa Senator Dick Clark's loss in 1978 has been attributed to voters' rejection of his pro-choice stance on abortion (Barone and Ujifusa 1981, 372; Wootton 1985, 221), and the same issue is said to have affected a large percentage of votes in the 1980 reelection efforts of Senators Bayh, Church, Culver, Leahy, McGovern, and Packwood (Hershey 1984). Acknowledging that such a conclusion was difficult to substantiate, Hershey asserted nonetheless that "it is clear that all six incumbents had been hurt by the pro-life targeting to some extent" (242). On the other hand, analysis of an Iowa state poll on the 1978 Clark-Jepsen Senate race found that the abortion issue played a minor role in people's voting decisions (Traugott and Vinovskis 1980).

It is so difficult, using national surveys, to investigate the impact of issues on Senate elections when the issues differ in importance and salience from district to district that it is not surprising that "[issues] show up so infrequently as having any measurable impact on individual voting [in congressional voting] once other variables have been taken into account" (Jacobson 1983, 121). Identifying the issues that were spotlighted in a given Senate campaign is all the more problematic when one examines these elections using the most accessible voter study, the National Election Study, for the reasons we have already discussed, namely, reduced sample size and skewed samples. What can be done, nonetheless, is to compare hard-fought and low-key campaigns on a case-study basis to analyze how and when issue voting is likely to be a major factor in the vote decision process. Is issue voting promoted by the considerable attention paid to hard-fought races and precluded by the light coverage characteristic of low-key races? That is, when there is very little information available to voters, how prominent a factor can issue voting possibly be in the vote decision? On the other hand, when issues are well defined and extensively covered in the news media, do voters appear to consider the candidates' positions on issues salient to them in making their vote choices?

Issue Voting in a Hard-fought Race: California, 1982

The 1982 California Senate contest between Governor Jerry Brown and San Diego Mayor Pete Wilson for S. I. Hayakawa's seat, described in chapter 4, was an "intensely bitter" campaign (*Los Angeles Times,* 17 October 1982, 20) that often focused on alleged improprieties and on personal attributes of the candidates, but issues of public policy were also prominently debated. Wilson had been considered a moderate as San Diego mayor but ran his Senate campaign as a conservative. Brown, while not easily labeled a traditional liberal (he was, for example, an early proponent of a constitutional amendment to balance the federal budget), was considerably more liberal than Wilson on the issues on which they differed. Moreover, since Brown was somewhat unpopular in the state, his advisers urged him to try to keep the focus of his campaign on policy issues and to stay on the offensive with continual attacks on Wilson's views.

To investigate the extent of issue voting in the Brown-Wilson race, we need to know which issues dominated the campaign. Both the *Los Angeles Times* and the *San Francisco Chronicle* covered the campaign extensively from the June primary on and almost daily starting in September. Both papers covered most of the candidates' major political functions, and since both candidates knew that representatives of the large-circulation papers were present, their major messages each day were transmitted well within earshot of these papers' reporters. It is probably safe to assume, therefore, that the campaign news coverage of these two papers generally reflects what Brown and Wilson had to say and how often they said it.[15]

The *Times's* and the *Chronicle's* coverage fell generally into two categories. One area was that of public policy issues, for which there are various policy alternatives and on which there is usually some disagreement both among political elites and in the general electorate. When we speak of "issue voting"—where the voter chooses the candidate closest to his view on the issues he cares about—it is to the public policy–type issues that we are generally referring. The second area of coverage comprised topics unrelated to public policy on which the candidates' views differed. These included charges and countercharges about competence, honesty, experience, personality, or judgment. They usually amounted to attacks by one side and defenses by the other on such questions as Brown's association with leftist activist Tom Hayden or Wilson's inexperience as a statewide candidate. These were not subjects on which voters could compare the candidates' views with their own, and thus they are not relevant to issue voting.

Table 21 lists all issues that were mentioned more than once by either the *Times* or the *Chronicle* between September 1 and November 1. The table separates policy-oriented issues from personally oriented topics and lists the number of times each was mentioned in a Senate campaign context by each newspaper.[16] Six subject areas appear to have dominated all others. Two were of the personal variety (Brown's accusation that Wilson had avoided paying federal income taxes in 1980 and had lived rent-free in a San Diego condominium and Wilson's continual assertions that Brown used "scare tactics" and deliberately lied throughout the campaign). The other four were policy-related issues. If issue voting was a factor in the Brown-Wilson election, one or more of the four policy issues was the likely focus.

One of the issues raised repeatedly by Brown was that of President Reagan's economic policies. Brown sought to associate Republican Wilson with the Reagan administration at a time of recession and high unemployment. A second issue, the nuclear freeze, was already controversial in California; an initiative had been placed on the upcoming November ballot calling for the United States and the Soviet Union to halt nuclear weapons production and testing. Brown not only stressed his unqualified support for the initiative but attempted to characterize Wilson's opposition to the initiative as support for nuclear weapons development and the arms race. Wilson, who opposed the initiative's specific content but not the notion of arms control (he wanted actual reductions rather than a freeze in place), attacked Brown as deliberately misrepresenting his position. Their differences were even more sharply drawn in late September, when Brown introduced a television spot showing an atomic mushroom cloud and a little girl saying, "I want to go on living," followed by the admonition to vote for Brown and "your life" as opposed to voting for Wilson. An "outraged" Wilson charged Brown with "graphic character assassination" (*Los Angeles Times,* 29 September, 1), and after "considerable editorial criticism"—even some of

TABLE 21
Coverage of Specific Issues by Two Daily Newspapers,
California Senate Race, 1982

Issues	L.A. Times	S.F. Chronicle	Total	Average
Policy issues				
Nuclear freeze	15	23	38	17.5
Social Security	17	18	35	19.0
Reaganomics	14	19	33	16.5
California Supreme Court/criminals' rights	10	11	21	10.5
High technology increases	2	5	7	3.5
Gun control	1	5	6	3.0
Support for business, agriculture	4	5	9	4.5
Elect all judges	5	3	8	4.0
Guest worker policy	3	1	4	2.0
Defense policy/conventional weapons	2	3	5	2.5
California highway policy	2	1	3	1.5
Trade	1	2	3	1.5
Personal/character/experience issues				
Brown's state budget deficits	5	9	14	7.0
Brown's use of scare tactics/lies	7	15	22	11.0
Brown's flipflops/flighty character	4	7	11	5.5
Brown's shady appointments/vetoes	7	5	12	6.0
Brown's shady contributions	3	3	6	3.0
Brown's presidency attempt	3	1	4	2.0
Brown's relationship with Hayden	2	5	7	3.5
Wilson's shady tax, rent deals	12	13	25	12.5
Wilson's lack of experience	1	4	5	2.5
Wilson's smear tactics	3	2	5	2.5
Wilson's shady contributions	1	3	4	2.0

Note: Figures represent the number of articles in each paper between 1 September and 1 November 1982. Issues mentioned at most once in each paper are not listed.

Brown's own supporters called it "overkill" and "heavy-handed" (ibid., 6 October, 3)—the Brown campaign withdrew the ad.

A third issue—what to do about Social Security—emerged as Brown attacked a suggestion by Wilson that the system be modified. Addressing the widespread concern that the system was in danger of going bankrupt, Wilson proposed in July that people under age 45 be allowed to choose alternatives to Social Security and that their mandatory contributions be reduced accordingly. Brown seized on this proposal as evidence that Wilson was not a friend of Social Security and made his own unqualified support of the system a campaign point for the next three months.

A fourth issue centered around Governor Brown's judicial appointments over the previous eight years. This issue, while not as prominent as the first three, preoccupied the two Senate candidates considerably more than any of the issues brought up during the rest of the campaign; it was also the one issue on which Wilson was the aggressor. Arguing that Brown's judicial appointments showed the governor to be "soft on crime," Wilson joined other conservatives in calling for the defeat of the three Brown-appointed state supreme court justices in November. (Wilson advocated the reelection of the fourth justice on the ballot, who had been appointed by former Governor Reagan and who had consistently voted with the minority on court decisions favoring the rights of the accused.)

Brown had also been criticized by conservatives for his appointment of a liberal, Rose Bird, as chief justice. Bird had already been the object of a recall effort and an organized drive to defeat her for reelection, and each of Brown's subsequent appointments to the high court occasioned renewed claims that he was weak on "law and order." (Indeed, Bird, along with two other Brown appointees, was recalled in the 1986 election.) When Wilson took up this charge, Brown only mildly defended his record in this area. But Wilson may ultimately have lost his advantage on the "law and order" issue by going so far on two side issues that even some Republicans repudiated his views. While the state supreme court was reviewing the recently passed "Victims' Bill of Rights" initiative, Wilson stated that any justice who ruled against its constitutionality— and particularly Chief Justice Bird—should be recalled from office. Wilson was immediately accused (and not only by the Brown campaign) of meddling with the court's functioning, and although he continued to attack Brown's appointees (and Brown himself for appointing them), he did soften his position. But later in the fall, Wilson took his objections about Brown's court appointees to extremes by calling for the election of all federal judges. When even Republicans rejected this idea, Wilson dropped it completely. But both incidents enabled Brown to take the offensive and make Wilson, rather than himself, the focus of the "law and order" issue.

THE CALIFORNIA ELECTORATE'S VIEW OF THE CAMPAIGN

A high-intensity race, the Brown-Wilson campaign was the subject of a great deal of news coverage, complemented by heavy campaign advertising.[17] We know from our earlier investigation of newspaper coverage of this race that the candidates differed sharply on a number of issues, and information about their positions was continually relayed to voters through news coverage. Were the issues the candidates were debating

TABLE 22
Importance to Californians of 25 Issues, October 1982

	Percentage Giving Issue a Rating of			
Issue	*10*	*6–9*	*5*	*1–4*
Cost of living	54%	36%	6%	4%
Unemployment	53	35	6	6
Crime	53	37	6	4
Taxes and government spending	50	38	6	6
Social Security	43	51	8	8
Danger of nuclear war	41	25	11	23
High interest rates	40	42	9	9
Price of energy	38	45	9	8
Supply of energy	38	50	8	4
Higher education	37	43	14	6
Housing	35	43	11	11
Public schools	34	44	12	10
Equal rights for women	33	36	14	17
Pollution	32	43	15	10
Judges and the courts	31	38	16	13
Illegal immigration	29	34	15	22
Water supply	27	49	13	11
Health care/Medi-Cal	26	46	15	14
Military issues	25	43	16	16
Abortion	24	25	18	33
Foreign relations	22	45	17	16
Race relations	22	40	20	18
Welfare	21	43	19	17
Public transportation	20	40	16	24
Highway and street maintenance	12	43	24	21

Source: California Poll 8206, 1–4 October 1982.

Note: The question read as follows: "I am going to read you a number of things that are of concern to people in California today. For each one I read we'd like you to think of a 10-point scale for your answer. If you think that this problem is of the utmost importance, would you say '10.' If you think the problem is of some importance but not of the utmost importance would you select a number somewhere between 1 and 10 for your answer."

salient and important enough to the public to be the basis on which they cast their votes? Three of the issues were considered important by most Californians; the fourth—Brown's judicial appointments—was considerably less salient. An October California Poll survey asked respondents to rate the importance of 25 issues on a 10-point continuum ranging from "of the utmost importance" to "not at all important." As table 22 shows, most issues were of some importance to respondents, but a few were clearly of greater importance than others.

"Reaganomics" was not offered by the pollster as one of the 25 issues, but "taxes and government spending" was fourth on the list, with half of those polled saying this was of utmost importance to them. ("Cost of living" and "unemployment," which were ranked first and second, were also related to Reagan economic policies, if less directly.) Social Security was also of high salience to Californians, as was the danger of nuclear war, and therefore, presumably, the nuclear freeze issue.[18]

In contrast with the Reaganomics debate and the Social Security and nuclear freeze issues, Brown's court appointees were considered highly important by a smaller percentage of Californians. The supreme court issue received a rating of 10 from fewer than a third of respondents and fell near the middle of the pack of 25 issues.[19] This is not to say that the underlying issue of crime was not important; crime was third on the California Poll list. But the majority of the debate in this area—fueled by the Wilson camp—focused not on crime but on Brown's court appointees, particularly those on the state supreme court.

The supreme court question. Four California Supreme Court justices were on the November ballot for confirmation, requiring a yes or no decision by the voters. Three were Brown appointees whom Wilson attacked throughout the campaign; the fourth, Frank Richardson, was a Reagan appointee and the type of judge whose appointment Wilson advocated. The last California Poll before the election showed that barely half of the respondents had an opinion on the question of the justices' retention. Fewer than 5 percent favored removing the three Brown appointees and retaining Wilson's favored Justice Richardson. Only 10 respondents out of 1,976 supported the three Brown justices and wanted Richardson removed. A substantial proportion favored retaining all four, but this does not indicate that they had been influenced by the Brown-Wilson debate, since supreme court justices had always been routinely confirmed in California elections.

Most of the respondents who favored retaining only Justice Richardson were Republicans, and 97 percent of these intended to vote for Wilson. As table 23 shows, of the few Democrats who favored keeping only Richardson, 68 percent indicated that they would vote for Wilson, and only 25 percent were for Brown. Thus in this one category (which constitutes 5 percent of those surveyed), respondents of both party affiliations stand out as overwhelmingly against Brown and for Wilson. But the vast majority of respondents either showed no awareness of the supreme court issue or showed no indication that it had anything to do with their choice of a Senate candidate. Evidently this issue, even though it played a central role in the two candidates' debate during the campaign, was too esoteric to register with most voters.

130

TABLE 23
Defections to Brown and Wilson, by Opinion on Recall of California Supreme
Court justices, October 1982

Respondent Voting for:	Opinion*					
	A	B	C	D	E	None
Democrats						
Brown	25%	46%	65%	75%	75%	64%
Wilson	68	43	24	18	13	20
Other	0	5	1	2	0	1
Undecided	7	5	10	5	13	15
(N)	(28)	(56)	(225)	(255)	(8)	(437)
Republicans						
Brown	3%	7%	14%	25%	—	12%
Wilson	97	79	78	69	—	78
Other	0	7	2	2	—	0
Undecided	0	7	8	3	—	11
(N)	(60)	(70)	(204)	(127)	(2)	(301)
TOTAL DISTRIBUTION (N = 1,976):	5%	8%	24%	22%	0%	42%

Source: California Poll 8207, 24–31 October 1982.
Note: Dashes indicate that the number of cases was insufficient to provide for an entry in
the cell.
* A = against recall of Richardson (appointed by Gov. Reagan); for recall of three Brown-
appointed justices
  B = for recall of all four justices
  C = no clear pattern
  D = against recall of all four justices
  E = for recall of Richardson; against recall of three Brown appointees

The nuclear freeze. The issue raised most often by Brown was whether
the United States should impose a freeze on the construction of nuclear
weapons. During the 62 days examined, the freeze was mentioned in a
Senate-race context by the *San Francisco Chronicle* in 23 articles and by
the *Los Angeles Times* in 15. Brown was unequivocally in favor of a
freeze and favored Proposition 12, the nuclear freeze initiative on the
November ballot. Wilson opposed both the idea of a freeze and the
initiative.

Advocates of the nuclear freeze voted for Brown over Wilson by a
margin of about two to one (57 percent to 31 percent), while opponents
of the freeze supported Wilson by an even greater ratio (63 percent to
26 percent). This finding alone does not speak directly to the existence

TABLE 24
California Voter Attitudes on the Nuclear Freeze, by Intended Vote for Brown or Wilson, October 1982

Intended Vote	Conservative		Leaning toward Conservative		Moderate		Leaning toward Liberal		Liberal	
	For	Against	For	Against	For	Against	For	Against	For	Against
Democrats										
Brown	56%	32%	57%	36%	77%	57%	79%	63%	87%	69%
Wilson	29	53	30	49	13	30	13	25	7	15
No opinion/other	15	15	13	15	10	13	8	12	6	16
(N)	(86)	(88)	(92)	(67)	(106)	(60)	(132)	(40)	(174)	(39)
Republicans										
Brown	17%	5%	19%	8%	27%	14%	44%	27%	32%	19%
Wilson	73	92	72	80	68	77	40	59	32	81
No opinion/other	10	3	10	12	5	9	16	14	36	0
(N)	(105)	(247)	(68)	(78)	(37)	(35)	(25)	(22)	(22)	(16)

Source: California Poll 8207, 24–31 October 1982.
Note: Ideology is self-designated. Percentages may not add up to 100% due to rounding.

or impact of issue voting, because most Democrats and liberals favored the freeze, while most Republicans and conservatives opposed it (the initiative passed by a slim margin). If we control for party and ideology, however, the strong relationship between voters' attitudes about the freeze and choice for senator remains (see table 24). Ninety-two percent of conservative Republicans opposing the freeze voted for Wilson, but only 73 percent favoring the freeze did so. Eighty-one percent of liberal Republicans opposing the freeze voted for Wilson, but only 32 percent favoring the freeze did so. Similar large differences existed among Democrats: 24 points separated proponents and opponents among conservatives, and 18 points separated liberals (in their support for Brown).[20]

Reaganomics. Immediately after the June primary, Brown began campaigning against President Reagan's economic policies, charging that Reagan's supply-side economic philosophy and the accompanying enormous federal deficit were direct causes of the recession that had put so many Californians out of work in 1982. Brown characterized Wilson as "a zealous advocate" of Reaganomics (*San Francisco Chronicle,* 12 October 1982, 1) and said that if elected, Wilson would be an automatic vote in the Senate to continue Reagan's economic policies in the future. In mid-October Brown said, "It is very clear to me that Reaganomics is a failure, and that this election is about that—do you want more of it or do you want a change?" He said that Wilson was a "man who was bought and paid for by the Republican high command. They own him" (ibid., 21 October 1982, 16). Inasmuch as the economic picture in California was not rosy, Wilson was not anxious to associate himself with Reagan's economic policies. But when he was questioned about his stance on those policies, he refused to repudiate them, opposed any tax increases, and blamed the deficit and unemployment on past administrations.

The relationship between Californians' views on Reaganomics and their choice for senator is shown in table 25. Both Democrats and Republicans who approved of President Reagan's economic policies preferred Wilson more than did those disapproving of those policies. Among Democrats this difference ranged from 54 percent for Wilson among the strongest advocates of Reagan's economic policies to only 8 percent for Wilson among those most strongly opposed. Among Republicans the figures were 85 percent and 60 percent, respectively. In addition, an exit poll conducted by Mervin Field showed that 21 percent of those voting for Brown "cited Brown's opposition to Reagan's policies as the first reason for supporting the Democrat" (*San Francisco Examiner,* 4 November 1982, B-1). And 20 percent of Wilson voters "said they voted for Wilson because he supports the Reagan administration policies" (ibid.). Controlling for voters' ideological identification, these differences remain, although the small sample and the skewed distribution of respondents across categories makes it difficult to place much confidence in the magnitude of the differences within each ideological grouping. The available evidence suggests, however, that Reaganomics was probably a factor for some voters as they made their choice between Brown and Wilson.

Social Security. As with the nuclear freeze and Reaganomics, the findings on Social Security are consistent with the proposition that people voted for the Senate candidate whose opinion was closer to their own on an issue of importance to them. This relationship is shown in table 26, controlling for party identification. Those believing that Social Security should be left alone preferred Brown to a considerably greater degree than did those who felt that alterations in the system were needed. This

TABLE 25
California Voter Attitudes toward Reaganomics, by Intended Vote for Brown or Wilson

Intended Vote	Very favorable	Favorable	Mixed	Unfavorable	Very Unfavorable
			Democrats		
Brown	39%	51%	57%	71%	82%
Wilson	54	44	25	19	8
Undecided	8	5	18	11	10
(N)	(26)	(39)	(49)	(95)	(154)
			Republicans		
Brown	9%	7%	11%	25%	40%
Wilson	85	90	89	69	60
Undecided	6	2	0	6	0
(N)	(112)	(94)	(35)	(16)	(10)

Source: Los Angeles Times Poll 61, 10–14 October 1982.
Note: An additive index was created from four items in the *Los Angeles Times* Poll (for item wordings see appendix 6): V26, V27, V53, V61. The index ranges from a score of 0 for those strongly supporting the Reagan view in all four cases to a score of 16 for those opposing Reagan in all four cases. The 0–16 scale was then evenly divided into the five categories shown above; e.g., respondents scoring from 0 to 3.2 are called "very favorable," and those scoring from 3.2 to 6.4 are called "favorable."
Percentages may not add up to 100% due to rounding.

TABLE 26
California Voter Opinion on Whether to Alter the Social Security System, by
Intended Vote for Brown or Wilson, October 1982

Intended Vote	Keep As Is	2	3	4	Favor Four Changes
		Democrats			
Wilson	23%	23%	26%	35%	45%
Brown	71	69	61	50	40
Undecided/other	7	8	14	15	15
(N)	(138)	(157)	(117)	(34)	(20)
		Republicans			
Wilson	68%	71%	78%	84%	100%
Brown	19	19	12	4	0
Undecided/other	14	10	10	12	0
(N)	(69)	(88)	(98)	(44)	(47)

Source: California Poll 8207, 24–31 October 1982.
Note: The items in the Social Security index were as follows:
V 65: We should keep Social Security benefits as they are now, even if it means having to raise Social Security taxes.
V 66: We should keep Social Security benefits as they are now, even if it means having to raise money from other taxes people pay.
V 67: If the Social Security fund is running short we should reduce Social Security payments to people who retire before age 65.
V 68: If the Social Security fund is running short we should reduce the cost of living increases to those now on Social Security.
Respondents in category 1 ("Keep as is") agreed with the first two statements and disagreed with the third and fourth; respondents in category 5 disagreed with the first two statements and agreed with the third and fourth; and categories 2, 3, and 4 fall between these two extremes.

pattern remains, although cell sizes are small, when self-proclaimed ideology is taken into consideration.

WAS THERE ISSUE VOTING?

The foregoing evidence, based on crosstabulations only, suggests the presence of issue voting based on three issues debated in the Brown-Wilson Senate race. Even controlling for party and ideology, however, does not rule out the possibility that the relationship between these variables and the vote may be spurious—because of the effects of still other variables or even because of possible interactions among the three issues.[21]

To address the possibility that other variables might be operating or

TABLE 27

The Effects of the Nuclear Freeze, Reaganomics, and Social Security on Voting in Senate Elections, California 1982 (least squares regression; unstandardized coefficients)

Poll	Intercept	Party	Ideology	Nuclear Freeze	Reagan-omics	Social Security	Age	Income	Gun Control	Text-books	Beverage Con-tainers	Redis-tricting	Water
California Poll	.183	.166 (.007)	.077 (.010)	.120 (.031)		.159 (.048)	-.002 (.0008)	-.018 (.004)	.052 (.030)	-.013 (.028)	.015 (.028)	-.053 (.031)	.044 (.032)
									($N = 777$; $R^2 = .42$)				
L.A. Times Poll 61	-.020	.082 (.009)	.042 (.016)	.087 (.034)	.369 (.064)		-.027 (.015)	-.042 (.022)	.047 (.031)		.012 (.031)		.079 (.034)
									($N = 661$; $R^2 = .43$)				

Note: For a description of the independent variables, see appendix 6. The dependent variable is vote the Senate (0 = Wilson, 0.5 = undecided, 1 = Brown). Education and sex were initially included in the regressions but were removed because they were statistically insignificant.

that the effects of three issues on the Senate vote were not unique and independent, I employ ordinary least squares regression of the three main issues on the vote, controlling for other variables that might show the relationships seen in the tables above to be spurious. Unfortunately, it is not possible to include in a single regression equation all three of the issues in which we are interested, because the California Poll asked questions about the nuclear freeze and Social Security but not about Reagan's economic policies, while the *Los Angeles Times* Poll asked about the nuclear freeze and Reaganomics but not Social Security. Therefore, the simultaneous effect of Reaganomics and Social Security on the vote cannot be analyzed.

Table 27 regresses the nuclear freeze and the Social Security variables, along with party affiliation, self-described ideology, and the additional controls of age and income on vote choice for senator (measured as a choice among three categories: Wilson, undecided, and Brown). Also included in the regression are variables tapping people's views on other issues. The two parts of table 27 are comparable, except that Reaganomics replaces Social Security in the lower portion. The unstandardized coefficients reported in this table indicate an effect consistent with the tabular findings. There is a statistically significant and fairly sizable relationship between voters' opinions about the nuclear freeze and their choices for senator. Specifically, the difference between opposing and supporting the nuclear freeze yields a difference of 9 percentage points (according to the *Los Angeles Times* data) or 12 percentage points (according to the California Poll data) in the likelihood of voting for Brown. The coefficients for Reaganomics and Social Security are likewise statistically significant and fairly sizable, as are those for party registration and self-described ideology.[22]

The effects of these issues are quite substantial. The California Poll shows that someone who favored a nuclear freeze and took a liberal position on Social Security was 28 percentage points more likely to vote for Brown than someone who opposed a freeze and favored the position on Social Security nearest to Wilson's. The *Los Angeles Times* Poll suggests that someone favoring a freeze and disliking President Reagan's economic policies was 45 percentage points more likely to support Brown. In both cases, the combined effects of the two issues was greater than the effects of party, ideology, age, and income combined.

In addition to the nuclear freeze, Reaganomics, and Social Security, as well as Brown's state supreme court appointees, other issues were debated during the fall of 1982 in California. Ballot initiatives called for placing deposits on the purchase of all cans and bottles, establishing water conservation programs, removing from the state legislature the power to redraw legislative district lines, and regulating handguns. While the Senate candidates took opposing positions on some of these initiatives, they did not concentrate on these questions in their campaigns, and their views on them were not covered widely by the press. For example, an initiative proposing limits on the number of handguns in California and the registration of all existing handguns was supported and publicly endorsed by Brown, while Wilson opposed it. Their positions on the issue, however, were rarely discussed in campaign news coverage: the *San Francisco Chronicle* referred to the candidates' stances on this issue six times, the *Los Angeles Times* only once. While people who felt very strongly about gun control may have known of the Senate candidates' views and voted accordingly, it is also likely, because of the scant press coverage of the issue, that few people knew how either Senate candidate felt about gun control. As table 27 shows, the coefficients on the gun-control variable in both polls are very close to zero and are not statistically significant. Views on gun control had no relationship to the vote for senator, even though the candidates had taken opposing positions. Indeed, none of the other "side" issues seem to have had much relationship to the Senate vote; only those that were heavily covered in the news media had any influence on the vote.

It appears from these data that issue voting in the 1982 California Senate race occurred only in connection with the issues that the candidates emphasized most strongly, that were, in turn, the focus of campaign press coverage, and that struck voters as salient. One issue in that race—the supreme court issue—met the first two of these criteria but not the third. Although it was continually debated and reported on, it was not particularly salient to voters and did not provoke issue voting.

Issue Voting in a Low-key Senate Race: Wyoming, 1978

We saw earlier that in low-key Senate races news coverage of campaigns and their attendant issues is very light, and we know that 43 percent of races from 1968 through 1984 were low-key. How likely is it that issue voting may occur in such Senate races? Data are not available to answer this question systematically, but it can be approached by comparing the hard-fought open-seat race between Brown and Wilson with a low-key open-seat race—that of Alan Simpson against Raymond Whitaker in Wyoming in 1978.

In June 1977, Wyoming Republican Senator Clifford Hansen an-

nounced that he would not run for a third term. Former state senator
Alan Simpson, who in 1976 had retired after 14 years in the state legislature (including a term as speaker *pro tempore* of the House) to pursue
the nomination for Hansen's seat, had little trouble defeating two opponents in the Republican primary. Considered a formidable legislator in
his own right, Simpson was also known as the son of former Governor
and Senator Milward Simpson. On the Democratic side, it appeared that
conservative political newcomer Dean Larsen would be the nominee until
two more liberal candidates, Casper attorney Raymond Whitaker and
Deputy Attorney General Charles Carroll, entered the race just before
the filing deadline. In a rather lifeless primary, Whitaker won with
46 percent of the vote, and the other two received 27 percent each. Like
Simpson, Whitaker was probably better known statewide than his opponents, but he was not necessarily held in as high regard given his
political win/loss record. After a stint as state Democratic chairman in
the 1950s, Whitaker had been an unsuccessful Democratic senatorial
candidate in 1960. He had been defeated in a primary bid for governor
in 1966, and two years he had lost in the primary for Wyoming's lone
House seat.

The general election campaign was a short one, since the Wyoming
primary occurs in early September. The intensity level of the campaign
was not much greater than that of the primaries. Simpson campaigned
daily, spending a considerable part of his time walking door-to-door
throughout the state. Whitaker, suggesting that Simpson "must have
seen 30 million antelope" (*Casper Star Tribune*, 20 October 1978, 10),
claimed that Wyoming was too large and too sparsely populated for
effective personal campaigning, and he limited his own campaigning to
occasional speeches, as well as television and radio spots. Overall, Simpson spent $439,805 on the campaign. Whitaker, whose reported per-
sonal worth was between $2 million and $5 million, spent $142,749.[23]

The Simpson-Whitaker race was covered by the Wyoming media, but
there were considerably fewer stories about the campaign than appeared
in the Brown-Wilson contest in California. As in the California race, the
state's two largest daily newspapers were examined, for the period from
September 1 until Election Day, to determine how often and in what
depth the media covered the Senate race.

Wyoming's two largest newspapers cover different parts of the state
and probably reach a greater proportion of the state's population than
the *Times* and the *Chronicle* reach in California. The *Casper Star Tribune* is by far the largest of the two, with a daily circulation of about
35,000. The *Wyoming State Tribune*, with a daily circulation of about

12,000, covers the Cheyenne and Laramie areas, in the southeast corner of the state.[24] Despite its expansive terrain, Wyoming is about two-thirds urban; moreover, Casper, Cheyenne, and Laramie together are more populous than Wyoming's 20 next largest cities combined. The campaign coverage by these two newspapers is assumed to represent the maximum coverage of this Senate campaign by all Wyoming newspapers and, for reasons discussed in chapter 3, to exceed television news coverage.

The *Casper Star Tribune* covered the Senate campaign slowly at first, at the rate of once or twice a week in September (36 mentions in all). By October the campaign was being mentioned almost daily, and the length of the articles had increased slightly. The Cheyenne-based *Wyoming State Tribune* devoted much less coverage to the race and in fact ran only 4 relevant stories in the late-campaign period between October 21 and November 6. Simpson was the subject of 24 headlines over the two-month period in the *Casper Star Tribune* and just 5 in the *State Tribune*. Whitaker's name appeared in nearly the same number of headlines but was mentioned in fewer stories overall. In the 66 days monitored, Simpson was prominently mentioned in 53 stories in the Casper paper and in 19 stories in the Cheyenne paper; the corresponding figures for Whitaker are 43 and 19.

While in the Brown-Wilson race in California the news media followed the candidates closely, with newspaper coverage seeming accurately to reflect the frequency (if not the depth and detail) of the messages put out by the two camps, in the Wyoming race news coverage was considerably less frequent. It is difficult to know whether the sparser coverage was due to failure by the newspapers to report what the candidates were saying or whether it reflected accurate coverage of fewer messages. The *Casper Star Journal* did print Simpson's campaign itinerary throughout the campaign (Whitaker did not provide his), so it is possible to note when a planned Simpson campaign stop went unreported. This happened occasionally, but generally the Casper paper covered all stops of two or more days' duration. On the occasions when Simpson was in Cheyenne, both papers covered the same story, an indication that the Casper paper was doing a complete job. It would therefore seem justified to assume that the *Star Tribune*'s coverage around the rest of the state was also fairly complete. Thus we may assume that the smaller number of overall news mentions of Whitaker reflects fewer messages put out by the Democrat rather than journalistic bias.

While some of the newspapers' attention to the Senate race focused on the probability that Simpson would win and on the size of his lead, considerable coverage was also devoted to the candidates' issue positions.

Most commonly, both papers quoted or paraphrased the candidates' stands on various issues but rarely spelled out these positions in detail. One paper sometimes gave details when the other did not, which suggests that the candidates were in fact saying more than the newspapers always reported. In any case, the typical news story in this race rarely did more than outline the candidates' positions on a given issue. This type of coverage differs strikingly from the coverage of the Brown-Wilson race in California, where the major issues were analyzed in considerable depth in the press.

The kinds of issues discussed by Simpson and Whitaker in the 1978 campaign may be categorized in the same way as those in the Brown-Wilson contest: as policy-oriented issues (those dealing either with potential legislation or policies otherwise debatable in a "pro-con" fashion) or personal topics (most of which involved one candidate attacking the other about past performance or behavior). Coverage of issues between September 1 and Election Day is presented in table 28. Simpson campaigned mainly on policy-oriented issues; the two that received greatest coverage by the newspapers concerned the proper role of the federal government in regulation of energy and the environment and how to reduce inflation. Simpson unequivocally favored federal deregulation of oil and natural gas, limits on federal intervention into Wyoming land policy, and less stringent regulation of the mineral industry in Wyoming. To tackle inflation, he called for a constitutional amendment to balance the federal budget, and he felt that cutting the deficit should involve cutting federal appropriations for non-defense programs rather than raising taxes.

Whitaker preferred to focus on a single, personal issue: Simpson's ties to special interests, particularly out-of-state interests. Throughout the campaign, Whitaker attacked Simpson's out-of-state contributions while reminding his audiences that he was accepting no contributions at all. Whitaker's message was that Simpson, if elected, would not be able to avoid having to repay his contributors (by voting as they would prefer), whereas Whitaker would always vote for the best interests of Wyoming. Simpson responded by asserting that he could not be bought and attempted to portray his opponent as a hypocrite by recalling that Whitaker had accepted contributions from special interests in all three of his previous statewide campaigns.

In some cases, Whitaker's views on policy issues were similar to Simpson's. For example, both candidates criticized President Carter's energy policy as unworkable in Wyoming. Both supported reductions in federal taxes. If Whitaker had a position on an amendment to balance the federal budget, it was not reported. There were two issues, though,

141

TABLE 28

Coverage of Specific Issues by Two Daily Newspapers, Wyoming Senate Race, 1978

| | Candidate Associated* | | | | | | | | |
| | Simpson | | | Whitaker | | | Both | | |
Issues	CST	WST	Total	CST	WST	Total	CST	WST	Total
Policy issues									
Federal regulation of environment, land	4	10	14	3	1	4	7	11	18
Oil and gas deregulation	4	1	5	4	1	5	8	2	10
Balanced-budget amendment/cut inflation, spending	5	4	9	1	1	2	6	5	11
Right-to-work legislation	5	1	6	2	0	2	7	1	8
Equal Rights Amendment	2	0	2	3	0	3	5	0	5
Federal campaign finance reform	0	0	0	6	0	6	0	6	6
Coal slurry pipeline	2	2	4	1	0	1	3	2	5
Wyoming needs a Democratic senator	0	0	0	4	1	5	4	1	5
Increase defense funds/cut waste	2	1	3	1	0	1	3	1	4
Abortion	1	0	1	2	0	2	3	0	3
Support working people	0	0	0	2	1	3	2	1	3
Decentralize Senate office	0	0	0	2	1	3	2	1	3
Other, assorted issues	4	8	12	2	5	7	6	13	19
Personal/character/experience issues									
Simpson's out-of-state vs. Whitaker refusal of contributions	8	3	11	9	3	12	17	6	23
Simpson's personal debts/ Whitaker's questionable property holdings	4	0	4	4	0	4	8	0	8

Note: Figures represent the number of articles in each paper between 1 September and 6 November 1978 in which a candidate is associated with an issue position.

* CST = *Casper Star–Tribune;* WST = *Wyoming State–Tribune.*

on which the two candidates definitely disagreed. As often as Simpson called for the complete deregulation of oil and gas, Whitaker called this proposal too extreme and advocated continued regulation. And where Simpson voiced support for right-to-work legislation, Whitaker opposed such legislation as unnecessary, telling the *Casper Star Tribune,* "I don't think it would make any difference if we kept it or passed it. . . . I don't know of one single action brought under it." He also stated that "labor leaders in the state don't consider the Right-to-Work law 'relevant any-more'" (18 October 1978, 10). Neither of these disagreements received much coverage. Unlike in the Brown-Wilson race, then, there were no issues in the Wyoming race on which the candidates were clearly divided *and* which received wide and continual coverage in the media—other than the matter of accepting campaign contributions. Of the issues on which the candidates were on record as opposing each other, according to table 28, only the question of federal intervention in Wyoming land and environmental policy received more than scant coverage, and even on this issue Whitaker had little to say.

THE WYOMING ELECTORATE'S VIEW OF THE CAMPAIGN

In the California race, most voters had become familiar with both candidates by the last month of the campaign. This was not the case in Wyoming in 1978. In a Wyoming statewide survey conducted three weeks before the election, respondents were asked to rate the two Senate candidates on six personal characteristics. This task did not require great familiarity with the candidates; respondents were asked whether each man was "honest or dishonest, weak or strong, intelligent or unintelligent, unpleasant or pleasant, good or bad, incapable or capable," and they were asked to "place an X on the scale to indicate your feelings about the candidate," with the first word in each pair scored as "1" and the second as "7." Even at this superficial level, few respondents could rate either candidate on all six sets of traits. Thirty-seven percent rated Simpson on all six, and 23 percent gave Whitaker ratings on all six pairs of adjectives. One-third were unable to rate Simpson at all, and nearly one-half failed to evaluate Whitaker (the rest evaluated the candidates on some, but not all, of the issues).

That these candidates were not well known is perhaps most sharply reflected by the fact that on a question asking how likely it was that each candidate was a Democrat or a Republican (a rating of "1" indicated a certain Democrat, a "7" a certain Republican, "4" was reserved for "don't know," and the other ratings represented lesser degrees of certainty), half of the respondents did not know that Simpson was a Republican, and even more (57 percent) were unaware that Whitaker was a Democrat. Assuming that there was as much correct as wrong guessing, not even three in ten respondents were certain of either candidate's party.

Given this lack of public familiarity with the two candidates at even the most basic level, it should be no surprise that the degree of the public's familiarity with the candidates' issue stances was even lower. The Wyoming Poll asked respondents to rate from "probable" to "improbable" the likelihood that each candidate held a given policy position during the campaign. A rating of "1" indicated the highest likelihood, a "7" the lowest, and a "4" that the respondent had no idea what the candidate's position was. On the issue of "forcing the government to balance the national budget each year except in time of war" only 9 percent of re-

143

TABLE 29
Identification of the Senate Candidates' Positions on Two Issues, Wyoming 1978
(in percent)

	Extremely probable (1)	Quite probable (2)	Slightly probable (3)	No opinion (4)	Slightly improbable (5)	Quite improbable (6)	Extremely improbable (7)
	1. "Favors removing federal controls on the price of oil and natural gas."						
Simpson	10	14	8	57	5	3	3
Whitaker	3	6	7	64	7	6	7
	2. "Favors retaining the provision in national law permitting states to enact right-to-work laws."						
Simpson	19	11	8	56	3	2	3
Whitaker	7	12	10	54	6	6	7

Source: Statewide Wyoming Election Survey, October 1978.
Note: The question was worded as follows: "Place an X on the scale in the position you believe to be accurate."

spondents felt it "highly likely" that Simpson favored this position. In fact, Simpson had taken exactly this position, and it had been reported clearly. Nevertheless, 49 percent offered no opinion on this question, and another 10 percent felt that it was improbable that Simpson favored a mandatory balanced budget. Nearly the same figures turned up on an item asking whether Simpson favored "a substantial cut in the Federal income tax," which he did. The electorate knew even less about Whitaker on these issues, in part because fewer of them knew anything about the Democrat in the Senate race and in part because Whitaker did not discuss these issues during the campaign nearly as extensively as Simpson did.

As noted above, there were two issues on which the candidates held clearly opposing views and on which, therefore, issue voting would have been possible: Simpson called for the complete deregulation of oil and natural gas by the federal government, whereas Whitaker, calling this view foolishly extreme, favored continued regulation; and Simpson called for the retention of right-to-work laws, while Whitaker viewed such laws as unnecessary and outdated. Respondents' impressions of the candidates' views on these issues are shown in table 29. Most respondents offered no opinion as to how either candidate stood. Some who did offer a position seem to have been guessing: 11 percent misidentified Simpson's position on oil and gas deregulation even though he was unequivocally and actively for it. Sixteen percent felt that Whitaker probably favored deregulation even though two weeks earlier he had called

Simpson's demand for complete deregulation "the most outlandish statement ever made in Wyoming politics," saying that such a move "would be a gross disservice not only to Wyoming but to the whole world" (*Casper Star Tribune*, 5 October 1978). On the right-to-work issue, 8 percent misidentified Simpson's stance, and 29 percent wrongly characterized Whitaker's.

Such figures suggest that some percentage of the correct responses also resulted from guesses (assuming that a guesser has an equal chance of being right or wrong). But even if we assume that respondents marking categories (2) and (3) as well as (1), or (5) and (6) as well as (7), actually knew the candidate's position and that the figures in the "correct" broadened categories include no random guessing, we still find very few respondents familiar with the candidates' positions on these issues. About one-third knew that Simpson favored deregulation of oil and gas, and one-fifth knew that Whitaker opposed it. Nearly four in ten knew that Simpson supported right-to-work legislation, but only 19 percent knew that Whitaker opposed it (29 percent actually said he favored it).

WAS THERE ISSUE VOTING?

Since all but a small percentage of respondents either were unaware of the positions of Simpson and Whitaker on the two issues on which the candidates sharply disagreed or misidentified their stances, it is difficult to see how any of these people could have been issue voting.[25] But what about those few who did correctly identify the positions of both candidates? The relationship between these voters' own positions on the two issues and who they voted for is shown in table 30. In the last column in the table there is a fairly large disparity in candidate choice between proponents and opponents of the two issues. Proponents of deregulating oil and gas and of retaining right-to-work laws were considerably more likely to vote for Simpson over Whitaker than were opponents of these issues. Controlling for respondents' party identification, however, diminishes these differences somewhat. Among Republicans, there were no differences in vote choice between proponents and opponents of these issues; both overwhelmingly favored Simpson. Among Democrats, those agreeing with Whitaker's position were clearly more likely to vote for him than those taking the opposing view.[26]

It seems clear, then, that there was very little issue voting in the Whitaker-Simpson campaign. One reason is that so little information got through about the issues that voters were unable to identify either Simpson's or Whitaker's positions. Simpson focused his campaign statements on the need for a balanced federal budget, the elimination of oil

TABLE 30
Wyoming Voters' Positions on Two Issues, by Their Vote for Simpson or Whitaker (in percent)

	Republicans			Democrats			Total		
	Favor	No Opinion	Oppose	Favor	No Opinion	Oppose	Favor	No Opinion	Oppose
1. "Removing federal controls on the price of oil and natural gas."									
Simpson	85	50	86	71	33	25	82	46	43
Undecided	14	50	14	5	50	18	13	46	16
Whitaker	1	0	0	24	17	57	6	9	41
(N)	(14)	(4)	(65)	(17)	(6)	(28)	(51)	(11)	(87)
2. "Retaining the provision in national law permitting states to enact right-to-work laws."									
Simpson	86	75	88	58	—	6	83	50	24
Undecided	12	0	13	25	—	19	13	17	17
Whitaker	2	25	0	17	—	74	3	33	59
(N)	(127)	(4)	(8)	(12)	(0)	(31)	(149)	(6)	(46)

Source: Statewide Wyoming Election Survey, 1978.
Note: Respondents were asked to place their opinion, ranging from "extremely good" to "extremely bad" on a 7-point scale; in this table "Favor" includes those responding 1, 2, or 3, and "Oppose" includes those responding 5, 6, or 7. Only those voters who correctly identified both candidates' positions are included in the table. Independents were excluded because there were too few for analysis.

and price controls, and retention of right-to-work laws. Whitaker limited himself essentially to criticizing Simpson's views on these issues (generally by saying Simpson "went too far"). Wyoming Poll data show that respondents were better able to identify correctly Simpson's views than they were Whitaker's on the issues the two debated, and they were better able to identify Simpson on the issues he stressed during the campaign than on issues that were not prominent (including increases in the defense budget and federal tax relief for business and industry rather than tax cuts for middle- and lower-income people). Among voters attuned enough to be able to identify correctly the issue positions of the candidates, these issues appeared not to have influenced Republicans' votes; Republicans preferred their candidate, Simpson, regardless of their own positions on the two issues that could be tested. While issue voting might have occurred among some Democrats, the percentage of such people was so small that even if issues did affect their vote choice, the overall incidence or importance of issue voting in this race was at most extremely slight.

Issue Voting and Voter Rationalization

It is important to remember that the likelihood of issue voting in a given race can be overestimated due to the presence of "voter rationalization." That is, in assessing policy voting in any election, the possibility must be considered that some survey respondents, instead of selecting a candidate on the basis of whether he took the "right" position on important issues, might be adapting the candidate's or their own issue positions to make them consonant with their already determined vote choice. "Voter rationalization" can take two forms: persuasion and projection. "Persuasion," according to Brody and Page (1972), occurs when a citizen alters or forms his own issue position to coincide with that of a favored candidate, and "projection" occurs when a citizen formulates his vote intention on some other grounds and then convinces himself that the preferred candidate shares his own position on an issue. As Brody and Page observed, "If causality runs from opinion to behavior for some citizens (the 'policy voters') and from behavior to opinion for other citizens (the 'rationalizers')," the resulting data will be indistinguishable. "If we cannot distinguish the rationalizers from those who . . . vote on the basis of policy considerations, we are in danger of overestimating the extent of policy voting by the number of such voters" (452).

Two research teams—Markus and Converse, and Page and Jones—

investigated this problem in the 1976 presidential election, using different models of the vote decision. They found not only that policy voting had occurred in that election but that projection and persuasion were to some extent factors as well. Markus and Converse (1979) took advantage of the availability of the CPS/NES panel design to develop a model that allowed for separate estimation of projection and persuasion. They tested for the differential impact of each on five issues, finding that projection was considerably more in evidence than persuasion and that on two issues—the "moral" issues of busing and women's rights—there was no apparent persuasion effect at all. They concluded that in the 1976 presidential election, the overall incidence of people rationalizing either their own or the candidates' issue positions on the basis of who they planned to vote for was slight: "However intriguing and plausible these side effects may be, the estimates we have derived from the model make clear that they remained no more than side effects in 1976. The policy differences consensually perceived to exist between the candidates, coupled with prior differences in voter positions on these issues [measured with panel data], had a noteworthy effect on voters' comparative assessments of the candidates, and through these invidious assessments, left their mark on final voting decisions" (1068).

Page and Jones (1979) focused on CPS/NES survey items tapping perception of the candidates' issue positions and of numerous other items that permitted the proper specification of a simultaneous causation model of voting. Their model did not permit estimation of the separate effects of projection and persuasion and used an issue index instead of analyzing various issues separately. They found strong evidence of policy voting in 1976, as well as strong "reciprocal effects," and speculated that most persuasion and projection comes when issues are not salient to voters and when information about them is lacking. Page and Jones also suggested that what at first may seem to be rationalization may in fact be *rationality:*

> The existence of strong effects of policy orientations upon candidate evaluations suggests that few voters, if any, rely exclusively upon simple rationalization in arriving at their final evaluations of presidential contenders' policies. It is much more likely that a given voter will have had at least some realistic notion of his or her comparative distances from the candidates which conditioned more general evaluations in the first place. Lacking perfect information, such voters might then combine what data they have on policy distances with party cues and judgments about the candidates' personal attributes into a preliminary compara-

148

tive evaluation of the nominees, which they then may use to infer their ultimate net distance from the candidates over a wider range of policy areas. (1085)

The nature of the available state-level data on the Brown-Wilson race in 1982 precludes the replication of either of these models; thus it is not possible to determine empirically how much projection and/or persuasion may have occurred among those respondents whose votes appear to have been related to the two Senate candidates' issue positions. It *is* possible, however, to speculate on the incidence of rationalization based on the specific circumstances of the Brown-Wilson campaign.

First, the issues analyzed—the nuclear freeze, Social Security, and Reaganomics—were salient to a large proportion of the California electorate. They were not cloaked in ambiguity; the Senate candidates took clear opposing positions on them, and the newspapers reported these opposing viewpoints continually. Thus, projection of their favored candidates' positions to match their own seems an unlikely possibility for most voters. Moreover, if projection were to occur, one would expect it to be operating on other issues as well; indeed, the more obscure the issue, the greater the possibility that the voter will not understand the candidate's true position and therefore may project. However, for issues other than the three most salient, there was little relationship between issues and the vote for senator.

Persuasion, according to Feldman and Conover (1983, 812), becomes more likely when ambiguity is low, that is, when voters know how the candidates stand. The process is: I like my candidate, I know he favors a certain viewpoint, so I'll favor that view too. This cognitive process might perhaps have been plausible for some people (e.g., younger voters) with respect to the Social Security issue: not having thought much about the pros and cons of changing the system, some people might have adopted their favorite Senate candidate's view. But for Reaganomics and the nuclear freeze, persuasion seems implausible, since these issues did not acquire their salience only through the Senate campaign. Voters' positions on Reagan's economic policies might have derived from their opinion of the president but would hardly have originated in their feelings about the 1982 Senate candidates. The nuclear freeze idea had a life of its own before Brown and Wilson began debating it and was already before the voters as a ballot measure. Moreover, it should be remembered that neither candidate's personal popularity scores were so high that people would be inclined to follow their lead on these issues just because they liked the candidates so much: many people disliked Brown, and

Wilson was not even particularly well known until the campaign was under way.

Like Markus and Converse, Feldman and Conover (1983, 835) found persuasion to be much less evident than projection in the 1976 election: "We found very little evidence of persuasion effects; there were no persuasion effects whatsoever for the two candidates and only marginal effects for the parties." If persuasion effects are negligible in a presidential race, it seems unlikely that two Senate candidates have created many new attitudes on the part of voters.

However much persuasion and projection may be entwined with issue voting in any election, what matters is the *relative* degree of issue voting resulting from hard-fought Senate campaigns, in which candidate issue positions are frequently and clearly transmitted to the public, as opposed to low-key elections, in which voters receive very little information at all. While it is difficult to pin down the *actual* degree of issue voting in either the hard-fought Brown-Wilson race or the low-key Simpson-Whitaker race, it is possible to conclude with some certainty that the ingredients that enable voters to choose between candidates on the basis of their policy positions were present in the one case and largely absent in the other. The low-key 1978 Wyoming Senate campaign was covered far less extensively in the press than was the 1982 Brown-Wilson race in California. There was some newspaper coverage of the Wyoming race, and in fact some of this coverage cast attention on issues raised during the campaign as well. Yet a large proportion of even the most attentive Wyoming voters failed to assimilate the messages conveyed through the press coverage. Wyoming Poll respondents were asked how attentive they had been to the various media, both generally and with respect to the 1978 campaign (which included a higher-intensity governor's race). On most issues, virtually all the respondents were unclear about how the candidates stood. At most 55 percent of even the most attentive voters were correctly able to identify the positions of the candidates on the issues most frequently reported on during the campaign.[27] These findings suggest two conclusions: first, that even in a low-intensity campaign, what the public knows about the campaign is tied to the nature of press coverage; second, that campaign messages must be relayed with much greater frequency than they were in Wyoming if they are to reach even the most attentive of the electorate. The evidence from the Brown-Wilson race shows that when an attentive public is saturated with information about the candidates through the news media, that public is capable of entering that information into their decision calculus; some of them actually use the information in deciding for whom to vote.

Undoubtedly, others balance this information against what they perceive to be the candidates' positions on other issues and vote on the basis of general political philosophy; that is, when these issues lie along a liberal conservative continuum, ideology voting is possible. A basic point here is that issues and ideology can be important in voting for a senator, but only under certain conditions: the candidates must differ significantly on the issues, their campaign must be a relatively hard-fought one, and information about their views must be transmitted to voters. Thus the large amount of information disseminated in hard-fought races, such as the 1982 race in California, tends to promote issue voting, while the light coverage characteristic of low-key campaigns, such as the 1978 Wyoming race, tends to preclude it.

7. The Effect of State-specific Factors on Senate Election Outcomes

In addition to campaign-specific factors—candidates' past political experience, the amount and type of coverage provided by the news media, and the level of voter information about the candidates and their views—there are also "external" factors beyond the influence of candidates or news reporters that may affect Senate outcomes. The most important of these external factors is the political environment in which campaigns take place. The political environment is fairly constant within a state from election to election but can vary considerably across states. This chapter focuses on three of these external, state-specific factors—population size, constituency diversity, and the distribution of party identification within states—and on the extent to which they affect Senate election outcomes.

It has been widely pointed out that more incumbent senators than representatives lose their reelection bids and that the average House incumbent's margin of victory is greater than that of Senate incumbents.[1] The larger number of safe House seats is often attributed to differences in the makeup of statewide versus district-level constituencies, particularly differences in constituency size and diversity, as well as to differences in the balance of partisan affiliation.[2] Generally, congressmen are seen to win more reelection bids, and by higher margins of victory, because of the similarity, or like-mindedness, of the people in House districts; House districts are much smaller and are, on average, more likely than entire states to include people with the same interests, the same social and cultural backgrounds, and, accordingly, the same political predispositions and identifications. House incumbents have an easier time, therefore, in identifying and making sure to represent these interests; it is a significant advantage, as well, for the representative to belong to the district's majority party. In contrast, the wider variety of interests represented in entire states presumably increases the likelihood that senators will alienate some portion of their constituents.

This line of reasoning for comparing districts and states should apply as well to states of different size and diversity: the larger and more heterogeneous a state, the more difficult it should be for a senator to please large proportions of his constituents and thus the smaller the average margin of victory of the state's Senate elections should be. Hibbing and Brandes (1983) argued that indeed, state size and variations in state party distribution both significantly affect Senate election outcomes, that these two "environmental" variables are in fact more important than "institutional" variables, such as the type of challenger a Senate incumbent faces or the office itself, in explaining not only why senators as a group are less safe than members of the House but also why some senators fare better than others. Examining Senate elections in the period 1946–80, and using only the two environmental variables of state population and party distribution, they accounted for "about three-fourths of the variance in the performance of incumbent senators" (814). Hibbing and Brandes concluded that solely on the basis of a state's population size and the partisan distribution of its voters, one can predict the size of the margin of victory in any Senate race where an incumbent is running for reelection. A closer look at the two variables, however, calls into question the importance of state size and demonstrates that the influence of the second external factor—the distribution of party identification of the electorate—is strongly related to the intensity of the campaign.

State Size and Senate Election Margin of Victory

Hibbing and Brandes hypothesized that "large constituencies mean difficult times for incumbent officeholders" and that "Senators from heavily populated states" should therefore "do substantially worse on election day than Senators from lightly populated states" (811). This hypothesis is the outgrowth of speculation regarding the varying abilities of legislators to please their constituents. According to Hibbing and Brandes, for example, "it could be argued that representatives, because of their smaller constituencies [and by extension of this logic, senators from small states], are able to meet personally virtually every politically

TABLE 3 I
Relationship Between State Population and Outcomes in Contested Senate Elections, Measured in Three Fashions, 1968–1984

	Number of Congressional Districts in State											
	1	2	3	4	5	6	7–8	9–11	12–15	16–25	26+	Total
I. Average margin of victory, percentage-point spread												
Races with incumbent running	21	19	15	15	23	16	17	18	24	12	7	17
(N)	(26)	(44)	(8)	(15)	(15)	(18)	(26)	(32)	(9)	(20)	(12)	(225)
All races, including open seats	19	18	16	20	21	15	18	16	15	11	6	16
(N)	(33)	(54)	(11)	(19)	(18)	(24)	(36)	(41)	(15)	(28)	(16)	(295)
II. Percentage of elections won by more than 20 percentage points												
Races with incumbent running	38%	39%	25%	27%	53%	44%	50%	47%	78%	30%	17%	41%
(N)	(26)	(44)	(8)	(15)	(15)	(18)	(26)	(32)	(9)	(20)	(12)	(225)
All races, including open seats	36%	35%	27%	32%	50%	37%	45%	42%	47%	25%	13%	37%
(N)	(33)	(54)	(11)	(19)	(18)	(24)	(36)	(41)	(15)	(28)	(16)	(295)
III. Percentage of incumbents who lost reelection race	8%	21%	13%	7%	20%	28%	31%	22%	11%	20%	42%	20%
(N)	(26)	(44)	(8)	(15)	(15)	(18)	(26)	(32)	(9)	(20)	(12)	(225)

significant person in the district, while Senators usually have no similar opportunity" (810). Meeting people translates into a positive image of the incumbent, and these "politically significant" people will convey this positive image to the voters for whom they are opinion leaders. An additional assumption is that challengers do not have the resources to reach these politically influential people. A slightly different version of this line of reasoning holds that a district's population size affects a legislator's ability to "pay assiduous attention to the needs of his constituents" (Jewell and Patterson 1977, 91). This reasoning focuses less on the politician's ability to meet constituents and more on the notion that the ability to take care of a larger proportion of their problems is what matters.[3] Such a view implies that casework and district service translate into votes and that members of Congress can offer only so much product with the time and resources at their disposal. Thus, the smaller the district, the larger the proportion of constituents the congressman can attend to.

Table 31 illustrates in three different ways the relationship between state population, measured by the number of congressional districts in a state, and the size of Senate election margins from 1968 to 1984. In the smallest states—those with one congressional district (which means a population of up to 550,000)—incumbents won by an average of 21 percentage points. According to the reasoning advanced above, this figure should decrease steadily as the number of constituents in a state rises. As constituencies double and triple in size, it becomes increasingly difficult to contact or attend to the needs of the same proportion of the people. The mean victory margin does drop by as much as six points for states in the three-district size range, but in states with five districts (about 2.5 million people) the average margin of victory jumps to 23 points. Incumbents from states with populations of 3–6 million people won by about the same margin as incumbents from states half that size, and the victory margin jumps to 24 points for incumbents from states with 12–15 districts. In states with 16 or more congressional districts, the margin of victory dropped again.

Although there is a modest overall relationship between state size and margin of victory, there is little direct relationship between state size and margin of victory for small and moderately populated states— the categories into which most states fall. Only in the very largest states does the connection between state size and margin of victory appear: the average margin of victory for incumbents from states with 16–25 congressional districts was 12 percentage points from 1968 through 1984, and for incumbents from the three states with more than 25 districts it was only 7 points.

Another way to analyze electoral competition is to see how often senators win by more than 20 percentage points, since the 20-point mark is often used as the breakpoint for distinguishing "safe" from marginal seats,[4] and senators with less than 60 percent of the two-party vote are generally considered to be justifiably worried about losing. In states with one congressional district, 37 percent of incumbents were reelected by at least 20 percentage points. Reelection margins were, however, just as large in two-district states. The margin drops to 25 percent for senators from states with three districts but shoots up as state size increases: over half of senators from states with a population of around 2.5 million enjoyed victories in the "safe" range. The figure remains around the 50 percent mark as state size increases to the 11-district level, and in states with 12–15 districts (6–7.5 million people), fully 78 percent of incumbents were returned with a margin of victory of more than 20 percentage points.

While elections in moderate-sized states are less competitive than those in small states, the pattern reverses itself at the high end of the state population scale. Senators from states with 16–23 congressional districts experienced about the same level of competitiveness as those from much smaller states; only 30 percent managed to win by 21 points or more. In the most heavily populated states—Texas, New York, and California—only 17 percent hit the "safe" level; the rest had competitive races. This last figure, which is clearly lower than for any other population level, finally conforms to the notion that senators from the biggest states have more difficulty winning reelection.

These findings apply only to the 225 races in which incumbents faced opposition for reelection, however. In the second rows of the first two sections of table 31 the 70 open-seat races in the period 1968–84 are added. As might be expected, most of the open-seat races were quite competitive, both because of the absence of any incumbency advantage and, not coincidentally, because of the more experienced candidates in both parties. Including these elections slightly lowers the average margin of victory across each population group, as well as the proportion of the races in each population level whose margin was greater than 20 points. But it does very little to alter the pattern of *differences* found above as we move from the smallest to the largest states. The races of senators from mid-sized states were roughly as competitive as those of senators from the small states, whereas senators from the three largest states faced considerably more competitive contests than anyone else.

156

A third way of viewing the relationship between state size and electoral outcomes is simply to look at the proportion of incumbents who lost their elections. The third section of table 31 arrays these data. While senators at the extreme ends of the state-size continuum lost reelection bids at very different rates—8 percent of one-district state incumbents lost in the period 1968–84, as opposed to 42 percent of incumbents from the very largest states—the pattern in between is anything but monotonic. Senators from states of 1 million people were just as likely to lose as senators from states of 2.5 million, 5 million, and even 8–12 million. But senators from states of 2 million or 6–7.5 million were only half as likely to lose as the previous group. In other words, with the exception of the very smallest and the very largest states, there was no relationship between state size and a senator's likelihood, over the period studied, of losing a reelection bid.

Senators from the very largest states do experience the closest elections. However, the evidence is insufficient to substantiate claims that variations in population size explain different Senate election outcomes. In the nine election years examined, the margin of victory in medium-sized states such as North Carolina, Indiana, or Massachusetts was, on average, greater than in smaller states the size of Connecticut or Colorado, while senators in the latter states faced no greater chance of electoral competition than did senators from the very smallest states. Hibbing and Brandes felt "safe in concluding that for incumbent legislators the more constituents there are, the more difficult they are to please" (817), yet the findings presented in table 31 suggest that this conclusion is not so safe. There appears to be no significant difference in the margin of victory of Senate elections whether a senator represents 550,000 constituents or 5.5 million. It is only in the very largest states—where constituents number more than 10 million—that a senator's average margin of victory is significantly lower than in smaller states. It is only in these few very heavily populated states, as well, that notably fewer elections are of the "safe" variety and that the chances of winning reelection are significantly reduced.

This evidence does not completely contradict the general notion that having huge numbers of constituents may reduce a politician's vote-getting ability by diluting any attempts to give voters the personal touch via casework. But if the idea has validity with respect to Senate elections, the threshold above which "assiduous attention to constituents' needs" fails to pay off would appear to be so high that only senators in the largest states are affected.[5] For most states, and therefore for most Senate elections, state size is not a sufficient explanation for electoral results.

Constituency Diversity and Senate Election Outcomes

Although population size and population diversity are often related, they are separate concepts. A number of observers have asserted
that the greater heterogeneity of states over congressional districts contributes to more competition in Senate races than in House races. This
assertion holds that it is much easier for political representatives to stand
for the views of particular interest groups within their constituencies
when there are relatively few constituents with opposing views. As a district becomes more heterogeneous, the likelihood increases that there will
be more voters on both sides of any issue, leaving the legislator (in our
case the senator) in a more vulnerable electoral situation no matter what
stand he takes. Froman (1963), using data from 1962, made this same
argument about House elections alone and concluded that "a lack of
competitiveness is a sign of greater homogeneity of constituency factors
within a district" (121). Fiorina (1974, 90–101) made a similar claim
for Senate elections and found some confirmation based on limited data.

The actual relationship between constituency diversity and the size of
the margin of victory for both House and Senate elections was tested by
Bond (1983) for the three elections in the period 1974–78. Using census
and other aggregate data, he calculated a diversity score for each congressional district and state on what he considered to be five of the most
important "politically relevant cleavages": the mix of urban, suburban,
and rural population; the mix of white-collar, blue-collar, service, and
farm occupations; income; race; and ethnicity ("native-born" as opposed
to "foreign-born"). Combining these variables in an index of diversity
first developed by Sullivan (1973) and employed by Fiorina (1974) as
well, Bond obtained a diversity score for each district and state and
analyzed the relationship between this measure and the winner's percentage of the two-party vote. In the case of Senate elections, he found
no relationship between the diversity of the state and the competitiveness of the election.[6] This finding held both in races with incumbent
senators running for reelection and in open-seat contests, and for a set of
Senate elections in the early 1960s as well as for the ones in 1974, 1976,
and 1978.

Bond expressed surprise at these findings, stating that "we normally
assume that social, ethnic, and economic diversity in a constituency
translate into political differences and that these result in electoral competition" (209). It may be, however, that these variables translate into
political differences after being filtered through the "political" variable of
party affiliation. That is, the party distribution within a particular con-

158

stituency may be based on social, ethnic, and economic differences, with heterogeneous districts (or states) featuring large numbers of both Democrats and Republicans and homogeneous ones more likely to produce one-party domination. Bond did not investigate the relation of state party distribution to Senate election outcomes, but an investigation of that relationship is in order.

State Party Distribution and Senate Election Outcomes, 1968–1984

In some states the distribution of party identification is evenly balanced between the two major parties, while in others the distribution is skewed in favor of one party, sometimes by a wide margin. The effects of state party balance on margins of victory were discussed by V. O. Key, who found that margins of victory in Senate elections of the 1940s and 1950s were determined in large part by a state's degree of party competition (1964, 547–48). More recently, Mann (1981, 33) wrote that "when the distribution of partisan voters across . . . states is uneven, some seats are safe for one party or the other." Kayden (1976, 22), referring to the existence of two strong parties in Indiana, stated that no candidate for statewide office "can expect to win by more than a few percentage points," making all elections in that state "hotly contested" and "uncertain in their outcome." Key, Mann, and Kayden were all making essentially the same point: that the size of an electoral outcome is determined in large part by the underlying distribution of partisanship in a state or district.

Variations in the distributions of party identification from state to state can lead to situations in which identical patterns of voter defection produce very different electoral results. In situations where both candidates manage to become well known to voters and where defections tend to be fairly equal among voters of both parties, a very close margin of victory is likely to result. A state such as Indiana, where Republicans and Democrats are about equal in number, might be the site of such races. In a state where Democrats vastly outnumber Republicans—such as Mississippi or Hawaii—campaigns exhibiting the same patterns of candidate awareness and defections that occurred in Indiana might nevertheless yield fairly substantial victories for the Democratic candidates. Defections from the two parties might be equal, but with so many more Democrats voting, the margin of victory for the Democratic candidate would still be large. Thus the effect of the state party distribution variable on Senate election results has the potential to be very strong.

Many different measures have been used over the years to assess the extent of one party's dominance over the other in each state. Until recently, most of these measures used a state's voting patterns in past elections as an approximation of current levels of partisan competition. For example, Ranney and Kendall (1954) combined the percentage of elections won by one party for president, senator, and governor with the mean proportion of the vote garnered by the runner-up party to create a measure of interparty competition; this procedure has been adopted by many others since. For Burnham (1970, 22–26 and passim) the average statewide vote for all partisan statewide offices over ten previous elections was a reasonable measure of the current ratio of the two major parties in the electorate.[7] Hibbing and Brandes (1983) calculated a single "party competition" score for each state: the mean percentage of the vote received by the state's Democratic House candidates in the period 1946–80. But because they "were not concerned with whether the state leaned toward the Democratic or Republican party but with how competitive the state has been in the postwar period," Hibbing and Brandes folded their figure at 50 percent, "so that a 75 percent mean Democratic vote was the same" in their regression equation as a "25 percent Democratic vote" (813). This is a curious choice, since it means that a state in which all of the Democratic House candidates won by large margins would be given a "competitiveness" score similar to that of a state where, whether due to gerrymandering or natural causes, half the Democratic House candidates won by large margins and half lost by similar amounts.

To the extent that such measures are intended to tap the underlying partisan predispositions of a state's voters, they are susceptible to considerable error, due particularly to the impact of incumbency on the vote choice (popular House incumbents may draw votes not only from identifiers of their own party but from identifiers of their challengers' party as well). Therefore, measures that rely on the vote for House candidates (or candidates for state legislature, or any other elective office) may inflate the actual proportion of their party's voters within a state. Of course, biases toward incumbents might balance out when there are incumbents of both parties in a state, especially over long periods of time, but they may not balance out well enough, as a closer look at Hibbing and Brandes's measure of state party distribution reveals. In New Mexico, for example, their measure—the mean Democratic percentage of the vote for all congressmen in a state in the period 1946–80—yields a 55–45 distribution in favor of the Democratic party. Considering that state party *registration* in New Mexico is about 2-to-1 Democratic,[8] and that a similar proportion of its state legislature was Democratic during the period studied, the actual two-party distribution is no doubt more heavily skewed toward the Democrats than the 55–45 figure implies. In fact, the 55–45 proportion largely reflects the popularity of Republican Congressman Manuel Lujan, who was reelected in the First District in every election from 1968 to 1980. Because New Mexico House members were elected at-large until 1962, the Hibbing-Brandes measure is essentially a function of Lujan's margins of victory averaged against the vote of the Second District's Democratic incumbent, Pete Runnels, and a couple of Republican incumbents before and after Runnels's five-term career.

By the same token, the Democratic proportions produced by Hibbing and Brandes's measure for many southern states are undoubtedly much too high. This is because so many Democratic House candidates, especially in the earlier part of the period, ran without Republican opposition in the general election. For example, the measure sets the two-party balance in Louisiana during the 34-year period at 88 percent Democratic. But in fully 69 percent of these elections the Democratic candidate had no Republican opponent at all. In Georgia, Mississippi, and Arkansas, the 88 percent, 87 percent, and 86 percent Democratic figures yielded by the Hibbing-Brandes measure are likewise influenced by the fact that in about two-thirds of the House races in each of these states the Democratic candidate received 100 percent of the vote. Even if it is assumed that the Republican percentage of the vote reflects the underlying level of Republican affiliation in a state, it is difficult to imagine that even the most heavily Democratic district would have fewer than 10 percent Republican identifiers; yet in two-thirds of cases the Hibbing-Brandes measure yields no Republicans at all in such districts. Granted, the justification for this measure is that the average of all the individual races over a long period of time approximates the actual underlying party breakdown. But when two-thirds of a state's elections are uncontested, leaving Republicans no option but to vote for the Democrat (or sometimes a third-party candidate), the "vote surrogate" measure loses credibility. It loses all meaning when *both* parties are running uncontested candidates at the same time. In Massachusetts 45 Democratic and 14 Republican candidates ran for House seats without opposition during 1946–80, the period Hibbing and Brandes examined. The Hibbing-Brandes score of "59 percent Democratic" may seem reasonable to knowledgeable observers of Massachusetts politics, but it is difficult to accept that the average of a series of district vote proportions is representative of the state's party affiliation as a whole when it includes 59 cases in which the district's election results were unrelated to the underlying distribution of party affiliation (100 percent Democratic in 45 districts and 0 percent Democratic in 14 others).

Until recently, surrogate measures tapping past voting patterns were often the only available way to assess the percentage of a state's electorate who identify with—and thus presumably are predisposed to vote for candidates of—the two major parties. Registration figures are another possible measure, but about half the states do not have partisan registration. Over the last few years, however, more and more state-level polls have provided direct measures of party identification. With the possible exception of private pollsters, there is no collection of state-level samples of all 50 states in any given year, so that it is still impossible to obtain wholly comparable data on the distribution of party identification from state to state. But Wright, Erikson, and McIver (1985) provided a reasonable alternative. They aggregated data on party identification from the four CBS/*New York Times* national election surveys in the period 1976–82. These polls, conducted just prior to the election in all four years, used a random-digit dialing sample technique, which means that respondents from each of the 48 contiguous states were randomly selected and that pooling respondents from the four surveys yields a reasonable cross section of each state's population (except in the case of the least populated states, where combining even four surveys fails to yield enough cases from which to obtain reasonable estimates). Since the same question tapping party identification was asked of all respondents in these state-level surveys, it is possible to obtain for all but the smallest states a comparable set of figures on the proportion of Democratic, Republican, and independent identifiers in each state.[9] I obtained party distribution figures for the smaller states from the state-level surveys at my disposal when available.[10]

To develop an assessment of state party distribution that will facilitate an examination of its relationship to margin of victory in Senate elections, I grouped states into five categories of mean partisan disposition. I calculated the two-party proportion of Democrats in each state and then distinguished between states that are at least 70 percent Democratic, states in which Democrats constitute 65 percent of the two-party distribution, states that are between 51 percent and 65 percent Democratic, states that are marginally Republican (51–55 percent), and the three remaining states, which are more solidly Republican.[11]

Between 1968 and 1984 there was a fairly strong relationship between the proportion of Democratic identifiers in a state and the average margin of victory in that state's Senate elections (see table 32). In the 12 "very Democratic" states (those in which Democrats outnumber Republicans by a ratio of 70 to 30), Democratic candidates outdistanced Republican candidates by 19 percentage points.[12] As the proportion of Democratic identifiers in a state decreases, the margin of victory for Democratic Senate candidates also decreases. The average margin for candidates in the "solid Democratic" states was 7 percentage points. In the states in which Democrats outnumbered Republicans by only a slight margin, the mean Democratic margin was 5 points. In states in which Republicans held a slight edge in party identification, Republican candidates won election by an average of 8 points. Finally, in the three states in which Republicans held a solid advantage in party distribution, Republican Senate candidates won by an average of 9 percentage points.

The diminishing Democratic margin of victory for Senate candidates across the various categories of state partisan distribution suggests the obvious: that the more voters of one's own party there are in a state, the easier it is to win an election. This conclusion is mediated, however, by whether or not the opponent is an incumbent. In the "very Democratic," "solid Democratic," and "leans Democratic" states, Democratic incumbents won election by large margins: 30, 20, and 16 points, respectively. The same was true of Republican incumbents in the two groups of states with a majority of Republican identifiers; the margins there were 21 points in the "leans Republican" category and 27 points in the "solid Republican" group. The more telling data about the power of incumbency are in the other five cells. Democratic senators who managed to win in the two groups of states populated by more Republicans than Democrats achieved average margins of 10 and 6 percentage points, respectively, over their Republican challengers. Republican incumbents running in Democratic states that were leaning won by an average of 9 points. What is more impressive, Republican senators racked up winning margins averaging 15 and 7 points, respectively, in the "solid Democratic" and "very Democratic" categories.

These patterns demonstrate two important points. First, in terms simply of winning or losing the election, the advantage of being an incumbent more than compensates for any disadvantage due to an adverse state party distribution. Even in states that overwhelmingly favor the other party, incumbents have managed to find the means to win reelection, if by narrow margins. Second, where party distribution is skewed in favor of their party, incumbents enjoy much less competitive races than senators running in states whose party balance favors the opponent's

TABLE 3.2
Democratic Margin of Victory, by States' Distribution of Party Identification, Senate Elections, 1968–1984

Seat Held by:	State Party Distribution				
	Very Democratic	Solid Democratic	Leans Democratic	Leans Republican	Solid Republican
Democratic incumbent	30 (33)	20 (24)	16 (50)	10 (15)	6 (8)
Republican incumbent	-7 (13)	-15 (13)	-9 (36)	-21 (25)	-27 (7)
Open seat	17 (20)	0 (11)	3 (21)	-5 (15)	-4 (3)
ALL RACES	19 (66)	7 (48)	5 (107)	-8 (55)	-9 (18)
	Alabama	Florida	California	Alaska	Idaho
	Arkansas	Minnesota	Colorado	Arizona	New Hampshire
	Georgia	Nevada	Connecticut	Iowa	Utah
	Hawaii	New Mexico	Delaware	Nebraska	
	Maryland	South Carolina	Illinois	North Dakota	
	Mississippi	Tennessee	Indiana	Kansas	
	Louisiana	West Virginia	Maine	South Dakota	
	North Carolina		Michigan	Vermont	
	Kentucky		Missouri	Wyoming	
	Oklahoma		Montana		
	Rhode Island		New Jersey		
	Texas		New York		
			Ohio		
			Oregon		
			Pennsylvania		
			Virginia		
			Washington		
			Wisconsin		

Note: Allocation of states into the five "party distribution" categories is detailed in Chap. 7, n. 9.

TABLE 33
Democratic Margin of Victory in Low-key Democratic, Low-key Republican, and Hard-fought Senate Races, by State Party Distribution, 1968–1984

Races	State Party Distribution				
	Very Democratic	Solid Democratic	Leans Democratic	Solid Republican	Very Republican
Low-key Democratic					
Incumbent running	40 (23)	36 (13)	29 (27)	27 (3)	15 (2)
Open seat	58 (5)	22 (2)	34 (1)	36 (1)	(0)
All races	43 (28)	34 (15)	29 (28)	29 (4)	15 (2)
Low-key Republican					
Incumbent running	−21 (4)	−26 (5)	−23 (14)	−33 (15)	−43 (3)
Open seat	(0)	(0)	−19 (1)	−33 (3)	(0)
All races	−21 (4)	−26 (5)	−23 (15)	−33 (18)	−43 (3)
Hard-fought					
Democratic					
Incumbent running	7 (10)	1 (11)	0 (23)	6 (12)	3 (6)
Open seat	3 (15)	−5 (9)	2 (19)	−1 (11)	−4 (3)
Republican					
incumbent running	0 (9)	−8 (8)	−1 (22)	−3 (10)	−15 (4)

party. Where party balance is tipped heavily in favor of Senate incumbents, landslide victories are the order of the day.

The individual-level survey findings in earlier chapters all pointed to the conclusion that factors central to the study of Senate elections become more meaningful when considered in the context of the hard-fought/low-key intensity distinction. Distinguishing between hard-fought and low-key races in examining the relationship between state party distribution and margin of victory produces two very different patterns. Table 33 arrays the mean Democratic margin of victory in the two types of elections across the five categories of state party distribution. In low-key races, a strong relationship between party distribution and margin of victory is evident. In low-key races with a Democratic winner, the margin of victory ranged from 43 points in "very Democratic" states to 34 points in "solid Democratic" states, 29 points in "leans Democratic" and "solid Republican" states, and down to 15 points in the "very Republican" states. The pattern is much the same in low-key races with a Republican winner, with the margin of victory averaging 43 points in "very Republican" states but decreasing as state distribution becomes more Democratic to a low of 21 points in the "very Democratic" states. Clearly, party distribution in a state has a strong bearing on the outcome of low-key races. With weak challengers unable to bring their messages through to

165

the electorate, incumbents receive large numbers of votes from the other party as well as from their own, resulting in landslides. However, the data also show that those landslides are far more monumental when the environmental factor of party balance is favorable than when it is unfavorable.

On the other hand, in hard-fought Senate races over the same period state party distribution had almost no impact on election margins. Democratic incumbents in "very Democratic" states won their hard-fought races by an average of just 7 percentage points. Margins of victory dropped to almost nothing in "solid Democratic" and "leans Democratic" states and climbed back to 6 and 3 percentage points, respectively, in the "solid Republican" and "very Republican" states. The margin of victory for Republican incumbents, which was 15 points in "very Republican" states, dropped to 3 points in "solid Republican" states and 1 point in "leans Democratic" states. In "solid Democratic" states, Democratic challengers enjoyed an average of 8 points, and the margin returned to nearly zero in the "very Democratic" states. In the open-seat hard-fought races there was also very little indication that party distribution influenced outcomes. In the "very Democratic" states, Democratic candidates had a 3-percentage-point advantage, and in the "very Republican" states, Republican candidates had a 4-point advantage. But Republican candidates in open-seat races actually held a 5-point advantage in the "solid Democratic" group. Overall, then, in hard-fought races the degree of dominance by one party over the other within a state seems not to affect the magnitude of Senate election margins of victory in any systematic way. In the period 1968–84 the margin of victory in all hard-fought races was small, and incumbency amounted to only a small advantage regardless of the distribution of party.

Most of the low-key Democratic races occurred in states in which Democrats outnumbered Republicans, just as most low-key Republican races occurred in Republican-dominated states. It is noteworthy, however, that the few times an incumbent enjoyed a low-key race in a state in which the other party was predominant, his margin of victory was nonetheless rather large; Democrat Frank Church's 20-point victory in Republican-dominated Idaho in 1968 and Republican Edward Brooke's 30-point victory in Democratic Massachusetts in 1972 are cases in point. In essence, then, the aggregate data in table 33 present evidence of the same patterns we saw when looking at individual-level vote decisions in chapters 5 and 6: the intensity of a Senate campaign influences the degree to which such factors as incumbency, party identification, and campaign-produced issues affect individual voters' choices; at the state level, intensity mediates the effect of a state's party balance on candidates' margin of victory.

We have seen that low-key political campaigns—which comprise almost all House races and 40 percent of Senate races—tend to produce large margins of victory, while hard-fought races—which comprise about 60 percent of all Senate races but only the occasional House race—produce close election results. In low-key races, where people know very little about the challenger, large numbers of voters from both parties may vote for the candidate (the incumbent) they know, and the resulting margin of victory will be affected by state party distribution. In hard-fought races, on the other hand, where both incumbents and challengers are likely to be familiar to voters, the effect of state party distribution decreases as factors evolving from individual campaigns take on increased importance. This difference between hard-fought and low-key election outcomes holds regardless of state size. Indeed, except in the very largest states, state population differences had very little influence on Senate election outcomes in the period 1968–84.

8. The Effect of Primary Divisiveness on Senators' Reelection Prospects

Primary divisiveness and incumbents' electoral vulnerability both can affect the election prospects of Senate candidates. The fallout from a divisive primary is one factor in the relationship between the contestedness of an incumbent's primary race and the closeness of general election results. At the same time, some of what appears to be the effect of primary divisiveness on the outcome of a Senate race may actually be a function of an incumbent senator's vulnerability *prior to* the primary. There are two approaches to investigating primaries' effects: one is by case-study examination of individual divisive Senate primaries, using state-level survey data to explore the relationship between voters' primary and general election vote decisions; the other is by multivariate analysis of aggregate data for the period 1968–84.[1]

The disruptive nature of primaries has often been noted, particularly their tendency to facilitate "rifts, splits, factions, [and] feuds" (Sorauf 1984, 220) and "sometimes [to] render the party incapable of generating a united campaign in the general election" (Keefe 1984, 4). Certainly in presidential politics, divisive primaries appear to have taken their toll on incumbents. Since 1900 every president who has been renominated without substantial opposition has won another term, but the four presidents who have faced "significant opposition for renomination" have lost in November (*Congressional Quarterly Weekly Report,* 4 February 1984, 224). A study by Kenney and Rice (1984) found divisive primaries at the senatorial and gubernatorial levels adversely to "affect a party's chances for general election victory" (904) to the extent that "the message to the parties is obvious. Hard-fought senatorial primaries will disadvantage your party's chances for victory in the fall" (913).[2]

The Incidence of Contested Senate Primaries

With the upper chamber generally perceived as more prestigious, and with fewer opportunities for politicians to run for the Senate than for the House, it is not surprising that Senate primaries are contested more often than House primaries. Most House primaries are completely uncontested, in fact, and in those races that are contested the victor wins by at least a 2-to-1 margin.[3] As can be seen in table 34, in the period 1968–84, 31 percent of Senate primaries were completely uncontested. Another 20 percent pitted a single serious candidate against token opposition, that is, a candidate or candidates who had no hope of winning and who spent virtually no time or money campaigning. Thus, in recent times, about half of Senate primaries have been essentially noncompetitive, compared with about 90 percent of House primaries.

During the same period 16 percent of Senate primaries were very close, with the top two candidates finishing 10 or fewer percentage points apart. Another 13 percent of the time, the second place candidate came within 10–25 points of the winner. The remaining 21 percent of contests constitute a middle group: not close but not quite token either. Incumbents are not as often involved in close primaries as are candidates in open seats, or candidates vying for nomination to challenge an incumbent. Since 1968, 44 percent of primaries involving an incumbent have been completely uncontested, and in another 29 percent the incumbent faced only token opposition. Challengers have come within 25 points of incumbents in 8 percent of all Senate primaries over this period, and in another 7 percent of cases challengers have actually defeated incumbents. Evidently, strong candidates, as well as the various contributors and workers whose money and time make a serious campaign possible, look carefully at their chances before committing to the formidable task of trying to defeat a sitting senator.

Challenger primaries are considerably more competitive. Only a quarter were completely uncontested, in 37 percent the victor won by 25 points or fewer, and in 17 percent of cases the margin of victory was within 10 points. As might be expected, the greatest number of competitive primary races occurred where there was no incumbent to face in the general election.

TABLE 34
Competitiveness of Senate Primaries, 1968–1984

Type of Primary	Incumbent Lost	Percentage-Point Distance between Nominee and Second-Place Finisher[a]					
		0–10	11–25	26–59	60–99	Uncontested	Total N
Incumbent running	7	3	5	12	29	44	241
Challenger primary		17	20	26	12	25	230[b]
Open seat		27	15	31	15	13	101[c]
TOTAL	3	13	13	21	20	31	572[b,c,d]

[a]Eight states held runoff primaries whenever one candidate failed to receive more than 50 percent of the vote. This was necessary 24 times in the period 1968–84. In each case, the narrower of the two margins of victory determined where the election was placed in this table.

[b]There were 11 fewer challenger primaries than incumbent primaries for the following reasons: (1) in 11 instances, no candidates ran in a challenger primary; (2) in South Carolina in 1986 and in Connecticut in 1974 the nomination was determined at a convention instead of in a challenger primary; (3) in West Virginia in 1970 the candidate was drafted; (4) in Virginia in 1970 and 1976, because incumbent Harry Byrd, Jr., ran as an independent, there was no incumbent primary, but there was a challenger primary in the Democratic primary in both years (the Republicans held a convention in 1970 and ran no candidate in 1976).

[c]There was an odd number of open-seat primaries because in Alabama in 1968 the Republican party held a nominating convention and the Democrats held a primary.

[d]There were 306 Senate elections in the period 1968–84. The nominee was chosen by convention in both parties in Indiana in 1968, 1970, and 1974; in Delaware in 1970; and in Virginia in 1978, 1982, and 1984. (Because of their unique nature, Louisiana primaries since 1978 are not included in the table either.)

What Constitutes a Divisive Senate Primary?

Primary divisiveness is usually measured strictly in terms of the closeness of the primary election results.[4] But is margin of victory a reasonable indicator of primary divisiveness? "Divisiveness" describes a situation in which observable animosity or unresolvable disagreement between two or more segments within a party (or between its candidates) produces the potential to alienate, or lessen the support of, a portion of the various individuals and groups—party workers, contributors, voters—that are essential to the party's success. In particular, party workers and/or voters may react in the general election either by defecting to the other party in November or by abstaining from working or voting in the general election.[5] In addition, resources otherwise allocated for the general election might have to be "wasted" on a primary battle, thus reducing the effectiveness of the eventual nominee's general election campaign.

The extent of the fallout from intraparty dissension during the primary campaign depends on a number of factors—the severity of the rift, how widely perceived it becomes, and whether it is possible to patch it up before the general election campaign begins. Perhaps the most clearly observable type of divisiveness, and therefore potentially the most damaging, occurs when a personal fight (as opposed to a factional battle based on ideology) develops between two serious rivals for a nomination. A certain amount of squabbling between candidates is to be expected, but when a campaign degenerates into a constant exchange of personal insults, voters previously inclined to support the nominee might become fed up and change their minds. Or there might be a less direct effect: bad feeling left by a primary battle, as Bernstein (1977) suggested, could "decrease the willingness of party workers to campaign in the general election. Having given of their time . . . party workers, especially those who supported the loser, may not be willing to volunteer to work again in the general election campaign" (540).

Studies of individual races in Iowa and Ohio found party workers who had been supporters of the loser of a divisive primary to be more reluctant than supporters of the winner to work in the general election (Johnson and Gibson 1974; Comer 1976). If such recalcitrance on the part of workers is shared by potential contributors, a nominee could lose part of the resources he had counted on for transmitting his issue positions or simply for developing name recognition. If grass-roots workers, contributors, and party influentials reduce their efforts on behalf of the nominee in the general election campaign, the reduced capacity of the nominee to make a positive impression on the electorate could lose him votes.

According to table 34, about half of Senate primaries in the period 1968–84 were more than marginally contested, and 29 percent of the time the second-place finisher came within 25 points of the winner. But closeness of the primary election results per se may not be an appropriate measure for the concept of divisiveness, as the following two examples illustrate.

In 1978 Kentucky's junior senator, Democrat Walter Huddleston, was considered by most observers, including state Republican party leaders, to be unbeatable. As a result, stronger candidates stayed away, and the May 23 Republican primary featured two little-known candidates, 32-year-old professor of government Oline Carmical and 34-year-old state assemblyman Louie Guenthner. By the end of March the two candidates together had collected less than two thousand dollars. Both candidates were conservatives, and they differed very little on issues. They did not attack each other; instead, as CQ put it: "with low budgets and little organization, they frequently campaign together across the state, both joining in attacks on Huddleston" (13 May 1978, 1188). In "a race that attracted a turnout of barely 30,000" (ibid., 27 May 1978, 1328), Guenthner defeated Carmical by 14 points.

In 1980 the reelection of two-term Maryland Republican Senator Charles Mathias was also perceived as assured. But in what CQ found a "puzzling" response to this widespread perception, eleven Democrats filed for the May 13 primary. None had statewide name recognition, none waged a particularly strong primary race, and there were no reports of animosity. (If there was animosity between the candidates, it probably was not perceived by voters, since there was very little press coverage of the campaign.) The result was that the top five candidates finished with 22 percent, 15 percent, 12 percent, 11 percent, and 10 percent of the vote, with the others splitting the remaining 30 percent. According to CQ, Edward Conroy probably won because two candidates each from the Baltimore and Bethesda–Silver Spring areas split most of the votes from those populous regions, and Conroy, from Prince Georges County, got most of his votes from his home base (CQ, 17 May 1980, 1329).

Both of these races, and many others like them, would be classified as "divisive" under any definition based exclusively on margin of victory, even though there is no reason to believe that party influentials or voters were embittered by these campaigns or that the candidates were forced to pour valuable funds into fighting their opponents that would otherwise have been available for the general election. By and large, the closeness of the challenger primary race tells us very little about the degree of divisiveness present. Thus, where challengers are concerned, indicators other than simple margin of victory need to be utilized. In challenger primaries one candidate is rarely perceived as having exclusive rights to the nomination. A spirited campaign is often expected, as each candidate attempts to convince the party rank and file and the voters that he is the best choice. Sometimes party influentials—or even the candidates themselves—look upon the primary campaign as a proving ground and move quickly to throw their support behind the winner no matter how close the race. Divisiveness is likely to exist only when candidates move beyond lively debate over issues and leadership ability to confrontational attacks that generate animosity and bitterness between themselves and among their supporters.

When an incumbent senator runs for renomination, however, the situation is a little different. Usually, the incumbent senator will have established a network of supporters around the state, both among party leaders and the rank and file. Any challenge to his renomination would be considered by many of them as an affront, and as a violation of norms of intraparty comity. Most serious challengers would probably attack the incumbent, and a confrontational campaign would undoubtedly be covered by the press. A proliferation of reports showing an incumbent in a campaign fight could deter some voters who ordinarily would have supported the incumbent. Murray and Tedin's (1983) claim about attacks on gubernatorial incumbents seems relevant, then, to senators as well: "If there is an insurgent challenge to an incumbent . . . the campaign must focus on the possible shortcomings of the existing administration. Party voters are unlikely to unseat a well known office holder from their own party unless given compelling reasons to do so. This means that serious challengers are necessarily forced to make a strongly negative case . . . that will likely guarantee a divisive primary" (14). Because a sitting senator is presumed to have a right to the nomination, even a challenge free of vitriolic attacks is likely (if it is a serious one) to engender resentment among the senator's followers, to lead a perked-up press to scrutinize the incumbent's record or raise questions about his level of support, and generally to raise doubts in the minds of some potential contributors and voters whose support had been guaranteed. The stronger the challenge, the greater the possibility that party support, previously united behind the senator, could erode.

The key difference, then, between incumbent and challenger primaries is that the same norms do not apply, and measures of divisiveness should vary accordingly. In incumbent primaries, the number of votes garnered by the challenger therefore seems to be a satisfactory indicator of the inroads made into a senator's previously unified support. It therefore seems reasonable to use margin of victory in an incumbent's primary as an approximation of divisiveness in that primary. On the other hand, the presence or absence of campaign vitriol is, as suggested earlier, a better measure of divisiveness in a challenger primary.

An examination of *CQ*'s descriptions of Senate primary campaigns in the period 1968–84 turned up 33 out of 231 challenger primaries that were characterized by antagonistic confrontations between the candidates. A few of these campaigns were described as vicious, or bitter. More commonly, the candidates in such races were not actually hostile toward each other, but they did call into question their opponents' personal integrity or accused their opponents of lying, conflict of interest, or personal indiscretion. These 33 races have been classified as divisive. The 198 nondivisive races are a varied group. There were 84 instances in which one strong candidate received united support from the party, gaining the nomination with either token opposition or no challenge at all.[6] In 105 challenger primaries none of the candidates was particularly strong. The two cases from Maryland and Kentucky cited above were typical of the races in this category; the most experienced of candidates in this group were state legislators, small-town mayors, or unelected party officials, none of whom were likely to be well known statewide and whose primary campaigns therefore were not likely to generate much interest, either among the press or in the electorate. In the remaining nine races two strong candidates faced each other without animosity, either by ignoring each other and concentrating on attacking the incumbent or by debating issues without resorting to personal attacks.

Assessing the Effects of Divisive Primaries: 1968–1984

As we have seen, 15 percent of Senate incumbents running for reelection in the period 1968–84 were unable to win a primary race by 25 percentage points or more; in fact, half of these lost the primary outright. Of the 19 senators who survived such close primaries, only 7 (32 percent) went on to win the general election.[7] By contrast, more than 80 percent of incumbent senators involved in "easy" primaries were subsequently reelected (see table 35). Thus, close incumbent primaries are associated with sharply reduced prospects of winning in November.[8] This initially suggests that a number of voters who might otherwise have supported the incumbent were influenced by a divisive primary to defect to

TABLE 3 5
General Election Fate of Incumbent Senators, by Primary Margin of Victory,
1968–1984

General Election Winners		Percentage-Point Primary Margin of Victory				
	Lost	*0–10*	*11–25*	*26–59*	*60–99*	*Uncontested*
Percentage		14	42	82	89	79
(*N*)	(16)	(7)	(12)	(28)	(71)	(107)

TABLE 3 6
Divisiveness of Incumbent and Challenger Primaries and the General Election
Outcome, 1968–1984

	Incumbent's Margin of Victory		
	Lost	*0–25 Points*	*26–100 Points*
Divisive Challenger Primary	(1/1)	(0/2)	(22/30)
	—	—	73%
Nondivisive Challenger Primary	(8/15)	(6/17)	(142/166)
	53%	35%	86%
		(14/32)	
		44%	

Note: The incumbent's victory rate in the general election, along with the ratios from which
the percentages were calculated, is reported in each cell. In the column marked "lost" the
figures are for the candidate who defeated the incumbent in the primary. Dashes indicate
that the number of cases is insufficient to provide for an entry in the cell.

the other party's candidate in the general election. The relationship between incumbent primary margin of victory and the general election outcome is striking, but it does not take into account the possible effects of
other factors on reelection chances, such as the degree of divisiveness in
the other party's primary.[9] How often incumbents (or the candidates who
defeated them in the primary) won the general election when both parties
had a divisive primary, when neither party had one, and when one but
not the other party had a divisive primary is shown in table 36. Since
there were only three instances in which both parties had a divisive primary, the "equalized" situation is represented almost entirely by the
lower right-hand cell, in which neither party suffered a divisive primary.
Under this condition, the incumbent won the election 86 percent of the
time. When only the incumbent primary was divisive, this figure dropped
to 44 percent, as seen in the lower left-hand cell. The low incumbent
victory rate in this cell is consistent with the findings of Bernstein (1977)

and Kenney and Rice (1984): controlling for the condition of the challenger primary, incumbents do better in the general election when they can avoid a divisive primary than when they cannot.

A perhaps unexpected finding emerges from the upper right-hand cell, however. When the incumbent primary was not divisive and the other party's primary was, it was not the incumbent but his eventual opponent who appeared to benefit. That is, the incumbent was 13 points less likely to win under this condition than when neither primary was divisive. One reason for this could be that the publicity arising from the contentiousness of the primary provided the winner of the challenger primary a boost in recognition not available to challengers whose primaries had been quiet. That recognition would very likely contain a substantial negative component, however. A more likely explanation is that the incumbents whose seats were the object of divisive challenger primaries were senators who were already more vulnerable to defeat in the general election than were other incumbents. If this is true, any harm done to the other party's nominee in his own primary might be dwarfed by the prior vulnerability of the incumbent in the ensuing general election. Such prior vulnerability would explain the low victory rates in the lower left-hand cell as readily as anything having to do with the divisiveness of the challenger primary.

This raises the question of the role of other potentially intervening factors and their relationship to divisiveness. Divisive primaries often occur in situations where an incumbent is already in some danger of losing his seat because of weaknesses developed during his tenure in office. The same political weaknesses that can leave a senator vulnerable to a general election challenge can also generate a strong primary challenge from within his own party. Therefore, in seeking to assess the impact of primary divisiveness on the general election, we must consider the effects of prior incumbent vulnerability separately.[10] Prior vulnerability was undoubtedly a factor, for example, in the case of Democratic Senator Herman Talmadge in 1980. Talmadge had been easily reelected several times to his Georgia Senate seat, but he was narrowly defeated in 1980 even though he had outspent his opponent by $1.7 million. He faced a rather stiff primary challenge that year, a year in which he had also admitted to being an alcoholic, undergone a highly publicized divorce, and been formally denounced by the Senate for using campaign contributions for personal purposes. All of these events occurred *before* his primary. It is thus difficult to assess how much Talmadge's difficult primary race ultimately contributed to his loss in November, or whether it contributed at all, since he might well have lost the November election even if his primary had been uncontested. The Talmadge example illustrates why any analysis of the effects of primary battles on Senate candidates' general election chances must take into account possible intervening variables, especially the possible prior vulnerability of an incumbent.

Three Divisive Incumbent Primaries: A Case-Study Approach

THE CALIFORNIA DEMOCRATIC PRIMARY, 1976

In 1970 Congressman John Tunney defeated incumbent Republican George Murphy by 10 percentage points to become the junior senator from California. Like his counterpart Alan Cranston, Tunney had a consistently liberal voting record in the Senate, averaging an 82 rating by the Americans for Democratic Action and a 5 from the Americans for Constitutional Action. Early in his term, Tunney endured some criticism for missing a key vote while traveling abroad. Generally, however, Tunney maintained a good attendance record, and his performance in the Senate appeared to satisfy most Californians. In each of three statewide California Polls from 1972 through 1975, an average of 72 percent of those who could rate his performance as a senator claimed to be satisfied.[11] In the third of these polls, conducted six months before Tunney's primary, 75 percent gave an opinion, and only 27 percent of these (mostly conservative Republicans) said that Tunney was doing a poor job. As for his standing in the polls, then, Tunney did not appear to be especially vulnerable as the primary season got under way in early 1976.

Another way to assess the extent of an incumbent senator's vulnerability is to see who is calling him vulnerable and how widespread such claims are. If California's political elites assumed that Tunney was vulnerable, evidence of this would very likely have surfaced in the six months prior to the start of the primary campaign. Between June 1, 1975 (a year before the primary), and January 1, 1976 (a point at which it becomes possible to consider that the primary campaign was under way), the *Los Angeles Times* carried 30 articles on various aspects of the approaching Senate race (about 4 per month). Most of them concerned either the jockeying of potential challengers (Democrat Tom Hayden as well as various potential Republican candidates) or statewide surveys covering the Senate race. In only one of these articles was Tunney referred to as potentially vulnerable, and that came in a statement in November 1975 by Congressman Barry Goldwater, Jr., son of the Arizona senator.[12] Goldwater was widely seen as Tunney's most formidable opponent after Governor Reagan removed himself as a possible candidate for the nomination, and as early as 1973 Tunney himself considered Goldwater to be his toughest potential rival.[13] But in late January 1976, Goldwater announced that he would not run for the Republican nomination, citing commitment to his family and a desire to remain as representative for California's Twentieth District. The *San Francisco Examiner* called Goldwater's reason for withdrawal "just buzz words, we presume, for 'I don't think I could win'" (1 February, 2-B).[14]

With Goldwater out of the picture, former Republican Lieutenant Governor John Harmer entered the race, and by March well-known former San Francisco State president S. I. Hayakawa seemed to have become the new frontrunner for the Republican nomination. A new California Poll in March showed that Hayakawa was the first choice of a plurality of Republicans and that he would do better than any of the other Republican hopefuls against Tunney in the fall. However, among those with a preference, Tunney was preferred in this match-up by a margin of 61 percent to 39 percent (16 percent responded "Don't know"). In the meantime, former antiwar activist Tom Hayden had decided to challenge Tunney from the left in the Democratic primary. Equipped with considerable funds—raised at rock concerts and from donations from his wife, Jane Fonda, and other Hollywood friends—Hayden was able to wage an aggressive, television-oriented campaign. Hayden attacked Tunney as "a militant waffler who flips and flops on the issues" (*San Francisco Examiner,* 6 June 1976, 29), and walked up and down the state promoting a 268-page plan for "America's future." In addition to disagreeing with Tunney on a number of issues—characterizing Tunney as "a conservative in liberal clothing" (*San Francisco Chronicle,* 20 January 1976, 8)—Hayden and Fonda attacked Tunney at a personal level. Fonda called the senator "a playboy and a dilettante" who enjoys "dating teenagers," and Hayden described Tunney as "a Chappaquiddick waiting to happen" (ibid., 25 March, 16). Tunney chose to ignore Hayden for several months, but in late May (by which time Hayden had pulled close in the polls) Tunney accused Hayden of "running a dishonest campaign" and publicly demanded that he and Fonda apologize for their "scurrilous personal attacks" against him (ibid., 28 May, 1). Tunney defeated Hayden in the June 8 primary by a margin of 54 percent to 37 percent. Not notably vulnerable prior to the primary season, Tunney had in fact kept his name before the public and clear of scandal and had established a generally liberal voting record without alienating any of California's major constituencies. Three potential Republican challengers had dropped out of contention for the nomination, with the strongest of these, Barry Goldwater, Jr., deciding not to give up his House seat for what he considered a long-shot bid. The eventual winner of the Republican primary, Hayakawa, had never before held elective office, and although he did have some statewide name recognition, he was just the sort of candidate who can win a nomination only when stronger candidates have declined to run.[15] Democrat Hayden, on the other hand, through his actions both during and after the primary campaign, seemed to inflict considerable damage to Tunney's reelection prospects. Although he had said early in the primary campaign that he would endorse Tunney, Hayden never officially did. He remained silent about his intentions for nearly three weeks after the primary and then finally in late June made it clear that he was not in a conciliatory mood. He told reporters: "I'll vote against Hayakawa. . . . It doesn't mean that John Tunney has been a better person this week than I said he was last week. I won't give any energy or time to someone who opposes national health security, opposes the farm workers, or has compared me to Nixon and other famous liars" (ibid., 23 June 1976, 9). Hayden kept a low profile throughout the general election campaign, and it was not until three days before the general election that he announced, "I'm voting for John Tunney." The *Los Angeles Times* called this Hayden's "strongest endorsement of the fall campaign" and confirmed that Hayden had done little to help Tunney's reelection effort (31 October 1976, 3).

Survey data from the California Poll support the conclusion that the divisiveness of the Democratic primary race seriously threatened Tunney's general election chances. Three months after the June primary, some of that divisiveness apparently was still evident among those who had supported Hayden. In September a survey asked respondents to rate Tunney and Republican challenger Hayakawa on 18 traits, such as responsibility, creativity, and leadership. While both candidates received more positive marks than negative, former Hayden supporters were much less favorable toward Tunney than were those who had supported Tunney in the primary. Thirty-nine percent of Hayden supporters scored Tunney as neutral or negative on the index, as opposed to 24 percent of Tunney primary backers. Hayden supporters did not prefer Hayakawa; they gave him even lower scores. Having taken sides earlier, four in ten continued to feel less than satisfied with their party's nominee.

This discontent also affected voter intentions in the general election. In polls taken in August, September, and October a consistent one-third of former Hayden supporters favored Hayakawa over Tunney. By October only 56 percent of Hayden voters were committed to voting for their own party's candidate for senator (see table 37). Some of these Hayden supporters identified themselves as moderates or conservatives, and their

TABLE 37
Intended General Election Vote of Tunney and Hayden Primary Voters, August, September, and October 1976 Polls (in percent)

Intended Vote	Tunney Voters			Hayden Voters		
	July–August	September	Early October	July–August	September	Early October
Tunney	70	77	81	62	62	56
Hayakawa	23	20	13	32	35	33
Undecided	7	3	7	6	3	11
(N)	(173)	(194)	(271)	(108)	(94)	(124)

Source: California Polls 7605 (24 July–2 August), 7606 (18–25 September), and 7607 (7–8 October).

vote for Hayakawa is perhaps not surprising given that Tunney had a solid liberal record, while Hayakawa's most notable political action had been to climb on the roof of a sound truck at San Francisco State University and disconnect the public address system of a group of radical demonstrators. Either these moderate and conservative Democrats had been entirely unaware of Hayden's own stances or they were following an "anyone but Tunney" strategy in the primary. But the September poll also revealed that 30 percent of moderate liberals who had supported Hayden planned to defect to Hayakawa (see table 38).

Liberals would be unlikely to support Hayakawa over Tunney on philosophical grounds, and it would therefore seem likely that these voters had developed such a negative view of Tunney during the primary campaign that they were now prepared to vote for a Republican in the general election. To this extent, it appears that even though he could not actually defeat Tunney in the primary, Hayden's constant and widely covered denigration of Tunney ultimately paid off for Hayakawa in the general election.

The Tunney case illustrates what can happen to an incumbent in the general election when he is damaged by a divisive primary. What is the impact on the general election when an incumbent is actually defeated in the primary? In the period 1968–84, 16 incumbent senators were defeated in primaries (five of them had not previously been elected but had been appointed to fill an unfinished term).[16] Of the 11 primary challengers who defeated full-term incumbents for the nomination, 7 were defeated in the general election. One reason for this high defeat rate is that these had become open seats, so that no candidate had any advantage of incumbency. Moreover, in some cases the opposition party had,

TABLE 38

Intended General Election Vote of Tunney and Hayden Primary Supporters, by Self-designated Ideology, September 1976

	Self-designated Ideology		
Intended Vote	Liberal, Moderate– Liberal	Moderate	Conservative, Moderate– Conservative
	Tunney Primary Voters		
Tunney	85	69	72
Hayakawa	12	26	25
Undecided	3	5	3
(N)	(72)	(42)	(76)
	Hayden Primary Voters		
Tunney	67	57	55
Hayakawa	30	36	45
Undecided	3	7	0
(N)	(57)	(14)	(22)

Source: California Poll 7606, (18–25 September 1976).

at the outset, undoubtedly been aware of the incumbent's vulnerability and had recruited a strong candidate for the general election fight.[17] There is evidence, however, that another reason for this high defeat rate in November was the divisiveness of the primary itself. Survey data are available in two races in which each challenger reached the general election by defeating an incumbent senator in the primary. These data suggest that injuries inflicted during a primary do not always heal by November and that heavy defections among supporters of the defeated incumbent can result.

THE FLORIDA DEMOCRATIC PRIMARY, 1980

In 1980, one-term Democratic incumbent Richard Stone, of Florida, was challenged in the September 9 primary by the same man he had defeated in the primary six years earlier, former Congressman Bill Gunter. In a campaign in which he and two other serious candidates began attacking Stone's Senate record months before the primary, Gunter concentrated on blaming Stone for voting to "give away" the Panama Canal, and he criticized Stone as well for his "lack of leadership."[18] Recalling the bitter campaign waged by Gunter and Stone six years earlier, one *Miami Herald* reporter summarized the primary this way: "This year [Gunter's]

181

incessant attacks on Stone . . . make the 1980 Democratic primary something of a grudge match" (7 September 1980, 5-M).

By August, Stone's popularity among Democrats was at the 50 percent mark, 12 points below Gunter's score on the same scale and well below the average rating of a sitting senator at this stage of a campaign.[19] Gunter and Stone were the top finishers in a four-man primary, and since neither received more than 50 percent of the vote, a runoff was held on October 7. Immediately after the September primary, Stone altered his unsuccessful strategy of ignoring his opponents and began to criticize Gunter for refusing to resign his post as state insurance commissioner while running for higher office, as called for in Florida's "resign-to-run" law. He also attacked Gunter's performance in Congress more than six years before. Gunter stepped up his attacks on Stone's record, and the two candidates also began assailing each other's personal integrity, each trying to "outshout and out-insult the other" (*Miami Herald*, 5 October, 1). For example, Stone accused Gunter of intentionally violating campaign finance laws (*Florida Times-Union*, 19 September, 1), and Gunter claimed that Stone had repeatedly lied to his constituents (*Miami Herald*, 18 September, 22-A).

All of the *Miami Herald* reporters covering the race called attention to the extreme animosity between the candidates. William Amlong described their exchanges as "vicious attacks" (18 September, 22-A). In an article entitled "Stone, Gunter Square Off, Pull No Punches," Robert Shaw wrote on September 19: "[They] escalated their bitter rivalry . . . into a full-fledged media event Thursday, trading tirades . . . and accusing each other. . . . Glaring at each other like two angry schoolchildren, they railed at each other's congressional absenteeism before Gunter ducked into his office. If their argument was more rhetorical than relevant . . . it did offer further proof of the deep-seated animosity between the two men" (10-A). Stephen Diog characterized Gunter as "eagerly . . . trading slurs with Stone blow for blow" and reported that the campaign staff of Paula Hawkins (the eventual Republican Senate nominee, who was enjoying a tranquil, nondivisive runoff) "couldn't be happier with watching Stone and Gunter tear each other apart" (22 September, 1-E). Just before the runoff, Shaw declared that the two candidates had "but one thing in common: Each thinks the other is vicious, sleazy, unprincipled, callow and basically unfit to be a U.S. Senator" (5 October, 1).

Stone lost the runoff by four percentage points and refused to endorse Gunter during the general election campaign. Polls taken in early and late September reported that one-fourth of Democrats planning to vote for

Gunter were not so much voting *for* Gunter as they were voting *against* Stone. Since Stone did not end up running in the general election, it is of course impossible to determine how much the divisiveness of the Democratic primary would have hurt him in November. But there is evidence that nominee Gunter's prospects did suffer as a result of the extreme animosity that had characterized his primary race against Stone. In a mid-October poll of probable November voters, only 45 percent of those who said they had supported Stone in the primary indicated that they planned to vote for Democratic candidate Gunter in November, while another 45 percent said they planned to vote for Republican Paula Hawkins. Ten percent were undecided, leaving fewer than half of the Stone Democrats likely to vote for Gunter. (Three-fourths of Gunter Democrats planned to vote for him in the general election.) Stone's and Gunter's primary supporters were also asked whether they were voting more *for* one candidate or more *against* the other. Of the very small proportion of former Gunter backers who now supported Hawkins, 93 percent were more for Hawkins than against Gunter, indicating that something positive about the Republican was causing the defection. However, of the sizable group of Stone supporters who were now backing Hawkins, 22 percent reported that they were more against Gunter than for the Republican. It is difficult to avoid the conclusion that the animosity toward Gunter that developed during the primary was a major source of defection for this group.

THE CALIFORNIA REPUBLICAN PRIMARY, 1968

Moderate-to-liberal two-term California Senator Thomas Kuchel was challenged in the June 1968 primary by archconservative superintendent of schools Max Rafferty. Rafferty attacked the incumbent's "liberalism" throughout the primary campaign, labeling Kuchel as "more of a left-wing Democrat than a Republican" (*Los Angeles Times*, 11 April 1968, 8) and "in effect a floor leader for the administration" (*San Francisco Examiner*, 5 May, 20). Rafferty attempted to link Kuchel with "the dreadful failures of the Johnson administration" (*Los Angeles Times*, 27 April, 15) and to blame his votes for Supreme Court justices for the decline in society's morals (*San Francisco Chronicle*, 8 May, 6). Kuchel did not campaign full-time until mid-April, and even then he deliberately refused to reply to Rafferty's attacks or even mention his opponent by name. Richard Bergholz, of the *Los Angeles Times*, provided this explanation: "The dangers of engaging in a public debate with a man of Rafferty's oratorical skills are obvious, particularly to a man like Kuchel who is clearly the leader in the fight at this stage and would have everything to lose and nothing to gain from such an encounter" (21 May 21, pt. 2, 4).

But after firing "salvo after salvo at the incumbent" (*Los Angeles Times,* 6 June, 18), Rafferty won the Republican primary by three percentage points. Although the campaign itself did not feature the same kind of public name-calling present in the Stone-Gunter primary in Florida, it was reportedly "no secret that Kuchel personally detests Rafferty" (ibid., 21 May, pt. 4, 1), and in fact Kuchel did not endorse Rafferty after the primary. The divisiveness of the campaign, which was clearly manifested in the actions of conservative Republican activists,[20] was evidently perceived by voters as well. A series of polls taken prior to the November election showed that while Rafferty retained the full support of voters who had favored him in the primary, Kuchel's primary voters now intended to abandon the Republican senatorial nominee in droves. At no time over the course of the general campaign did Rafferty command the support of more than 45 percent of Kuchel Republicans, and by October, when Rafferty might have hoped that fences would be mended within the party, his support among former Kuchel voters had dropped to 39 percent.[21] Rafferty ultimately lost by 5 points a seat that Kuchel had won by 13 points in 1962.

Of course, when a primary candidate who is closer to his party's ideological extreme defeats a more moderate senator, some voters may switch to the other party's candidate in November for ideological reasons rather than as a result of any animosity between their party's primary candidates. The other party's candidate in November might in some cases match more closely a voter's own views on salient issues. For example, when Jeffrey Bell defeated liberal Senator Clifford Case in New Jersey's Republican primary in 1978, many liberal Republicans may in fact have preferred Democratic candidate Bill Bradley to Bell, who was very conservative. Data from California surveys in 1968 indicate that liberals who had supported Kuchel in the Republican primary were considerably more likely to support Democrat Alan Cranston in November than were conservative supporters of Kuchel. As in New Jersey in 1978, the ousted Republican incumbent in the 1968 California race had probably been closer to the Democrat on most issues than to the newly nominated conservative Republican. Because of the ideological distance between Kuchel and Rafferty, it is more difficult than in the 1980 Florida race to know whether the liberal and moderate defections to the other party in the general election were due to ideology or to primary divisiveness.

However, even conservatives who had supported Kuchel were prepared to desert Rafferty. In July, loyalty to Rafferty among Kuchel conservatives was 59 percentage points less than it was among Rafferty conservatives (99 percent versus 40 percent). This difference narrowed to 47 points in September (92 percent versus 45 percent), presumably as the stances of Rafferty and Cranston became better known, but was still a wide 33 points just before the election (93 percent versus 60 percent). In most other cases of divisive primaries over the period examined, the ideological positions of the primary contestants were closer to each other than to those of the challenger from the other party. Moreover, there is usually reason to assume that the number of voters who have even a sketchy awareness of the philosophical differences between primary candidates is quite small. Thus, the amount of defection based on ideology is likely to be small in most instances. Nonetheless, because comparable survey data are not available for other Senate races, it is unfortunately not possible to generalize from analyses of state-level surveys about the overall amount of voter support lost either by Senate incumbents or by their victorious primary challengers when bruises are sustained in a divisive primary contest. We turn, therefore, to an alternative means of addressing the question: a multivariate analysis of aggregate data covering the period 1968 to 1984.

A Regression Analysis of Effects of Primary Divisiveness

As stressed earlier, an investigation of the effect of primary divisiveness on general election outcomes needs to account for the impact of any prior vulnerability of the incumbent and for possible compensating divisiveness in the other party's primary. I do so here by investigating the 200 Senate elections from 1968 to 1984 in which there was both an incumbent primary and a general election. The dependent variable is the incumbent party's margin of victory in the general election, which is regressed on the two divisiveness variables. For the incumbent's party, the measure of divisiveness is the margin of victory for the winner of the incumbent primary.[22] For the challenger primary, divisiveness is a dichotomous variable measured as described above; when there was evidence of bitterness or other forms of animosity between the candidates, the primary was rated as divisive.

In addition to primary divisiveness, we need to account for incumbent vulnerability prior to the primary. One indication of vulnerability is whether or not the incumbent has been the subject of *scandal*. Examples of scandal include conflict-of-interest or ethics charges, problems with

185

alcohol, or messy divorces. Another indication of vulnerability is notable agedness, frailty, or disability. I combined these two types of vulnerability into a dichotomous variable in which an incumbent was scored "1" if descriptions of the race in *Congressional Quarterly Weekly Report* included mention of scandal involvement or of notable agedness,[23] and "0" otherwise.

Three additional measures tapping vulnerability were included in the equation: *previous electoral trouble, temper of the times,* and *ideological incompatibility.* If an incumbent comes close to losing his seat, he may be perceived as weak when he next enters an election campaign. Conversely, an incumbent's landslide victory is often an indication to would-be challengers that he is not vulnerable electorally. Thus an incumbent's margin of victory in his last election may be considered a measure of vulnerability on the grounds that senators who did very well in their last election might draw a less serious challenge in their next election than those who barely eked out a victory. In some years, the electoral atmosphere is better for one party than for the other. High inflation or unemployment, an unpopular president, or a scandal in the administration can lead to a change in the public's relative perceptions of the two parties from year to year, just as times of prosperity or a popular president can. A variable indicating the number of House seats won by the incumbent's party in the current election represents a measure of the temper of the times; such a measure could be expected to account for such effects as how the economy is doing, the popularity of the president, and a host of other influences (most of them beyond the incumbent senator's control) that might incline voters to favor one of the parties more or less than they ordinarily would.

A third measure of incumbents' vulnerability is their distance from their state's "ideological center." A measure of this distance may be derived from estimates by Wright, Erikson, and McIver (1985), on a scale ranging from -1 to $+1$, of the average ideological position of the electorate in each of the fifty states. As a measure of the incumbent's ideological position, I averaged six yearly conservatism ratings, based on CQ's conservative coalition scores.[24] After transforming the incumbent ideology measure to make it compatible with the Wright state-ideology scale, I created an "ideological distance" index by calculating the absolute value of the difference between the incumbent's and the state's ideological position.[25] Such a measure should serve to control for some of the vulnerability an incumbent might suffer if his voting record has been incompatible with the views of his constituents.

Finally, we include in the equation the measure developed in chapter 7 to estimate the distribution of party identification in a given state.[26] This mean partisanship score, adjusted to reflect the party of the incumbent,[27] is included as a control for the electoral advantage one candidate enjoys due to a favorable balance of state party distribution. Our equation, then, is:

$$G = b_0 + b_1 Dinc + b_2 Dchal + b_3 V + b_4 L + b_5 H$$
$$+ b_6 I + b_7 P + u$$

where

G = the incumbent's margin of victory in the general election;

$Dinc$ = the incumbent's margin of victory in the primary;

$Dchal$ = 1 if the challenger primary was divisive, and 0 if it was not (with divisiveness measured as described above);

V = 1 if the incumbent was vulnerable due to scandal, notable age, or other potentially damaging events prior to the primary campaign, and 0 otherwise;

L = the incumbent's margin of victory in his previous general election;

H = the number of seats won by the incumbent's party in the current election;

I = the incumbent's ideological distance from the average position of the electorate of his state;

P = the incumbent party's advantage due to the distribution of party identification in the state; and

u = the error term.

The unstandardized ordinary least squares regression coefficients, along with their standard errors, are arrayed in table 39. The coefficients on each of the four measures of vulnerability and the control for state partisanship are substantively and statistically significant. For instance, being the subject of scandal or appearing old or frail carries the penalty of 13 percentage points in the general election, other factors held constant. An incumbent fairly far out of step with his constituency—say, by 20 points on the ideological distance scale—stands to have his margin of victory reduced by about 8 points more than if his voting record closely reflected the general ideological position of his constituents.

The distribution of party identification in a state can also be a substantial influence, depending on how skewed the advantage is toward one party. For highly Democratic states—e.g., states having a Wright score of around -0.2—the advantage in the general election margin of victory of a Democratic incumbent over a Republican incumbent comes to nearly 10 percentage points. In states in which the two parties are more balanced, of course, the impact is less.

TABLE 39
The Effect of Incumbent Primary Divisiveness and Other Variables on the General
Election Outcome: Ordinary Least Squares Regression

Independent Variable	Range	Unstandardized b	Standard Error
Intercept		6.45	
Incumbent's primary margin of victory	0–100	.150	.041
Challenger primary divisiveness	0/1	−3.68	3.00
Incumbent vulnerability due to scandal, notable age	0/1	−13.11	3.47
Incumbent's margin of victory in previous election	0–100	.237	.063
House seats gained by incumbent's party this election	−49–+49	.240	.045
Incumbent's ideological distance from state electorate	.00–.39	−39.54	12.09
Incumbent's advantage due to state party distribution	−1–+1	24.38	8.37
		$\bar{R}^2 = .36$	$(N = 200)$

Note: Dependent variable = incumbent's general election margin of victory.

The coefficient of .15 on the incumbent primary divisiveness variable indicates that, controlling for conditions in the challenger primary as well as for various aspects of vulnerability, every percentage point an incumbent gives up in his primary produces the loss of less than two-tenths of a point off his margin of victory in November. Point for point, this may not seem to be a large impact. But perhaps a more realistic way to view the significance of the effect is to compare the general election fate of an incumbent who had had only token opposition (and had avoided a divisive primary) with that of an incumbent who weathered a stiff primary challenge. If the margin for the first incumbent were, say, 70 percentage points, and the margin for the second were 5 points, the difference between their margins in the general election due to the difference in their primaries would be just less than 10 percentage points. In many races this margin is not the difference between actually winning and losing the general election, but it is worth noting that from 1968 through 1984, 44 incumbents won by 10 points or less, and another 34 lost by this amount or less.

There is a problem with the ordinary least squares (OLS) approach, however. There is every reason to believe that aspects of incumbent vulnerability not captured by the four variables in the equation influence both the general election outcome and primary margin of victory for the incumbents.[28] In such a situation, the error term is correlated with both the causal variable of interest and the dependent variable (general election margin). Unless we can purge the divisiveness variables, particularly the incumbent divisiveness variable, of that portion of the error term that is correlated with it, the coefficients produced by OLS may be biased. The standard procedure for correcting this problem is two-stage least squares regression.

A TWO-STAGE LEAST SQUARES APPROACH

If it were possible to measure initial vulnerability perfectly, the result would be a recursive model, with vulnerability causing divisiveness, and vulnerability, divisiveness, and various other variables causing the general election outcome (assuming that no other variables cause both vulnerability and primary divisiveness). But vulnerability cannot be measured perfectly. We can identify certain weaknesses, such as scandal, notable age, and a few other factors that are likely to weigh against an incumbent in the minds of voters. And we can take into account how well the incumbent did in his last election as an indication of his strength as a candidate six years later. But six years is potentially long enough to repair a weak image or ruin a strong one, and scandals and notable frailty, while an important influence, are rather uncommon. Even after other sources of an incumbent's potential vulnerability are taken into account—such as his ideological distance from his constituency, the general standing of his national party in light of recent economic news, or the public's approval of the president—there remain intangible, or at least difficult-to-measure, factors that probably contribute to his vulnerability. The incumbent may be perceived to be indecisive, or a weak leader, or too little interested in his constituents' concerns, or to possess any number of other negative traits.

Just such a combination of negatively perceived characteristics is illustrated by the case of former California Republican S. I. Hayakawa. Soon after entering the Senate in 1976, Hayakawa acquired a reputation as something of a loafer. Stories about his falling asleep in the Senate chamber or in committee appeared often in the news, to the point where Hayakawa became a recurring subject of jokes in Johnny Carson's "Tonight Show" monologues. These stories—along with his penchant for wearing a tam-o'-shanter, the fact that he was in his seventies, and his rather negligible legislative record—contributed, by the end of his term, to the impression that Hayakawa was not a serious senator. While it is difficult to know for certain what factors led to Hayakawa's consistently low ratings with Californians (for example, in a February 1980 California Poll, Hayakawa was perceived as doing a "poor" job by 44 percent of those respondents having an opinion on his performance level), by the middle of his term reports were surfacing that he would be strongly opposed not only in the general election but also in the 1982 Republican primary. By December 1981 it appeared likely that Hayakawa could lose to any number of Republican challengers, and in January 1982 he announced his intention to retire after one term. While it is true that Hayakawa's age would be accounted for by one of the variables in the equation, other characteristics that made him vulnerable would not. Yet such factors may in fact influence both primary and general election outcomes, presenting the kind of correlated errors problem that is usually corrected with the two-stage least squares approach.

In the first stage, divisiveness is estimated as a function of the various measures of vulnerability plus at least one other variable not present in the OLS equation above. The coefficients on each of these independent variables, when multiplied by their respective values and added to the intercept, produce a new version of the divisiveness variable—one that has been purged of the left-out aspects of vulnerability and indeed all other components contained in the error term in equation 1. This surrogate for divisiveness may now be substituted into equation 2 along with the measures of prior vulnerability. The coefficient produced in the second stage should no longer be biased due to correlated errors.

In order to estimate an instrument for divisiveness in the incumbent primary, it is necessary to identify one or more variables that affect primary divisiveness but that have no independent impact on the general election vote. One possibility is to examine the incumbent's vulnerability within his own party. Perhaps incumbents who stray from their state party's ideological center are more likely to draw strong primary challenges than incumbents who are careful to stay close to the party rank and file. For example, in a state where Democratic elites and most of the rank and file are fairly liberal, a conservative Democratic senator might draw more primary competition—which could lead to divisiveness—than would a senator with a fairly liberal voting record. Likewise, a Republican with a liberal voting record might draw a primary challenge from more conservative candidates representing closer ties to the mainstream of the party, whereas an incumbent with a conservative record in the Senate would not. In neither case would the incumbent's ideological distance from the party necessarily affect the general election outcome independently of the effect of that distance on primary divisiveness. In fact, an incumbent who strays from the center of the party in order to be closer to the state electorate as a whole might, as a result, be a stronger general election contender.

190

Bartels (1983) constructed indices of Democratic party liberalism and Republican party conservatism for each of the fifty states.[29] If we take the incumbent ideology measure described above (and in note 24), transform this variable to make it compatible with the Bartels indices, and then subtract this transformed mean rating from the state party score, the result is an approximate measure of the distance of each incumbent senator from the mainstream of his or her party.[30] This "party distance" variable, which ranges from 0 to 31 for the senators in this study, proved to have a substantial impact on divisiveness, controlling for the various measures of vulnerability.[31]

A second factor influencing a primary's divisiveness might be the degree of party cohesiveness within a state. For example, some state parties exert more control than others over the nomination process. State law in Connecticut, New York, Utah, and several other states requires that nominating conventions be held prior to the statewide primary. At these conventions, candidates appear before party representatives from local party organizations around the state to seek official party endorsement. The rules for each of these states vary, but the effect of each is to allow potentially fractious disagreements over which candidate best represents the party to be ironed out in relative privacy and in a short period of time. The various party factions may then emerge united behind one candidate. Non-endorsed candidates may, under certain circumstances, challenge the endorsed candidates in the primary, but presumably the endorsed candidates will enjoy the advantage of whatever resources the party organizations have to offer (Jewell 1984, 52). Morehouse (cited in Bibby et al. 1983, 82) classified all 100 state parties as strongly, moderately, or weakly cohesive on the basis of each state's pre-primary endorsement laws or traditions. With a few changes, I included this three-category index as a second new (excluded) variable in the first-stage equation.[32]

A third variable that is likely to affect the margin of victory in the incumbent's primary is the political experience level of the incumbent's primary opponent. Political experience is likely to be an advantage for several reasons. First, elected officials are more likely to be known than most other candidates. Familiarity typically produces attention, and it is likely that the press will cover a governor or congressman more than a state legislator or a small-town mayor, and any elected official over a candidate with no prior political experience. One reason for such differing coverage is that the actions of politicians, especially those who have statewide visibility, are perceived by the press as more newsworthy than those of unknown, private citizens. When it comes to primary elections, this could be the difference between a candidate's receiving some coverage and no coverage during a campaign. Second, as discussed in chapter 2, candidates with political experience are probably better able to put together a campaign organization, have better ties to potential contributors, and can bring to bear their previous experience to run a more efficient campaign than can candidates who have not held office.

To measure political experience, I first distinguished between candidates who have never held political office and those who have and then divided the latter group into three categories. All candidates who had never held elected office were scored 0. This group consisted mostly of attorneys but included members of a variety of professions, including teachers, salesmen, contractors, and physicians. State legislators and former state legislators, small-town mayors, and city council members were scored 1; anyone who had been elected to a statewide office, speaker or other leaders of the state legislature, large-city mayors, and congressmen were scored 2; and governors were scored 3.

In addition to the three new variables and the vulnerability measures, I included the measure of state party distribution in the first-stage equation. Key (1964, 437–39) proposed, and Hacker (1965) and Bernstein (1977) affirmed, that the more dominant a party is within a state, the greater advantage that party has in the general election; as Bernstein put it, "Increasing the chances of victory in the general election encourages primary competition" (542). Table 40 contains the coefficients and standard errors for the variables in the first-stage equation. We see from the coefficients for the four measures of vulnerability that whether an incumbent is likely to have a divisive primary depends a great deal on whether he has been involved in scandal or appears notably aged or frail. Whether he is in step with the ideological tendencies of his state's electorate also has an impact, as does the margin of victory in his last election. Only the "temper of the times" variable does not have a significant impact here, and this is not surprising. The condition of the economy, the current perception of the president, and the other current political conditions picked up by the "House seats" measure are conditions that should affect the incumbent's chances for reelection rather than renomination. Since the same conditions that hurt (or help) the incumbent will hurt (or help) any potential challenger from the incumbent's party in exactly the same way, this variable should have no bearing on a decision to challenge the incumbent in the primary.

Both the measure of ideological distance from the party and the cohesiveness variable appear to influence the incumbent's primary margin. The coefficient −.61 indicates that for each point an incumbent deviates

TABLE 40
The Effect of Incumbent Primary Divisiveness on the General Election Outcome:
Two-Stage Least Squares

Independent Variable	Range	Unstandardized b	Standard Error
Stage 1 (dependent variable = incumbent's primary margin of victory)			
Intercept		77.01	
Incumbent's distance from mean state party ideology	0–31	−.61	.235
State party cohesiveness	0–2	5.76	2.04
Strength of incumbent's primary opponent	0–3	−29.33	2.84
Scandal, notable age	0/1	−17.14	4.76
Incumbent's margin of victory in previous election	0–100	.157	.086
House seats gained by incumbent's party this election	−49–+49	−.065	.065
Incumbent's ideological distance from state electorate	.00–.39	44.65	22.23
Incumbent's advantage due to state party distribution	−1–+1	−15.62	11.71
		$\bar{R}^2 = .52$	$(N = 221)$

Stage 2 (dependent variable = incumbent's general election margin of victory)			
Intercept		6.69	
Instrument for incumbent primary divisiveness*		.150	.069
Challenger primary divisiveness	0/1	−3.90	3.07
Scandal, notable age	0/1	−12.36	3.96
Incumbent's margin of victory in previous election	0–100	.230	.065
House seats gained by incumbent's party this election	−49–+49	.233	.046
Incumbent's ideological distance from state electorate	.00–.39	−39.48	12.48
Incumbent's advantage due to state party distribution	−1–+1	23.82	8.80
		$\bar{R}^2 = .33$	$(N = 200)$

*The "House seats gained" variable was removed from those listed in the Stage 1 equation (previous table) before the instrument was created.

from the ideological mean of his party, he loses just over a half-point in his primary victory margin. This relationship exists even after controlling for the incumbent's distance from the mean ideological position of the statewide electorate, which includes voters in the other party plus independents. Whereas this latter variable has a fairly strong impact on the general election vote, the party distance measure's correlation with the general election vote is .01. It should be noted that the strong impact of the party distance variable on the primary margin of victory does not necessarily imply that primary voters are consciously punishing incumbents who deviate from the mainstream of the party. The substantial coefficient could just as easily be explained at the elite level: incumbents whose ideologies differ greatly from the party norm attract strong challengers, whereas these same strong challengers are less inclined to go to the trouble when the incumbent is close to the mainstream.

The degree of party cohesiveness also partially explains the extent of primary divisiveness. Incumbents from strongly cohesive states have, all other factors controlled, an advantage of about 11 points over incumbents from weak parties in their primary margin of victory. Finally, the political experience of the incumbent's challenger has a very strong impact on the incumbent's primary margin of victory. The difference between a congressman or statewide official and someone without any political experience results in a difference of nearly 60 points in the primary outcome.

Our instrument for incumbent primary divisiveness, then, has four main components: the incumbent's prior vulnerability with respect to the general election, the incumbent's distance from the ideological center of his state party, the degree of cohesiveness of the party in his state, and the strength of the primary challenger. Substituting this instrument for incumbent divisiveness into the original equation yields the coefficients shown in the second part of table 40. The coefficient for incumbent primary divisiveness, which was .15 in the OLS equation, is again .15. That the two-stage least squares approach produces the same coefficient permits us to be more confident that our assessment of the impact of primary divisiveness on the general election outcome is accurate. To return to our earlier comparison, the difference between a nondivisive primary won by 70 points and a divisive one won by 5 points is a loss of about 10 points to the incumbent in November.

How substantial is this effect? One way of answering this question is to determine how may senators who experienced a divisive primary and lost in the general election might have survived if primary divisiveness had had no effect at all. In other words, how many of the senators who lost in the period 1968–84 were denied reelection because of a divisive primary? Over this period, 34 of the 46 incumbents defeated in the general election lost by fewer than 10 percentage points. Of these, 9 had also lost a primary by fewer than 25 points and thus could be considered to have suffered a divisive primary. If we look at all general election losers, no matter how many points they lost by, and if we allow that any primary won by fewer than 55 points was divisive, we still find that only 17 senators lost general election contests as a direct result of a divisive primary. Thus, under the most liberal definition of divisiveness, about one-third of the defeats since 1968 can be attributed to divisive primaries.

Does Divisiveness Matter?

We have seen that Senate races that include a closely contested primary tend to be associated with general election trouble for the incumbent party, whoever its nominee may finally be. This finding remained when the divisiveness of the challenger primary was taken into account, and it is similar to the results reported by Bernstein in his analysis of Senate elections in an earlier period. Taking into account the independent effect of prior incumbent vulnerability, we have seen that, indeed, most divisive primaries occur when the incumbent is vulnerable to begin with, and this prior vulnerability contributes strongly as well to the poor success rates of these incumbents in general elections. Primary divisiveness itself appears to have a modest independent effect on general election outcomes. This conclusion must, however, be qualified for two reasons. First, the standard error on the two-stage least squares estimate of the effect of divisiveness is large. This leaves open the possibility that the real effect of divisiveness is zero or that the impact is as great as or greater than the moderate estimate of .15. Second, analysis of individual races—such as the three reviewed in this chapter—suggests that on at least some occasions, primary divisiveness per se can have a substantial impact. The evidence from survey data for the Tunney-Hayakawa race indicates that even a well-regarded incumbent senator can suffer in the general election as a result of a stiff primary challenge. In Tunney's case, some Tom Hayden supporters appear to have switched to Republican Hayakawa, and it is difficult to believe that they did so just because they were impressed with either Hayakawa's politics or his assets as a candidate. Evaluated in light of past studies of primary divisiveness, these results suggest that the prior vulnerability of incumbents is a more important influence on general election outcomes than is incumbent primary divisiveness (which itself is caused, in part, by vulnerability). They also suggest that both the Bernstein and the Kenney and Rice studies, which did not take into account prior vulnerability of senators, probably overestimate the effect of divisiveness per se. But even if the effect of divisiveness is not large in absolute terms, incumbents struggling to overcome the effect of notable age, scandal, or other political weaknesses will undoubtedly consider the sacrifice of even four percentage points a formidable additional burden.

The findings of this chapter also underscore the complexity of the dynamics that produce Senate election outcomes. Senators not only have to concern themselves with taking care of constituents' needs and with preparing for the other party's challenge every sixth year; their electoral well-being also depends on their ability to appear vigorous, to stay out of trouble, to avoid divisive challenges from within their own party, and—in attempting all of this—to remain mindful of the risks of straying too far from their state's ideological center. They must weigh all of these factors against the ever-changing backdrop of the national and state economic pictures, and the popularity of the current president.

9. Conclusion: New Directions for Senate Elections Research

Efforts to explain U.S. Senate elections are confounded by seemingly contradictory or inconsistent outcomes within or across election years. Within individual states, results from year to year often defy generalizations as well. In many instances, a state's two senators are of similar political profiles, yet one incumbent may breeze to reelection time after time, while the state's other senator, even though he or she has similar partisanship and general ideology, faces a series of uphill struggles. On the other hand, in many states the two senators are from different parties or have different ideological points of view. Some such pairs of senators are reelected repeatedly even though they differ dramatically in ideological outlook. It may be tempting to explain such occurrences by claiming that voters are ideologically fickle or that they prefer to have "balanced" representation in Washington. And indeed, ideology and partisanship sometimes play a significant role in Senate elections. But the extent of that role is a function of other factors, such as initial candidate quality, capacity to raise campaign funds, and skill in attracting favorable media attention. The key to understanding the remarkable diversity of Senate election outcomes is to look beyond static features of the political landscape—the ideological and partisan composition of Senate electorates, state size and geographical location, and the ideology and party identification of incumbent senators—and to widen our perspective to include, as well, the *interaction* between voters and Senate campaigns. This means focusing on the nature of Senate campaigns themselves and

197

on the particularly important fact that some Senate campaigns are high-intensity, hard-fought affairs, while others are much more low-key. The effects on voters of such factors as the incumbency advantage, the influence of national factors, and the extent of party-based voting all depend on campaign intensity and on the resultant amounts of information voters receive in individual campaigns.

The focus of this book has been the necessity for candidates to become known if they expect to attract votes on the basis of their own merits rather than simply on the basis of party identification. Whether voters base their decisions on comparisons of candidates' personal attributes, issue positions, general ideology, or other factors (apart from national conditions), they must first have information about the candidates. When they are aware of only one candidate, a different type of vote decision results, one based much more on party identification or on incumbency. In such situations identifiers of the out-party generally defect to a known incumbent over an unknown challenger. Therefore, if one of the candidates—most often the challenger—is not known at the start of a campaign, he must make himself known, and he must do so within a few months via the media. The amount of information hard-fought and low-key Senate campaigns manage to direct at voters varies, and on their end, voters absorb varying amounts of information to bring to bear on their vote choices.

The distinction between hard-fought and low-key races is also central to the effect of state party distribution on Senate election outcomes. While neither state size nor homogeneity per se appears to have much systematic influence on Senate election outcomes, the impact of a given state's party balance may well do so, depending on the intensity of the race. A party's numerical voter advantage in a state seems to be dwarfed in importance by the impact of a hard-fought campaign, so that no matter how skewed a state's party distribution is, either candidate may win. On the other hand, in a low-key race the impact of state party balance on the margin of victory can be considerable.

What is noteworthy about Senate elections as a class of elections is that depending on the level of intensity of the Senate campaign in a given election year, very different decision processes might be employed by voters. Moreover, different processes may predominate in the same state from one election to the next. The availability for study of large numbers of Senate campaigns of differing intensities presents an opportunity for developing an understanding of elections generally that does not present itself in either of the other two major types of elections. Presidential elections feature wide variation in personality- and issue-related elements but

198

occur infrequently and feature a constant, high level of campaign intensity; House elections are very numerous but offer little variation in electoral context. Many steps, however, lie ahead in the pursuit of the opportunity that Senate election study presents.

Expanding Research into Senate Elections

Many aspects of Senate elections need to be investigated further, and our knowledge of what happens in individual Senate races, particularly how the news media cover Senate campaigns, needs to be expanded. The extent to which news coverage is generated by candidates' actions and decisions, as opposed to those of news organizations, could be investigated by comparing Senate candidates' campaign itineraries with the actual news coverage their activities received. A candidate's initial credibility in the eyes of the press and potential contributors, which may be based to some extent on perceptions of the candidate's previous experience, may also, as political polling proliferates, be based on the candidate's initial standing in polls. Such standing depends in part on voters' perceptions of how well the candidate might do against potential opponents, but it also is likely to depend on how well known he is to begin with. Thus a candidate's initial electoral prospects—or lack thereof—may become a self-fulfilling prophesy as the decisions of others about political support and news coverage exert their influence on subsequent poll results: candidates with initial recognition and thus promising poll results (especially against an incumbent) receive additional news coverage and campaign contributions. Their recognition rates continue to increase, resulting in better poll standing in subsequent match-ups with incumbents. Candidates with little or no initial recognition, on the other hand, look like losers in initial polls and are likely to receive little news coverage and fewer contributions and to show no marked gains in subsequent polls. Two questions that thus remain to be investigated are how a challenger breaks the pattern of low recognition and light news coverage, and where the threshold between a low-key candidacy and the achievement of a hard-fought race is located. Access to state-level polls, combined with data on contributions and press coverage, would provide a basis for investigating such questions. Chronicling the actions and decisions of incumbents during the campaign, particularly those provoked by challengers' campaign moves, would allow us to explore the extent to which campaign intensity is affected either by candidate decisions and actions or by decisions made by members of news organizations.

Simply increasing monitoring of the news media in Senate races would produce important data. In this study I examined newspaper coverage of 12 Senate races, and while this provided the basis for a number of generalizations about Senate campaigns, systematic investigation on a larger scale is in order. Monitoring a sizable but manageable number of newspapers in many more states would be one approach to the problem of obtaining data on news coverage. It would also help in evaluating whether Senate campaign intensity is actually bimodally distributed (essentially hard-fought *or* low-key) rather than spaced intermittently along an intensity continuum. Basic "observational" research on news coverage could also involve monitoring a few Senate campaigns, strategically selected; Goldenberg and Traugott's work on a single election in Michigan, in which they catalogued both television news and newspaper coverage in all sections of the state, heads in this direction. Case studies comparing hard-fought and low-key campaigns in the same state, looking at the same news organizations and the same constituent populations, would provide a useful basis for generalizations, since the problem of controlling for potentially contaminating factors due to different campaign environments could be minimized.

In the case of hard-fought Senate races, we need to continue research into what constitutes the information voters have about candidates and campaigns beyond the fact of mere recognition of candidates' names. What do voters know about candidate views on matters of national policy? What do voters think about candidates' "leadership," "competence," or other personal characteristics? With such information, a much fuller assessment of the impact on the vote choice of issues, candidate personality, and of course party identification—similar to the work done for years on presidential elections—could be undertaken.

Data for such analysis, not now readily available, would need to be obtained in one of two ways. One would be to design a national random sample that draws enough respondents from the states in which Senate elections are taking place to permit state-by-state analysis. The other approach would be to coordinate individual state-level polls so that identical questions could be asked in each state. Each approach has its advantages and drawbacks. If done via random-digit dialing, the former method would be far simpler and more economical. But designing a questionnaire from a national, or centralized, perspective would tend to preclude the kind of individualized probes that are essential for investigating the issues and events of particular Senate campaigns. Failed past efforts to organize a network of state polls offer testimony to the problems of coordinating even a minimum questionnaire schedule; lack of funding as well as disagreements over the best questions, or question wordings, are among the difficulties of a decentralized effort. Moreover, most polling organizations are in business to serve candidates, newspapers, or private corporations and are thus not particularly interested either in expanding their questionnaires or in cooperating with organizations in other states, and currently only a few university-affiliated state data organizations do statewide polling.

The advantages and disadvantages of comparing currently available statewide polls are seen in the comparison of California and Wyoming races in chapter 6. When Social Security, Reagan's economic, and the nuclear freeze initiative dominated the campaign in California, polls were designed that reflected the fact that these were key issues in the state, and the voters' positions on these issues were tapped. However, one of the polls contained no questions on Social Security, and another had no items tapping people's views on Reaganomics, even though these were both salient to the voters and were being hotly debated by the Senate candidates at the time. The Wyoming poll tapped opinions on different issues that were central to the Wyoming Senate campaign. It is doubtful that any national poll with questions common to all respondents could easily provide the depth made possible by either of the two state polls; using the two state polls made it possible to investigate voters' reactions to the very different issues that were salient in the California and the Wyoming campaigns. However, using the two different state polls also created severe limitations as far as analysis is concerned: because the same questions were not asked in both surveys, direct comparison was impossible. A coordinated state-poll project would have to produce a single question schedule allowing for flexibility within basic subject areas so that the idiosyncrasies of individual campaigns could be addressed. "Experts" in each state would be responsible for establishing the key issues, events, and candidate-oriented characteristics that constitute the campaigns, and these individual components could then be incorporated into an overall questionnaire design that would ensure a common set of background data on all respondents and standardized techniques for rating candidates and relaying respondents' opinions.

It would also be useful to determine whether voters in one part of a state receive the same information, the same quantity of information, or the same slant on information as people in other parts of the state; this would be particularly interesting in the case of states that are geographically split, such as Pennsylvania, Idaho, Vermont, New Jersey, California, Tennessee, or Colorado. States such as these tend to have several major media markets; in these cases, a newspaper in one part of the state may provide more thorough coverage or more prominently placed cam-

201

paign stories than in another, and it is important to know whether respondents who read the first paper are differently informed—controlling for other factors—than readers of the other paper. Contextual data on which newspapers respondents read and which television shows they watch may provide important data linking the information they receive (through both news coverage and paid advertising) with the opinions they have about Senate candidates.

The quality of challengers appears to be a central factor in determining whether a race will be hard-fought or low-key. We need therefore to investigate further *why* potential candidates decide to run or to wait. Jacobson and Kernell (1981), noting the findings of much research that the state of the economy and the popularity of the president are important factors in the *voters'* calculus, have proposed that candidates and the political elites who have a hand in selecting them also assume that these factors are on the voters' minds, and make their decisions accordingly. Jacobson and Kernell therefore argued that political scientists modeling the vote should use measures of such factors as the state of the economy and the president's popularity *in the spring,* which is when the candidate selection process is under way, rather than in the fall at the time of the election. But many candidates make decisions on whether to risk a Senate challenge long before spring, often announcing more than two years before an election. This points up the need for further study of the political vulnerability of incumbents. How do potential challengers gauge the likelihood of beating an incumbent (either in the primary or in the general election) long before anyone knows what the state of the economy or the popularity level of the president at election time will be?

The Place of Senate Election Studies in General Election Theory

Political scientists devote considerable attention to presidential and congressional elections in order to understand the vote decision process in elections in general. If the amount of information voters have is central to their choice between political candidates, as I have asserted, then the empirical study of voters—and elections—is best served by the development of a sample of situations where the level of information disseminated (and presumably assimilated by voters) *varies.* The set of elections to be studied should include enough instances of high- and low-intensity campaigns, existing side by side, to permit meaningful comparison of how this variable affects the vote decision process. Senate elections, because of their broad range of campaign intensities, provide the best laboratory for such a general study of elections, and this is why there is such a serious need for a national survey or a coordinated set of state-level surveys. Presidential elections, although they were the basis of the *American Voter*'s seminal theories of voting behavior, are a constraining type of election. Occurring only once every four years, they constitute a very small sample of elections in America (there have been only 10 since the first comprehensive national surveys were undertaken in 1952). However important as subjects of study in their own right, presidential elections are unique in that they are the only kind in the United States in which the candidates' names become household words, and in which most voters are exposed to a great deal of information not only about candidates' personal attributes but also about their general philosophies and their positions on specific policy issues. In-depth study of presidential elections and campaigns thus may produce a thorough understanding of voting behavior in one type of election—where considerable information is disseminated about both candidates—but this situation does not describe most other elections.

House elections are much more plentiful than the high-visibility presidential elections. Indeed, one feature of House races that makes them ideal for systematic investigation is the regularity and frequency with which they occur and the similar size of constituencies from one district to the next. However, with some exceptions, House races pit a well-known incumbent against an invisible, often politically inexperienced challenger. The level of information disseminated during House campaigns is—again, with some exceptions—generally quite low, and voters tend either to vote for the candidate they know (the incumbent) or to vote on the basis of the one piece of information they do have, which is party label. Voters' inclination to favor the incumbent, combined with the fact that the partisan balance in many districts is skewed toward the incumbent's party, results in comfortable victories for House incumbents in most cases. Systematic study of House elections using national random samples thus allows an understanding of voting behavior in low-intensity, light-information campaigns. But as we have seen, not all elections are such low-key affairs, and generalizations made on the basis of House races cannot be applied across the board.

It is the range and distribution of Senate elections that sets them apart from either presidential or House elections. Some Senate campaigns are in the spotlight throughout the election season and even receive national attention; commentators and journalists from the national news media analyze these races individually, evaluating the candidates and the issues dominating their campaigns. And each year there is also a fairly sizable group of practically invisible races, with very little news coverage or paid political advertising, where (as in so many House races) a familiar incumbent faces an invisible challenger whose campaign never gets off the ground. Because the proportions of hard-fought and low-key Senate races are generally even, looking at Senate elections allows a general investigation of how and why campaigns of different intensity affect the way people vote. Moreover, because Senate constituencies differ greatly in their size and composition, and because they offer a unique opportunity to compare the campaigns of two different sets of candidates targeting the same constituency, Senate elections allow for a rich variety of comparisons and controls.

Appendixes

Hard-fought and Low-key Races, 1968–1984

In the following table, sp = special election, H = hard-fought, L = low-key, and o = open-seat. D and R indicate the party of the candidate who won the election.

State	1968 (N=34)	1970 (N=35)	1972 (N=33)	1974 (N=34)	1976 (N=35)	1978 (N=35)	1980 (N=34)	1982 (N=33)	1984 (N=33)
Alabama	oL(D)	—	H(D)	L(D)	—	spoH(D) oL(D)	oH(R)	—	L(D)
Alaska	oH(D)	spL(R)	L(R)	H(D)	—	L(R)	oH(R)	—	L(R)
Arizona	oH(R)	H(R)	—	L(R)	oH(D)	—	H(R)	L(D)	—
Arkansas	L(D)	—	L(D)	oL(D)	—	oL(D)	L(D)	—	H(D)
California	oH(D)	H(D)	—	L(D)	H(R)	—	L(D)	oH(R)	—
Colorado	L(R)	—	H(D)	H(D)	—	H(R)	H(D)	—	L(R)
Connecticut	H(D)	oH(R)	—	L(D)	L(R)	—	oH(D)	H(R)	—
Delaware	—	oL(R)	H(D)	—	H(R)	L(D)	—	H(R)	L(D)
Florida	oH(R)	oH(D)	—	oH(D)	L(D)	—	oH(R)	L(D)	—
Georgia	L(D)	—	oH(D)	L(D)	—	L(D)	H(R)	—	L(D)
Hawaii	L(D)	H(R)	—	L(D)	oH(D)	—	L(D)	L(D)	—
Idaho	H(D)	—	oH(R)	L(D)	—	L(R)	H(R)	—	L(R)
Illinois	L(R)	spH(D)	L(R)	L(D)	—	H(R)	oH(D)	—	H(D)
Indiana	H(D)	H(D)	—	H(D)	H(R)	—	H(R)	L(R)	—
Iowa	oH(D)	—	H(D)	oH(D)	—	H(R)	H(R)	—	H(D)
Kansas	oH(R)	—	L(R)	H(R)	—	oH(R)	L(R)	—	L(R)
Kentucky	oH(R)	—	oH(D)	H(D)	—	L(D)	L(D)	—	H(R)
Louisiana	L(D)	—	oH(D)	L(D)	—	L(D)	L(D)	—	L(D)
Maine	—	L(D)	H(D)	—	H(D)	H(R)	—	H(D)	L(R)
Maryland	H(R)	H(R)	—	L(R)	H(D)	—	L(R)	L(D)	—
Massachusetts	—	L(D)	L(R)	—	L(D)	H(D)	—	L(D)	oH(D)
Michigan	—	L(D)	H(R)	—	oH(D)	H(D)	—	L(D)	H(D)
Minnesota	—	oL(D)	L(D)	—	L(D)	spH(R) oH(R)	—	H(R)	H(R)
Mississippi	—	L(D)	L(D)	—	L(D)	oH(R)	—	H(D)	H(R)
Missouri	oH(D)	H(D)	—	L(D)	oH(R)	—	H(D)	H(R)	—
Montana	—	L(D)	H(D)	—	oH(D)	oH(D)	—	H(D)	L(D)
Nebraska	—	L(R)	L(R)	—	oH(D)	oL(D)	—	L(D)	H(D)
Nevada	H(D)	H(D)	—	oH(R)	L(D)	—	L(R)	H(R)	—
New Hampshire	H(R)	—	L(D)	oH(D)	—	H(R)	H(D)	—	H(R)
New Jersey	—	H(D)	L(R)	—	L(D)	oH(D)	—	oH(D)	L(D)
New Mexico	—	H(D)	oH(R)	—	H(R)	L(R)	—	H(D)	L(R)
New York	L(R)	H(R)	—	H(R)	H(D)	—	oH(R)	L(D)	—
North Carolina	L(D)	—	oH(R)	oL(D)	—	L(R)	H(R)	—	H(R)
North Dakota	L(R)	H(D)	—	H(R)	L(D)	—	oL(R)	H(D)	—
Ohio	oH(R)	oH(R)	—	oL(D)	H(D)	—	L(D)	L(D)	—
Oklahoma	H(R)	—	oH(R)	H(R)	—	oH(D)	oH(R)	—	L(D)
Oregon	H(R)	—	H(R)	H(R)	—	L(R)	L(R)	—	L(R)
Pennsylvania	H(R)	H(R)	—	H(R)	oH(R)	—	oH(R)	L(R)	—
Rhode Island	—	L(D)	H(D)	—	oH(R)	L(D)	—	H(R)	L(D)
South Carolina	L(D)	—	L(R)	L(D)	—	H(R)	L(D)	—	L(R)
South Dakota	H(D)	—	oH(D)	H(D)	—	oL(R)	H(R)	—	L(R)
Tennessee	—	H(R)	H(R)	—	H(D)	H(R)	—	L(D)	oL(D)

State	1968 (N=34)	1970 (N=35)	1972 (N=33)	1974 (N=34)	1976 (N=35)	1978 (N=35)	1980 (N=34)	1982 (N=33)	1984 (N=33)
Texas	—	oH(D)	H(R)	—	H(D)	H(R)	—	L(D)	oH(R)
Utah	H(R)	H(D)	—	oH(R)	H(R)	—	L(R)	H(R)	—
Vermont	L(R)	H(R)	—	oH(D)	H(R)	—	H(D)	H(R)	—
Virginia	—	H(D)	H(R)	—	H(D)	oH(R)	—	oH(R)	L(R)
Washington	L(D)	L(D)	—	L(D)	L(D)	—	H(R)	L(D)	—
West Virginia	—	L(D)	L(D)	—	L(D)	H(D)	—	H(D)	oH(D)
Wisconsin	L(D)	L(D)	—	L(D)	L(D)	—	H(R)	L(D)	—
Wyoming	—	H(D)	L(R)	—	H(R)	oL(R)	—	H(R)	L(R)
116 Hard-fought	11H	18H	12H	11H	14H	12H	13H	15H	10H
118 Low-key	13L	11L	13L	14L	11L	10L	12L	15L	19L
57 open-seat Hard-fought	9oH	4oH	8oH	6oH	8oH	8oH	8oH	3oH	3oH
13 open-seat Low-key	1oL	2oL	0oL	3oL	0oL	5oL	1oL	0oL	1oL
304 races									

Number of Newspaper Stories Mentioning Senate Incumbents and Challengers in Six Hard-Fought and Six Low-key Races

Every page of each newspaper listed was examined (except the *New York Times*, where only the Index was consulted) from August 1 to but not including Election Day in November. Each article containing the candidate's name was counted, including editorials but excluding letters to the editor and paid advertisements.

In the following tables, the column headed October includes days in November prior to Election Day. *H* represents when the candidate's name appeared in a headline, and *NH*, when the candidate's name appeared in an article but not in a headline. In Hawaii, North Dakota, and Wisconsin, the Senate primary occurred during August or September. Data for the hard-fought race in North Dakota in 1974 and the low-key race in New Jersey in 1976 are presented in table 5.

Hard-fought Races

Newspaper	August–September		October		All 3 Months		
	H	NH	H	NH	H	NH	Total
South Dakota 1968							
Senator George McGovern							
Sioux Falls Argus Leader	27	42	31	48	58	90	148
Archie Gubbrud							
Sioux Falls Argus Leader	18	42	18	48	36	90	126
Incumbent's advantage	+9	0	+13	0	+22	0	+22
Wisconsin 1980							
Senator Gaylord Nelson							
Milwaukee Journal	11	25	29	37	40	62	102
Former Representative R. Kasten							
Milwaukee Journal	13	11	20	24	33	35	68
Incumbent's Advantage	−2	+14	+9	+14	+7	+27	+34
California 1982							
Governor Edmund G. Brown, Jr.							
Los Angeles Times	36	54	25	41	61	95	156
San Francisco Chronicle	34	54	49	39	79	92	176
San Diego Mayor Pete Wilson							
Los Angeles Times	41	34	30	36	71	70	141
San Francisco Chronicle	29	47	36	46	65	93	158

Hard-fought Races

Newspaper	August–September		October		All 3 Months		
	H	NH	H	NH	H	NH	Total
*Florida 1980**							
Paula Hawkins							
Miami Herald	15	22	28	18	43	40	83
Florida Times-Union	12	29	30	32	42	61	103
Bill Gunter							
Miami Herald	24	27	29	26	53	53	106
Florida Times-Union	24	29	33	37	57	66	132
Indiana 1980							
Senator Birch Bayh							
Indianapolis News	19	35	31	61	50	96	146
Lafayette Journal and Courier	31	22	28	36	59	58	117
Representative Dan Quayle							
Indianapolis News	17	34	28	57	45	91	136
Lafayette Journal and Courier	18	22	18	39	36	61	97
Incumbent's Advantage							
Indianapolis News	+2	+1	+3	+4	+5	+5	+10
Lafayette Journal and Courier	+13	0	+10	−3	+23	−3	+20

* The 1980 Florida primary was September 9; both parties had run-offs on October 7.

Low-key Races

Newspaper	August–September		October		All 3 Months		
	H	NH	H	NH	H	NH	Total
California 1974							
Senator Alan Cranston							
Los Angeles Times	7	12	25	11	32	23	55
San Francisco Chronicle	4	11	5	12	9	23	32
H. L. Richardson							
Los Angeles Times	9	4	11	11	20	15	35
San Francisco Chronicle	2	6	2	16	4	22	26
Incumbent's Advantage							
Los Angeles Times	−2	+8	+14	0	+12	+8	+20
San Francisco Chronicle	−2	+5	+3	−4	+5	+1	+6

Low-key Races

Newspaper	August–September		October		All 3 Months		
	H	NH	H	NH	H	NH	Total
Wisconsin 1974							
Senator Gaylord Nelson							
Milwaukee Journal	4	11	6	16	10	27	37
State Senator Thomas Petri							
Milwaukee Journal	8	10	4	14	12	24	36
Incumbent's Advantage	−4	+1	+2	+2	−2	+3	+1
North Dakota 1976							
Senator Quentin Burdick							
Grand Forks Herald	3	16	12	23	15	39	54
Fargo Forum	4	13	10	21	14	34	48
Robert Stroup							
Grand Forks Herald	7	10	8	17	15	27	42
Fargo Forum	17	9	10	10	27	19	46
Incumbent's Advantage							
Grand Forks Herald	−4	+6	+4	+6	0	+12	+12
Fargo Forum	−13	+4	0	+11	−13	+15	+2
Hawaii 1980							
Senator Daniel Inouye							
Honolulu Star-Bulletin	6	22	5	15	11	37	48
E. Cooper Brown							
Honolulu Star-Bulletin	3	13	1	9	4	22	26
Incumbent's Advantage	+3	+9	+4	+6	+7	+15	+22
Texas 1982							
Senator Lloyd Bentsen							
Dallas Morning News	12	19	11	17	23	36	59
Representative Jim Collins							
Dallas Morning News	11	22	8	19	19	41	60
Incumbent's Advantage	+1	−3	+3	−2	+4	−5	−1

State-level Data Sources and Sample Sizes

Alabama: 1968
Comparative States Election Project (CSEP), post-election survey conducted by the Institute for Research in Social Science and the Louis Harris Political Data Center, University of North Carolina, Chapel Hill. *Source:* State Data Program, University of California, Berkeley. $N = 756$.

California: 1968, 1970, 1974, 1976, 1980, 1982
California Poll, conducted by the Field Institute, San Francisco. *Source:* State Data Program, University of California, Berkeley.
1968: Survey 6806, October 1968. $N = 1,139$.
1970: Survey 7007, October 1970. $N = 1,123$.
1974: Survey 7407, October 1974. $N = 1,077$.
1976: Survey 7606, September 1976. $N = 1,044$.
Survey 7608, October 1976. $N = 1,245$.
1980: Survey 8006, October 1980. $N = 1,018$.
1982: Survey 8206, early October 1982. $N = 1,218$.
Survey 8207, late October 1982. $N = 1,976$.

Colorado: 1974, 1980
Denver Post poll, conducted by Research Services, Denver.
1974: poll conducted 25–30 October 1974. *Source: Denver Post,* 3 November 1974, 1. $N = 1,056$ (likely voters only).
1980: poll conducted 22–29 October 1980. *Source: Denver Post,* 2 November 1980, 20. $N = 1,019$ (registered voters).

Florida: 1968, 1980
1968: CSEP (see Alabama above). $N = 602$.
1980: poll conducted for candidate Bill Gunter, October 1980. *Source:* William R. Hamilton & Staff, Washington, D.C. $N = 2,107$.

Georgia: 1980
Market Opinion Research Poll, 16–18 October 1980. *Source: Florida Times-Union,* 26 October 1980, B-1. $N = 800$ (likely voters only).

Illinois: 1968, 1984
1968: CSEP (see Alabama above). $N = 471$.
1984: *Chicago Sun-Times* poll, 22–25 October 1984. *Source: Chicago Sun-Times,* 30 October 1984, 4. $N = 1,014$ (registered voters).

Indiana: 1980
Poll conducted for candidate Birch Bayh, October 1980. *Source:* William R. Hamilton & Staff, Washington, D.C. $N = 1,191$ (likely voters).

Iowa: 1968, 1972, 1984
1968: Iowa Poll, 29 October 1968. *Source:* The Roper Center, University of Connecticut, Storrs. $N = 600$ (likely voters).
1972: Iowa Poll, 28–30 October 1972. *Source:* The Roper Center, University of Connecticut. $N = 599$ (likely voters).
1984: Iowa Poll, 30 October–2 November 1984. *Source: Des Moines Register,* 4 November 1984, 1. $N = 804$ (likely voters).

Maryland: 1976
Sun Poll, conducted by Hollander Cohen Associates, Baltimore, 23–25 October 1976. *Source: Baltimore Sun,* 31 October 1976, 1. $N = 1,000$ (likely voters).

Massachusetts: 1978, 1984
1978: Massachusetts Survey 3, October 1978. *Source:* Public Affairs Research Center, Clark University, Worcester. $N = 1,004$.
1984: Boston Herald Poll, 8 October 1984. *Source: Boston Herald,* 12 October 1984, 6. $N = 400$ (registered voters).

Michigan: 1978
Market Opinion Research Michigan Poll 3, 27 September 1978. *Source:* William Bradshaw, Department of Communications, University of Michigan, Ann Arbor. $N = 714$.

Mississippi: 1982
Social Science Research Center poll, Mississippi State University, 7–18 September 1982. *Source: Jackson Clarion-Ledger/Daily News,* 26 September 1982, 1-A. $N = 613$.

Missouri: 1980, 1982
1980: Selection Research poll, 10–12 October 1980. *Source: St. Louis Post-Dispatch,* 21 October 1980, 1. $N = 400$ (registered voters).
1982: Market Shares Corporation poll, 25–26 September 1982. *Source: St. Louis Globe-Democrat,* 30 September 1982, 1-A. $N = 451$ (likely voters).

Nebraska: 1982
Selection Research poll, October 1982. *Source: Omaha World Herald,* 31 October 1982, 1. $N = 872$ (likely voters).

New Jersey: 1976, 1978
Eagleton Poll, conducted by Eagleton Institute of Politics, Rutgers University, New Brunswick.
1976: New Jersey Poll 23, October 1976. $N = 800$.
1978: New Jersey Poll 34, October 1978. $N = 1,205$.

New Mexico: 1976, 1978
Zia General Election Surveys. *Source:* Zia Research Associates, Albuquerque.
1976: General Election Survey 3, October 1976. $N = 975$.
1978: General Election Survey 3, October 1978. $N = 809$.

New York: 1976
CBS News/*New York Times* Presidential Election Day Survey. *Source:* Inter-University Consortium for Political and Social Research, Ann Arbor, Michigan. $N = 1,038$ (registered voters).

North Dakota: 1974, 1976, 1980
North Dakota Citizens Advisory Surveys. *Source:* Bureau of Governmental Affairs, University of North Dakota, Grand Forks.
1974: Citizens Advisory Survey 1, September 1974. $N = 1,057$.
Citizens Advisory Survey 3, November 1974. $N = 690$.
1976: Citizens Advisory Survey 2, October 1976. $N = 510$.
1980: North Dakota State Survey, October 1980. $N = 836$.

Ohio: 1968
CSEP (see Alabama above). $N = 476$.

Pennsylvania: 1968
CSEP (see Alabama above). $N = 480$.

South Dakota: 1968
CSEP (see Alabama above). $N = 485$.

Tennessee: 1982
Paul Keckley poll, conducted "late September." *Source: The Political Report*, Washington, D.C., 8 October 1982. Sample size not available.

Texas: 1972
Belden Associates Texas Poll, September 1972. *Source:* The Roper Center, University of Connecticut, Storrs. $N = 1,038$.

Utah: 1982
Bardsley and Haslacker poll, 20–26 September 1982. *Source: Salt Lake City Tribune*, 3 October 1982, 1. $N = 811$ (likely voters).

West Virginia: 1982, 1984
West Virginia Poll, Charles Ryan Associates, Charleston.
1982: poll conducted 10–14 October 1982. *Source: Charleston Daily Mail*, 18 October 1982, 1. $N = 1,695$ (registered voters).
1984: poll conducted 24–25 October 1984. *Source: Charleston Daily Mail*, 29 October 1984, 1. $N = 501$ (likely voters).

Wisconsin: 1964
Statewide Survey 5, Project 175. *Source:* Survey Research Laboratory, University of Wisconsin, Madison. $N = 702$.

Wyoming: 1972, 1976, 1978
Statewide Wyoming Election Surveys. *Source:* Center for Government Research, University of Wyoming, Laramie.
1972: poll conducted October 1972. $N = 868$.
1976: poll conducted October 1976. $N = 978$.
1978: poll conducted October 1978. $N = 1,033$.

Awareness of Candidates:
Questionnaire Wordings and Coding Schemes

Alabama: October 1984
Source: Birmingham News/Capstone Poll, conducted 14–18 October 1984, published in *Birmingham News* 22 October 1984, 1.

The table from which the awareness percentages were taken was entitled "How voters felt . . . about Heflin . . . about Smith." For each candidate, the response categories were "Very Positive," "Positive," "Neutral," "Negative," "Very Negative," and "Don't Know/Didn't Answer."

Respondents answering "Don't Know/Didn't Answer" were coded as "not aware"; all other respondents were coded as "aware."

California: October 1968
Source: see appendix 3.

"Would you look at this list of items for a moment. They are descriptions that might apply to any of the candidates for Senator. First, let's take the Republican candidate, Max Rafferty. Which items do you think best apply to Rafferty—you can just tell me the numbers of them. Pick as many or as few as you think apply to Rafferty." (The question was repeated for Democratic candidate Alan Cranston.) For both candidates, respondents were presented with a card listing 18 descriptive phrases.

Respondents choosing any of the 18 responses were coded as "aware"; those unable to choose from the 18 attributes (and coded "Don't know" by the interviewer) were coded as "not aware."

California: September 1976
Source: see appendix 3.

"I'd like you to give me your impressions of some of the candidates who are running in the November election. This card shows a list of words and phrases that can describe different personality traits. I'd like you to rate [John Tunney/ S. I. Hayakawa] on each of these traits. For each phrase I'd like you to circle one number from one to ten which tells how much of that trait you think the candidate has. A "1" would be the lowest amount possible and a "10" would be the highest amount possible. Use your intuition . . . there are no right or wrong answers. Your feelings are what we are interested in." (Twenty traits were listed, some positive and some negative.)

Respondents responding "Don't know" to at least 10 of the 20 items were coded "not aware"; respondents who rated the candidates on 10 or more traits were coded "aware."

California: October 1980
Source: see appendix 3.

"I am going to read you the names of several people and I am going to ask you if you recognize his name or not. First, have you heard or read anything about Alan Cranston? Have you heard or read anything about Paul Gann?"

A response of "Yes" was coded as "aware"; a response of "No" or "Not sure" was coded as "not aware."

215

Florida: October 1980

Source: see appendix 3.

"Now I'd like to ask you your impression of some people in public life. As I read each one, just tell me whether you have a favorable impression of that person, a somewhat favorable impression, a somewhat unfavorable impression, or a very unfavorable impression. If you don't recognize them, just say so." (The order of the names was "alternately reversed.")

Respondents who said they did not recognize a candidate's name were coded as "not aware"; all other respondents were coded as "aware."

Indiana: October 1980

Source: see appendix 3.

Same as Florida: October 1980.

Maryland: October 1982

Source: *Sun* Poll, conducted by Hollander Cohen Associates, Baltimore, published in *Baltimore Sun*, 10 October 1982.

The table from which the awareness percentages were taken was entitled "Recognition Factor." For each candidate, the response categories were "Know a good deal about," "Know some," "Know a little," "Know almost nothing," and "Undecided."

Respondents answering "Know almost nothing" or "Undecided" were coded as "unaware"; all other respondents were coded as "aware."

Massachusetts: October 1978

Source: Becker Poll, conducted 20–21 October 1978, published in *Boston Herald American*, 26 October 1978, 1.

The table from which the awareness percentages were taken was entitled "Senatorial Candidate Popularity." For each candidate the response categories were "Favorable," "Unfavorable," and "Never heard of/No opinion."

Respondents answering "Favorable" or "Unfavorable" were coded as "aware"; those in the "Never heard of/No opinion" category were coded as "not aware."

Minnesota: September 1982

Source: Minnesota Poll, conducted 16–17 September 1982, published in Minneapolis Star and Tribune, 3 October 1982, 4-A.

For each candidate, the response categories were "Favorable," "Unfavorable," "No impression," and "unaware." Respondents responding "Unaware" were coded as "not aware"; all others were coded as "aware."

New Jersey: October 1976

Source: see Appendix 3.

"There is a U.S. Senate election in New Jersey this fall. Do you know who the Democratic candidate is? Do you know who the Republican candidate is?"

The correct answer was coded as "aware"; an incorrect answer or a response of "Don't know" was coded as "not aware."

New Jersey: October 1978

Source: see appendix 3.

"Can you recall the name of the Democratic candidate for Senate in New Jersey? Who is it? What about the Republican candidate for Senate? Do you know his name? Who is it?" If a candidate was not recalled, the respondent was asked, "Have you heard anything about [Jeff Bell/Bill Bradley]?"

Respondents who could recall or recognize a candidate were coded as "aware"; respondents who answered "No" or "Don't know" to both the recall and recognition items were coded "not aware."

New Jersey: October 1984

Source: Eagleton Poll, conducted 8–10 October 1984, published in *New York Times*, 15 October 1984, B-4, and 18 October 1984, B-6. $N = 600$ (likely voters).

The figures in Table 5-6 refer to the percentage of likely voters who had heard of the candidate.

North Dakota: September 1974

Source: see appendix 3.

"By using a check (X) mark, rate the performance of the following government officials and former officials in their jobs . . . Senator Milton Young . . . Governor William Guy. . . ." For each candidate the response categories were "Excellent," "Good," "Poor," and "Don't know."

Respondents answering "Don't know" were coded as "not aware"; all other responses were coded as "aware."

Wyoming: October 1972

Source: see appendix 3.

"I would now like to ask you a few questions about the two United States Senatorial candidates, Mr. Hansen and Mr. Vinich. Is there anything you like about Mr. Hansen? Is there anything you like about Mr. Vinich? Is there anything you dislike about Mr. Hansen? Is there anything you dislike about Mr. Vinich?

Respondents answering "No" or "Don't know" to both questions about a candidate were scored "unaware"; those responding affirmatively to either question were scored "aware."

Wyoming: October 1976

Source: see appendix 3.

"Using the terms included in the following scales, we want you to describe Gale McGee and Malcolm Wallop, candidates for the U.S. Senate. Just place an "X" in the position which best describes your own feelings about the candidates." Respondents were shown a card with six paired antonyms (e.g., honest-dishonest) and asked to rate candidates between 1 and 7.

Respondents who gave the "no opinion" response ("4" on each scale) for all six attributes were coded as "not aware"; respondents who gave at least one valid positive or negative response were coded as "aware."

Wyoming: October 1978

Source: see appendix 3.

Same as Wyoming: October 1976, substituting names of candidates Alan Simpson and Raymond Whitaker.

Construction of the Ideology Index in Chapter 6

The ideology measure in chapter 6 was created by combining ideology indices from the 1972, 1974, and 1976 CPS/NES surveys. The survey items that make up the three indices, including the variable numbers from the corresponding NES codebooks, are summarized below. For each of the three indices, respondents were divided into five equal-sized categories, from most liberal to most conservative. Each of these quintiles was then pooled with the corresponding quintile from the other two surveys, forming the five groupings found in the ideology measure in chapter 6.

The 1972 Index

The 1972 ideology index contains 11 areas of focus, of which 6 were measured with a single item and 5 were measured by combining two or more items on the same subject. Respondents were assigned a single score for each of the 11 topic areas; these 11 scores were then weighted equally in an additive index. Respondents who failed to answer or had no opinion on more than 5 of the 11 topics were omitted from the 1972 index.

1. Women's rights (7-item scale)
V239: Companies should first lay off women whose husbands have jobs. vs. Companies should treat male and female employees the same.
V240: Men are born with more drive to be ambitious and successful than women. (agree/disagree)
V242: Women are usually less reliable on the job than men because they tend to be absent more and quit more often. (agree/disagree)
V244: By nature women are happiest making a home and caring for children. (agree/disagree)
V246: Men are more qualified than women for highly responsible jobs. (agree/disagree)
V248: Women have just as much chance to get important jobs as men; they just aren't interested. (agree/disagree)
V251: Women should stay out of politics. (agree/disagree)

2. Protest (3-item scale)
V275: Approve/disapprove of taking part in protest meetings or marches permitted by the local authorities.
V276: Approve/disapprove of a person going to jail rather than obeying a law he doesn't believe is just.
V277: Approve/disapprove of a person who tries to stop government from its usual activities with sit-ins, mass meetings and demonstrations, all other methods having failed.

3. Racial issues (6-item scale)
V104: The federal government should assure blacks fair treatment in jobs. vs. These matters should be left up to the states and communities.
V106: The federal government should see that black and white children attend the same schools. vs. The government should stay out of this area.

V110: The government should support the right of blacks to go to any hotel or restaurant. vs. The government should stay out of this area.

V112: Civil rights leaders are trying to push too fast. vs. Civil rights leaders are not pushing fast enough.

V115: Whites have a right to keep blacks out of their neighborhoods. vs. Blacks have a right to live anywhere they can afford.

V118: Are you in favor of desegregation, strict segregation, or something in between?

4. Vietnam policy (2-item scale)

V50: Did the U.S. do the right thing in getting into the fighting in Vietnam? (yes/no)

V1069: What should the U.S. do now, ranging from immediate withdrawal to achieve complete military victory?

5. Social welfare benefits (2-item scale)

V696: All but the old and handicapped should have to take care of themselves without social welfare benefits. (agree/disagree)

V941: Same item, asked later in the survey.

6. V196: Where do you stand between making marijuana legal and setting higher penalties?

7. V202: Where do you stand between busing to achieve racial integration and keeping children in neighborhood schools?

8. V621: Where do you stand between protecting the rights of the accused and stopping crime regardless of the rights of the accused?

9. V629: Where do you stand between the government helping minority groups and minority groups being responsible for helping themselves?

10. V1067: Where do you stand between the government having to assure everyone a job and good standard of living and each person being responsible for getting ahead on his own?

11. V1068: Where do you stand between having the tax rate even higher for those with higher incomes and everyone having the same tax rate?

The 1974 Index

The 1974 ideology index comprises 10 areas of focus, 2 of which were measured by combining more than one item on the same topic. Respondents were given a single score for each of the 10 areas; these 10 scores were then weighted equally in an additive index. Respondents who failed to answer or had no opinion on more than 4 of the 10 areas were omitted from the 1974 index.

1. Protest (3-item scale)

V2238: Identical to V275 in 1972 index.

V2239: Identical to V276 in 1972 index.

V2240: Identical to V277 in 1972 index.

2. Women's rights (2-item scale)

V2302: Women and men should have an equal role in running business and government. vs. A woman's place is in the home.

V2370: How warmly do you feel about the women's liberation movement?

3. V2264: Civil rights leaders are trying to push too fast. vs. Civil rights leaders are not pushing fast enough.

4. V2265: Where do you stand between the government having to assure everyone a job and good standard of living and each person being responsible for getting ahead on his own?

5. V2273: Regarding urban unrest, where do you stand between using all available force to maintain law and order and correcting the problems of poverty and unemployment that give rise to the disturbances?

6. V2281: Where do you stand between protecting the rights of the accused and stopping crime regardless of the rights of the accused?

7. V2288: Where do you stand between busing to achieve racial integration and keeping children in neighborhood schools?

8. V2296: Where do you stand between the government helping minority groups and minority groups being responsible for helping themselves?

9. How warmly do you feel about "big business?"

10. How warmly do you feel about "radical students?"

The 1976 Index

The 1976 ideology index comprises 15 topics of focus, 3 of which were measured by combining more than one item on the same subject. Respondents were given a single score for each of the 15 topics, and these scores were then weighted equally in an additive index. Respondents who failed to answer or had no opinion on more than 7 of the 15 topics were omitted from the 1976 index.

1. Women's rights (5-item scale)
   V3787: Where do you stand between women and men having an equal role in running business and government and women remaining in the home?
   V3798: Companies should first lay off women whose husbands have jobs. vs. Companies should treat male and female employees the same.
   V3808: It's more natural for men to have the top responsible jobs in a country. vs. Sex discrimination keeps women from the top jobs.
   V3813: Men have more of the top jobs: because they are born with more drive to be ambitious and successful. vs. Our society discriminates against women.
   V3839: How warmly do you feel about the women's liberation movement?

2. Racial attitudes (5-item scale)
V3205: Do you favor or oppose busing to integrate the schools?
V3213: Civil rights leaders are trying to push too fast. vs. Civil rights leaders are not pushing fast enough.
V3214: Whites have a right to keep blacks out of their neighborhoods. vs. Blacks have a right to live wherever they can afford to.
V3217: Are you in favor of desegregation, strict segregation, or something in between?
V3257: Where do you stand between busing to achieve integration and keeping children in neighborhood schools?

3. Government role in assuring jobs (2-item scale)
V3241: Where do you stand between the government having to assure everyone

a job and good standard of living and each person being responsible for getting ahead on his own?
V3758: Same item later in survey.

4. V3248: Where do you stand between protecting the rights of the accused and stopping crime regardless of the rights of the accused?

5. V3264: Where do you stand between the government helping minority groups and minority groups being responsible for helping themselves?

6. V3273: Where do you stand between government providing an insurance plan to cover all health expenses and these expenses being covered by individuals and private insurance programs?

7. V3353: The government should spend less even if it means cutting back on programs like health and education. (agree/disagree)

8. V3357: Military spending: should be cut. vs. Should continue at least at the present level.

9. V3565: The government should have the power to wiretap phones for national security reasons. (agree/disagree)

10. V3767: Regarding urban unrest, where do you stand between using all available force to maintain law and order and correcting the problems of poverty and unemployment that give rise to the disturbances?

11. V3772: Where do you stand between legalizing marijuana vs. increasing penalties for using marijuana?

12. V3779: Where do you stand between having the tax rate even higher for those with higher incomes and everyone having the same tax rate?

13. V3821: How warmly do you feel toward "big business?"

14. V3827: How warmly do you feel toward "radical students?"

15. V3909: A person who tries to stop government from its usual activities with sit-ins, mass meetings and demonstrations, all other methods having failed. (approve/disapprove)

Text of Items Used in Creating Indices in Table 25 and Descriptions of Independent Variables in Table 27

TABLE 25.

The additive index in table 25, "California Voter Attitudes toward Reaganomics," was created from the following four items in *Los Angeles Times* Poll 61, 10–14 October 1982.

V 26: There are a number of factors which shape our state's economy, and certainly the President plays an important role in that process. What effect do you think President Reagan's policies are having on the economy? Are Reagan's policies making the California economy very much better than it would have been, or somewhat better, or somewhat worse, or are President Reagan's policies making the California economy very much worse than it would have been without his policies?
   1. Very much better   4. Somewhat worse   6. Not sure about effect
   2. Somewhat better   5. Very much worse   7. Refused
   3. Same

V 27: And what effect do you think these policies are having on your own or your family's financial situation? Are Reagan's policies making your personal financial situation very much better than it would have been, or somewhat better, or somewhat worse, or are President Reagan's policies making your personal financial situation very much worse than it would have been without his policies?
   1. Very much better   4. Somewhat worse   6. Not sure about effect
   2. Somewhat better   5. Very much worse   7. Refused
   3. Same

V 53: Generally speaking, would you say you are a supporter or a critic of President Reagan's economic ideas? (IF SUPPORTER) Are you a supporter because you think his ideas are right, or because nobody else seems to *have* any ideas? (IF CRITIC) Are you a critic because his ideas are wrong, or because his ideas aren't working?
   1. Supporter because ideas are right
   2. Supporter because nobody else has ideas
   3. Critic because ideas are wrong
   4. Critic because ideas aren't working
   5. Neither supporter nor critic (volunteered)
   6. Not sure which
   7. Refused

V 61: Considering the nation's economy as a whole, do you think President Reagan is going in the right direction today . . . or do you think he has gotten off on the wrong track . . . or do you think he's somewhere in between?
   1. Right direction   3. Wrong track   5. Refused
   2. In between   4. Not sure which

TABLE 27.

The independent variables in California Poll 8207 were measured as follows:

Party:
    0. Registered Republican
    1. Decline to state
    2. Registered Democratic

Ideology:
    0. Conservative
    1. Leans conservative
    2. Middle-of-the-road
    3. Leans liberal
    4. Liberal

Nuclear freeze:
    0. Will vote NO on Proposition 12, the freeze initiative
    0.5. Still undecided
    1. Will vote YES on freeze initiative

Social Security:
    0. Favors four changes in current system (see table 26)
    0.25: Favors three changes
    0.5. Favors two changes
    0.75. Favors one change
    1. Keep as is (favors none of the four changes)

Age:
    Variable is actual age

Income:
    1. Less than $7,000
    2. 0 to $10,000
    3. $7,000–10,000
    4. $10,000–15,000
    5. $10,000–20,000
    6. $15,000–20,000
    7. $20,000–25,000
    8. $20,000–30,000
    9. $25,000–30,000
    10. $30,000–40,000
    11. Over $30,000
    12. Over $40,000

Gun control (Proposition 15); textbooks (Proposition 10); beverage containers (Proposition 11); redistricting (Proposition 14); water (Proposition 13):
    0. Will vote NO on this Proposition
    0.5. Still undecided
    1. Will vote YES on this Proposition

TABLE 27. (*continued*)

The independent variables in *Los Angeles Times* Poll 61 were measured as follows:

Party:
0. Strong Republican
1. Weak Republican
2. Independent Republican
3. Independent
4. Independent Democrat
5. Weak Democrat
6. Strong Democrat

Ideology:
0. Very conservative
1. Somewhat conservative
2. Middle-of-the-road
3. Somewhat liberal
4. Very liberal

Nuclear freeze:
0. Will vote NO on Proposition 12
0.25. Lean toward voting NO
0.5. Still undecided
0.75. Lean toward voting YES
1. Will vote YES on Proposition 12

Reaganomics: The 4-item additive index (see above for item wordings) ranges from 0 (completely pro-Reaganomics) to 1 (completely anti-Reaganomics)

Age: Variable is actual age

Income: 0. Less than $10,000
1. $10,000—30,000
2. Over $30,000

Gun control (Proposition 15), beverage containers (Proposition 11), water (Proposition 13):
0. Will vote NO on proposition
0.25. Lean toward voting NO
0.5. Still undecided
0.75. Lean toward voting YES
1. Will vote YES on proposition

Notes

1. Patterns and Anomalies in Senate Elections

1. See also Miller and Stokes 1963.

2. Among the published studies finding an influence of one or more of these candidate activities on reelection advantage are Fiorina 1977, 1982; Parker and Davidson 1979; Cover 1980; Parker 1980a, 1980b, 1981; Alford and Hibbing 1981; Jacobson 1981b; Yiannakis 1981; Cover and Brumberg 1982; Cain, Ferejohn, and Fiorina 1984; and Parker and Parker 1985. Johannes and McAdams 1981; and McAdams and Johannes 1983, 1984, and 1985 offer a dissenting view, arguing that casework, trips home, and mailings have a minimal effect on House elections.

3. An increase during the 1960s and 1970s in defections toward incumbent House candidates by voters identifying with the out-party was documented in Arseneau and Wolfinger 1973; Cover 1977; Ferejohn 1977; and Nelson 1978–79. See also Fiorina 1977; Mann 1978; Alford and Hibbing 1981; Cover and Mayhew 1981; and Campbell 1983.

4. Abramowitz (1980), Mann and Wolfinger (1980), Hinckley (1980b, 1981), Jacobson (1981b, 1983, 1985), and Kazee (1983) have called attention to challenger quality and capability as important to understanding voting in House elections.

5. Three studies in the early 1970s documented the advantages of incumbency in Senate elections: Hinckley 1970; Kostroski 1973; and Cowart 1973.

6. These points have been made by a number of scholars; see, e.g., Mann and Wolfinger 1980, 618, on the 1978 election.

7. In the period 1960–84, 92 percent of House incumbents and 85 percent of Senate incumbents have sought reelection.

8. A small number of studies have concerned themselves with how senators' incumbency advantage has compared with House incumbents' advantage *over time*. While there is general agreement that the advantages of incumbency for congressmen have increased over the years, there is, as Alford and Hibbing

(1983) pointed out, a "disconcerting . . . diversity of findings" with respect to Senate incumbents. Alford and Hibbing, as well as Cooper and West (1981), argued that the incumbency advantage of senators has declined since the 1960s. Cover and Mayhew (1981) and Tufte (1973) claimed that the incumbency advantage, while consistently smaller than that enjoyed by congressmen, has neither increased nor declined since the 1950s. And Kostroski (1973) found the incumbency advantage to be increasing, although Alford and Hibbing have suggested that Kostroski's findings were almost entirely a function of the earlier period (1948–70) he examined.

9. Hibbing and Alford (1982, 506), among others, also have asserted that senators have greater individual visibility than do congressmen. And Foote and Weber (1984) found that in 1981 and 1982 senators were much more visible than congressmen on network television news (see also Robinson and Appel 1979), but they also found that the average coverage of any member of Congress was "quite low" (3). However, as I show in chapter 5, survey research has revealed that both senators and congressmen are widely recognized in their own district.

10. Others who have related higher visibility of senators to disadvantages associated with greater accountability include Michael Barone and former Maine Senator William Hatheway (quoted in *Congressional Quarterly Weekly Report*, 1980, 906) and Jacob (1985, 115). Note, however, that such notice could just as well work in their favor. Tuckel (1983, 286) argued that "television committee hearings, talk shows, and interviews have placed many senators . . . in the limelight, thus providing them with free publicity" and boosting their chances of reelection.

11. See also Jacobson 1983, 72–74, on this point.

12. See, e.g., Jewell and Patterson 1977, 91; Abramowitz 1980, 633; Dodd 1981, 407; and Hibbing and Brandes 1983, 810–13.

13. Moreover, gerrymandering, which often deliberately increases or optimizes an incumbent's advantage in terms of party affiliation of the voters, is irrelevant to a senator's constituency.

14. It is possible, but unlikely, that these outcomes are due to different voters' alternately voting and staying home. Evidence from studies of turnout indicates that Americans do not vote in such a pattern.

15. The one area where the data in table 1 are consistent with a realignment explanation is the South. In the 1950s all twenty-two southern Senate seats were Democratic. As table 1 shows, the number of split states rose from four in 1968 to a high of eight after the 1980 election. After the 1982 elections there were two states, North Carolina and Virginia, in which both senators were Republican. However, changes have not been exclusively in one direction. Tennessee's Senate seats, both held by Republicans in the early 1970s, were back in the hands of Democrats by 1985.

16. Using an index of population diversity, Bullock and Brady (1983, 31) found that between 1947 and 1978 the most heterogeneous states were much more likely to have split-party Senate representation than the most homogeneous states.

17. See Fiorina 1978, 440; Jacobson 1983, 1985; Hinckley 1980b, 1981; Goldenberg and Traugott 1984; and Eismeier and Pollock 1986.

18. Others who have made claims based on this assumption include Hinck-

ley (1980a, 1980b, 1981), Ragsdale (1981), Luttbeg (1983), and Davidson and Oleszek (1984, 637). Voters' knowledge of Senate candidates and resultant voting decisions will be discussed in detail in chapter 5.

19. Of course the importance of the concept of campaign intensity, and of the nature of the information flow in a campaign, is by no means limited to Senate elections. The dynamic examined in this study could apply equally well to House, presidential, or any other type of election, but the lack of variation in the independent variable—campaign intensity—precludes such study in these types of elections. Senate elections, because they vary so widely in campaign intensity, therefore provide the best opportunity to study the effects of campaign intensity on the vote.

20. Although other avenues of dissemination, such as personal contact, speeches, mailings, and via campaign workers, labor leaders, and friends, also enter the picture, they are of minor importance compared with mass media exposure, a point stressed by both Fenno (1982) and Hershey (1984, 168–69).

2. Hard-fought and Low-key Senate Races

1. These claims will be addressed in detail in chapter 5.

2. Fenno (1982, 11, 13), for example, wrote: "Senate campaigns seem to be more dependent on the media than House campaigns. Senate campaigners recognize their greater potential for attracting free media, and, to varying degrees, depend on them. . . . Senate candidates . . . worry constantly about finding media outlets through which they can present themselves to the people indirectly. For House candidates, the people they meet are real people, real voters. For Senate candidates, the people they meet are extras who play walk-on roles in media production."

3. Whether voters *receive* the information is a separate consideration. In theory, an enormous amount of information could be imparted but never received, either because nobody attended to the news or because those who did forgot what they heard or read. Voters' attention to news about elections and their recognition of candidates and campaign issues will be discussed in later chapters.

4. Mansfield (1976, 62) made the same observation about several candidates vying for the Democratic Senate nomination in Florida in 1974: although they worked hard, those candidates who traveled around the state by car found it impossible to compete successfully with those who were able to travel the great distances between the state's urban centers by plane.

5. Although this study is largely concerned with the information available to voters and the subsequent choices they make (i.e., whether to defect from party affiliation), I will look in later chapters at the effect of the intensity of Senate campaigns on election margins of victory, controlling for the distribution of party identification in a given state. Using margin of victory as a measure of intensity would come close to defining an independent variable in terms of a dependent variable.

6. Sorauf (1988, 152) makes the same point: party contributions are clearly a part of individual campaign efforts, but expenditure reporting for them is not well-documented.

7. Conclusions reached in subsequent chapters are based on data from the

period 1968–84, although in some instances generalizations about Senate elections are likely to hold for earlier periods as well.

8. See Jones 1982, 122, for a replication of Matthews's analysis for the Senate of 1977–79.

9. Independent and minor party candidates receiving less than 10 percent of the vote were omitted. Except when explicitly comparing races in which incumbents are running with open-seat races, the term "challengers" will be used to refer not only to incumbents' opponents but to candidates for open seats as well.

10. A closer look at this category shows that candidates whose tenure in office had ended many years before tended to be the ones who could not manage a hard-fought campaign. For example, it had been six years since Stephen McNichol had been governor of Colorado when he challenged incumbent Peter Dominick in 1968; it had been ten years since Wesley Powell had been governor of New Hampshire when he challenged Senator Thomas McIntyre in 1972; it had been thirty-eight years since Terry Carpenter had been a congressman when he challenged Nebraska Senator Carl Curtis in 1972. All three were involved in low-key campaigns. Presumably, name recognition had diminished statewide for these and other challengers whose public exposure had recently been negligible. Such was the case, Ornstein wrote (1985, 254), for Alaska Senator Ted Stevens's 1984 challenger, former attorney general John Havelock, "who had been out of public office for more than a decade and was neither well known nor aggressive."

11. Rohde (1979, 9–10) argued that representatives from smaller states are more likely to run for Senate than those from larger states, because their greater visibility to the statewide electorate gives them a better chance of winning. The data in table 4 offer modest confirmation of this proposition: House members from smaller states are slightly more likely than large-state congressmen to *win* Senate race challenges; however, they are notably more likely than large-state congressmen to achieve a *hard-fought* challenge.

12. Three candidates with only city or county experience—from St. Louis, Detroit, and Wilmington—managed hard-fought races. They may have been better known statewide than many of the state legislators because of local news coverage in areas containing a large proportion of the statewide electorate. Statewide data were not available to test this possibility.

3. Political Campaign Coverage and the Public's Sources of News

1. See, e.g., Leary 1977, 19–20; Sabato 1981, 194; and Ranney 1984, 90–91.

2. See, e.g., Rubin 1981, 152–60; and Polsby and Wildavsky 1984, 79–82.

3. Graber 1976b, 1984, 1985; Hofstetter 1978; and Robinson and Sheehan 1983 on the subject of network news programs. Stempel 1961, 1965, 1969; Graber 1971, 1976a, 1984; Hofstetter 1978; and Stempel and Windhauser 1984 on major daily newspaper coverage. For a synopsis of newspaper and television coverage studies discussing presidential elections from 1952 through 1984, see Westlye 1986, 68–71.

4. For more on the "automatic" coverage afforded presidential campaigns by the press, see Patterson and McClure 1976, 29–30; Arterton 1978, 51–52; Ostroff 1980; and Linsky 1983, 50, 56.

5. Carey (1976) compared House and Senate campaign coverage by three national newsmagazines and what he called three "national" newspapers—the *Los Angeles Times,* the *New York Times,* and the *Washington Post*—for the last four weeks of the 1974 election campaign. Since all three papers but none of the magazines covered state and local news in addition to national news, it is perhaps not surprising that the three newspapers contained over five times as many congressional campaign stories as did the newsmagazines (52).

6. Clarke and Fredin (1978, 150) examined newspapers and local news broadcasts in 67 media markets across the United States and reported that "topic emphasis by a few stations that have been analyzed correlates highly with the same-city newspaper coverage."

7. Bagdikian 1971, 139, 143–44; Epstein 1973. Gormley (1976) and Leary (1977, 58–59, 62) also found a clear tendency for television to rely on newspapers and noted an occasional dependence in the other direction as well.

8. Fenno (1982, 11), Davidson and Oleszek (1984, 637), and Hershey (1984, 166) refer to the role of "statewide media" or "statewide press" in campaigns, but without elucidation.

9. See Drew and Wilhoit 1976, 435; and Ryan and Owen 1976, 671. Winter (1982, 1) observed that "in recent years newspapers have increasingly shifted to local news as their mainstay."

10. Tunstall and Walker (1981) also concluded that California local television news does not extend coverage beyond the local community and that "newspaper coverage of [state] politics and government is stronger" but still "full of gaps" (138).

11. Comparing local news coverage in one daily metropolitan newspaper with that of two local television news stations in the same city, Sasser and Russell (1972) found that over a 10-day period, the newspaper carried 323 local news stories (168,646 total words), while the television stations carried 131 and 130 stories (25,030 and 20,980 words), respectively.

12. For a discussion of news executives' dilemma over ratings versus news importance, see Epstein 1973, 100–112; Powers 1977, 72–73; and Bicker 1978, 85–95.

13. Vermeer (1982, 78) found that only 10 editors out of a sample of 168 claimed never to use candidate press releases. In his study of one gubernatorial and two congressional campaigns, Vermeer found that in each instance, over 70 percent of the candidates' press releases were printed (in full or in part) by at least one newspaper in the state or district (89).

14. All pages of the *Dispatch* were inspected, and stories about the gubernatorial contest were divided into the following categories: stories directly concerning the campaign; stories primarily about other topics but mentioning the gubernatorial campaign; editorials; letters to the editor; the "Voting Machine Poll" (a nonscientific, intermittently published tally of the intended vote choice of people in various shopping centers), and stories involving either of the gubernatorial candidates in a non-campaign context. Ostroff did not include weekend news coverage in his report, possibly because there were no local weekend news programs. I did review the Saturday and Sunday newspapers during this period and have included weekend coverage in the figures presented below. It seems unrealistic to remove weekends from an analysis of this kind, since people who

read the paper during the week are just as likely, and perhaps even more likely on Sunday (according to the 1981 *Ayer Directory,* over 130,000 more households subscribe to the *Dispatch* on Sundays than on weekdays), to read it on the weekend. Removing the weekend data from the figures does not change the order of magnitude of the differences between newspaper and television coverage.

15. Leary (1977, 21) suggested that this notion of displacement might have pertained to television news coverage of the 1974 California gubernatorial campaign. Pointing to an "extraordinary sequence of sensational crimes that occurred in 1974 in California, such as Patricia Hearst's kidnapping and subsequent adventures with the Symbionese Liberation Army, and the unprovoked series of street killings in San Francisco that came to be known as the Zebra murders," Leary observed that "such sensational (and visual) events dominated public interest and, against such lurid fare, the political contestants seemed pallid. The news scales were weighted against the politicians."

16. Distinguishing between paid advertising and free news coverage, Ranney (1984, 90–91) stated that "both forms are vital to any well-run campaign in a large (national or statewide) constituency" but that free television is generally thought to be more desirable.

17. See Fenno 1982 for examples of candidates who see the impact of television news this way.

18. See Roper 1983. In addition, Stevenson and White (1980) found that respondents tend to overreport the amount of television news they watch and that this bias is reflected in responses to the Roper item. Carter and Greenberg (1965) also asserted, although with less evidence, that the Roper item is biased toward television overreporting.

19. For a list of these studies and their findings, see Westlye 1986, 101–2.

20. When presented with a list of state-level news items, 68 percent of respondents said that newspapers would be their primary source for learning of such news, while only 26 percent chose the local television or radio news. Other studies focusing on state-level news have not produced consensus. In some cases, newspapers were the primary source of people's information; in other cases it was television, and sometimes the two were rated equally. See also Stempel's (1973) study of three Ohio cities; Tipton, Haney, and Basehart's (1975) study of Kentucky residents; Ducey and Reagan's (1981) and Reagan and Ducey's (1983) analyses of two Michigan cities; and Latimer and Cotter's (1985) study of Alabama.

21. Quarles (1979), using different data from the 1972 election, came to the same conclusion: consumers of print media acquired accurate perceptions of the candidates' issue stances, whereas "network news-viewing has no effect" (427).

22. See Blumler and McQuail 1969; McLeod et al. 1977; and Lemert et al. 1983.

23. Data confirming this will be presented in chapter 5.

24. For example, races with three serious candidates, those with incumbents suffering from major scandal or frailty, and those in which celebrities from other walks of life were running were avoided as races for which the press might conceivably adopt coverage criteria different from the usual.

25. It was especially important as well to avoid choosing all of the hotly contested races from midterm years and all others from presidential years. This

would have left open the possibility that findings of light coverage in the latter races resulted from the need to allow reporters and newsspace to go to the more salient race at the top of the ticket, rather than from characteristics of the Senate campaign itself.

26. Whether to include letters to the editor when counting "stories" is a difficult decision. On the one hand, they contain information about the campaign and thus potentially contribute to reader awareness just as news stories do. On the other hand, the number of published letters in a given newspaper depends on formatting and space allotment policies and varies greatly from paper to paper, not necessarily according to the intensity of the Senate race. For example, between August 1 and Election Day, the *Los Angeles Times* and the *San Francisco Chronicle* ran only 6 and 10 letters, respectively, about the intense Senate race in 1982 between California Governor Jerry Brown and San Diego Mayor Pete Wilson. However, in South Dakota in 1968, the *Sioux Falls Argus Leader* ran 150 letters to the editor in October and November alone about the race between Senator George McGovern and former Governor Gubbrud. About two-thirds of these were very short, simply endorsing one of the candidates. Forty-nine others were in direct response to the paper's October 9 endorsement of Gubbrud, either praising or objecting to this decision. As late as 25 editions later, *Argus Leader* continued to run such letters. Presumably, other newspapers in South Dakota were not doing this to such an extent, and it therefore seems unreasonable to include these letters in our count.

27. For example, in presidential years, comments from incumbent senators attending the national party conventions are often reported. In 1980 the *Honolulu Star Bulletin* mentioned the name of Senator Inouye, who was spokesman for the Hawaii delegation, five times during coverage of the Democratic convention in August in a context unrelated to the race back home. Sometimes the stories are even unrelated to politics. For example, during the 1976 campaign in New Jersey, Senator Harrison Williams was the victim of a burglary; this was reported in several of the papers examined. The frequency of these kinds of news stories was typically very low and could not, therefore, afford incumbents a measurable advantage in public recognition beyond what they received from campaign coverage. Two ongoing stories of a seemingly non-campaign nature were in fact counted. One was George McGovern's presidential try in 1968. During August McGovern made a late move for the Democratic presidential nomination and received considerable local coverage for his effort. And in 1980 Senator Birch Bayh chaired the Senate committee that was looking into possible improprieties by the President's brother, Billy Carter, while he was a lobbyist. As spokesman for the committee, Bayh received national coverage almost daily during August, including a thinly veiled guest appearance in the "Doonesbury" comic strip. These stories were counted because the challengers in both races used the incumbents' actions in their campaign attacks, in both cases arguing that the incumbent was spending too little time in the state. Some papers also keep track of how state legislators, the local congressmen, and the state's two senators vote while Congress is in session. Typically, these votes are listed in a "box score" fashion once a week. Mentions of the incumbent (or the challenger, when he was a congressman or state legislator) were included in the non-campaign category.

28. When a candidate's name was not in a headline, it was usually because

his opponent's name was. There were only a few stories about the campaign in which neither candidate's name appeared in a headline. Some of these had other topics or candidates as the main focus and mentioned the Senate race only peripherally; more often they focused directly on the Senate campaign, with headlines such as "Senate campaign heats up."

29. Cohen (1963) found that the press often perceive stories as ongoing and have a tendency when determining the day's priorities to follow up on the previous day's story before looking for new stories. This leads, he argued, to stories published as follow-ups that would not have been published at all had they been new that day. This norm did not appear to dictate coverage of particular Senate events or episodes; for the most part, individual events or statements were not followed up by the press unless the candidates themselves reacted with charges or countercharges.

30. Nearly all studies of presidential media coverage have concluded that networks and newspapers give candidates (or their parties) very nearly equal amounts of coverage.

31. Shaw and Clemmer (in Shaw and McCombs 1977) reported that attentiveness to the news media on the part of the citizens of Charlotte, North Carolina, increased slightly over the course of the 1972 presidential campaign.

32. Hale (1985) quantified coverage in the categories of "contest" and "substantive" coverage for the 1984 Senate race and found that the two types were "equally provided in September." He noted, however, that most of the issue coverage was simply passive recounting of candidate statements, which "allows the candidates to emphasize what they want about issues." Hale claimed that the issues "grew old" as a result; because reporters failed to "delve into the issues in more detail," no new angles developed and the same old charges and countercharges by the candidates were reported less and less. Hale suggested this as a reason why the "contest" coverage increased to 60 percent of total coverage in October and to 63 percent during the final six days of the campaign (33).

33. Clarke and Evans (1983) looked at coverage from September 27 through Election Day in each of 82 districts with contested races. I calculated the frequencies presented here from data in different parts of the book. Clarke and Evans claimed on pp. 12–13 that their analysis was based on 731 articles from newspapers in 82 districts—71 where an incumbent faced a challenger, plus 11 openseat districts. However, on pp. 37–38 they stated that their analysis was based on 731 articles from newspapers covering just the 71 incumbent/challenger races. Using this second citation yields 10.3 articles per paper, 0.25 articles per day, and 1 article every 4.08 days.

4. A Closer Look at Four Senate Campaigns

1. All newspaper quotations in this section are from the *Milwaukee Journal*.

2. As part of his campaign for the 1974 Democratic gubernatorial primary in California, underdog Jerome Waldie, four-term congressman from the San Francisco Bay Area, walked the length of the state during August 1973. As Leary (1977, 17) described this tactic, Waldie "in an unassuming style ... could (and did) command attention from local newspapers, radio and television. He left in his wake a ripple of stories and pictures ... the publicity may not have been spectacular, but for the brief passage through town, Waldie was news."

3. See Mann and Wolfinger 1980 for a discussion of the difference between recall and recognition rates in the 1978 U.S. House elections.

4. As with the prior Wisconsin case study, all subsequent quotations about the 1980 Wisconsin race are from the *Milwaukee Journal*.

5. The role of these and other issues in the Brown-Wilson race is discussed in an analysis of issue voting in Senate elections in chapter 6.

6. It is even theoretically possible that a hard-fought race would not receive much press coverage: a candidate could flood the airwaves with ads designed to disseminate a high level of information statewide. However, as we saw in chapter 2, the relationship between campaign spending and the hard-fought/low-key intensity variable is quite strong. And in assessing whether the race is newsworthy, the press may well take into account information such as how much a challenger is spending.

7. In his study of press coverage of state government, Wolfson (1985, 141) concluded that "governors get blanket coverage." See also Dunn 1969, 26.

8. California Democratic gubernatorial candidate William Roth certainly felt that this was the case during the 1974 primary campaign: "I found [that the] media automatically discount the candidate who lacks the aura of officialdom" (in Leary 1977, 25).

9. See, e.g., the *Columbia Journalism Review*'s survey of journalists' views regarding the early coverage of the 1980 presidential election (19, no. 2 [1980]: 41–46).

10. Nor does it explain why, following the release of a *Milwaukee Journal* poll on October 27 showing that Nelson led Kasten by a margin of 53 percent to 33 percent, Kasten's name appeared in only 2 *Journal* headlines (out of 11 stories) in the last six days before the election.

11. For example, Jamieson and Campbell (1983, 18) list the essential qualities of a newsworthy event as "(1) personalized—it happened to real people; (2) dramatic, conflict-filled, controversial, violent; (3) actual and concrete, not theoretical or abstract; (4) novel or deviant; and (5) treats issues of ongoing concern to the news media." Paletz and Entman (1981, 32) state that "reporters and editors want news—defined as conflict, controversy, duplicity, scandal."

12. See, e.g., Leary 1977, 37–42; Kayden 1978, 126–27; Sabato 1981, 154; and Goldenberg and Traugott 1984, 113. In the Ohio gubernatorial race described by Ostroff, for example, he reports that the television news organizations in Columbus, Ohio, cited their intentional avoidance of obvious "media events" as one of the reasons for their light news coverage of the Rhodes-Celeste gubernatorial race in 1978 (1980, 418).

13. Rosenbloom noted that Bush's opponent, Lloyd Bentsen, won nevertheless, and he conjectured that the coverage from this Republican effort led to higher turnout than otherwise would have occurred—which benefited the Democrats: "Had fewer people voted, the Republicans might well have won in Texas" (1973, 40). However, had the race been low-key, without the concerted effort by the Republican Party, a more likely result would have been an even larger Bentsen margin, with many Republican identifiers defecting to the known candidate over the relatively unknown one. Data on this point are presented in chapter 5.

14. The transmission of information via paid political advertisements remains to be studied systematically for Senate elections.

5. The Effect of Campaign Intensity on the Vote Decision

1. The ambiguity of this item's referent is not the only problem here. There are fundamental problems as well with using the 1978, and indeed any, national election survey to analyze the electorate's attitudes and behavior with respect to Senate elections. The important thing to note in the data presented here with respect to respondents' media contact with Senate candidates is the *differences* between hard-fought and low-key races, and not the absolute levels of contact.

2. Abramowitz 1980; Hinckley 1980a, 1980b, 1981; Mann and Wolfinger 1980.

3. For a discussion of problems with pre-1978 surveys, see Mann 1978, chap. 3; and for a discussion of biases in the 1978 CPS/NES survey concerning House elections, see Jacobson 1981a, 240–45.

4. Two elections in the low-key group may appear to have been misclassified. In North Carolina, incumbent Jesse Helms outspent his opponent by about 28 to 1 in a race in which *Congressional Quarterly* (14 October 1978, 2875) described challenger Ingram's operation as "disorganized, almost haphazard." Likewise, in New Mexico, the closeness of Senator Domenici's victory was a surprise to many. He outspent his opponent by 5 to 1, and as the *Almanac of American Politics* (1979, 566) reported, "New Mexico politicoes stayed out [of the campaign] because they disliked [challenger Anaya]; national Democrats assumed Domenici was a shoo-in . . . no one knew how vulnerable he was." The final results in Tennessee and South Carolina might also call into question their placement in the hard-fought category. However, *CQ* reported tough fights from challengers who spent a lot of money and who campaigned hard around their states.

5. Hinckley (1980a, 644), looking at the same data, found this rate to be 85 percent.

6. Jacobson (1981a, 242) suggested that the challenger recognition rates on the House side are too low in the 1978 survey, because, coincidentally, "unusually weak challengers—or unusually strong incumbents—were sampled."

7. Communications with candidates, pollsters, and university archivists indicate that for many races (especially those before 1970) no surveys were conducted, that the results of many polls that *were* conducted have been mislaid or discarded, and that many senators who have commissioned polls prefer not to make them available. The data here comprise all the state-level surveys that were available.

8. These conclusions were based on data tapping recall, not recognition. Stokes and Miller found that only about half of their adult sample could recall their congressman's name, and this figure rose only slightly when only voters were polled. Despite increased education levels, these recall figures did not increase significantly over the next two decades (Glenn 1972; Arseneau and Wolfinger 1973; Freedman 1974; Ferejohn 1977; Nelson 1978–79). Gallup polls from the 1940s and 1950s indicated that the public's ability to recall their senators was at around the same level (Erskine 1963, 135–37).

9. In addition to studies of the increased impact of incumbency in House elections (Erikson 1971; Cover 1977; Ferejohn 1977; Nelson 1978–79), several studies (Hinckley 1970; Cowart 1973; Kostroski 1973) found that Senate incumbents had such advantages as well.

10. Since most of the surveys analyzed here were conducted prior to the elec-

tion, there are three possible vote choice responses instead of the usual two. Respondents may remain loyal, defect, or be undecided. In the following analysis defections are calculated as a fraction of all three responses. Since it is likely that many of the undecideds will choose to defect on Election Day, the absolute defection figures reported here may be lower than the actual figures. When possible, "partisans" were defined to include strong and weak identifiers, plus those independents leaning toward one of the two major parties. In the New York, Michigan, and North Dakota surveys, as well as in the data obtained from newspapers, independents were not separated into three types, and thus leaners could not be included among partisans.

11. The method used here to calculate the incumbent's advantage in awareness is not the only one that produces the pattern of findings in table 14. For example, if instead of comparing the differences between incumbent and challenger familiarity we calculate the awareness of a challenger as a percentage of the awareness of the incumbent, the mean figures corresponding to those in table 14 are: hard-fought, incumbent running, .923; all nine hard-fought, .960; low-key, incumbent running, .586; all seven low-key, .621.

12. Froman (1966, 6) noted that people who "already have actual or latent predispositions to support one party over another . . . will tend to expose themselves disproportionately to the communications of the candidate and party they already support. . . . In other words, the candidate toward whom they already lean will be more effective in reaching them with his communications than will the candidate of the other party."

13. Examination of the candidate-preference ratings for those surveys in which this question was asked indicates that most people who could rate a candidate rated him or her positively. Very few rated either the incumbent or the challenger negatively.

14. As did Jacobson (1978, 479) for 1972 and 1974 and for the 1974 Senate races.

15. Eubank and Gow (1983) found that these patterns, noted by Ferejohn and Nelson for earlier years, held through 1980—with one notable exception: in 1978 and 1980 about half of respondents of the challenger's party who could not recall the names of either candidate defected to the incumbent (130). Eubank and Gow attributed this change from earlier years to a "proincumbent bias" caused by changes in the NES survey. Questions placed before the congressional vote choice item "focus the attention of the respondent on the incumbent" by supplying his name and generally bringing him to mind and "thereby prompt voters to subsequently report that they voted for their representative."

16. The exceptional case here is Massachusetts in 1978, where Senator Brooke had a recognition advantage over Tsongas of 14 points (see table 13). Fewer than half of the Democrats who knew only Brooke defected, however. Since Brooke's financial affairs had brought him criticism in connection with his well-publicized divorce, people may have been voting more *against* Brooke than *for* Tsongas. If this was indeed the case, it might explain why so many people voted for Tsongas without recognizing him.

17. It should be noted that an advantage in defections to a candidate does not necessarily result in a correspondingly large margin of victory. Margin of victory may be related to the distribution of party identification among a state's voters.

18. That so many Democrats who were aware of neither Hansen nor Vinich voted for the incumbent in the 1972 Senate race in Wyoming suggests that the measure of awareness may fail to pick up a number of people who recognize the incumbent but cannot specify likes and dislikes about him.

6. Ideology, Issue Voting, and Senate Campaign Intensity

1. Campbell et al. 1960; Stokes and Miller 1962; Miller and Stokes 1963.

2. This finding originated with the research of Stokes and Miller (1962). Looking at the 1978 House elections, Abramowitz (1980) found no relationship between ideology and the vote. Abramson, Aldrich, and Rohde (1983, 215) did find "a systematic relationship between issue positions [as measured by a voter's ideology] and the vote," although this finding must be viewed with some caution, since their analysis assumed that all Democratic candidates were more liberal than their Republican opponents.

3. Abramowitz also pointed out that constituents were more likely to know something about their senator's voting record than about that of their congressman. He allowed that "these findings may also reflect greater involvement of ideological or single-issue interest groups in Senate campaigns" (1980, 639). And he found that "when they were given clearly defined alternatives, voters generally chose a candidate whose ideology was consistent with their own. When they were given ambiguous or indistinguishable alternatives, voters were forced to use other criteria to make their choice" (1981, 118). Wright and Berkman (1986) found for the 1982 elections that "Senate candidates' policy positions systematically influence voters' decisions" (567) and that in particular, "as the candidates become more polarized, the effects of voter ideology increase" (577).

4. Because the questions asked in the three surveys differed slightly, the content of the items in the index differs slightly from year to year. The construction of the indices is described in appendix 5.

5. Pooling data does not eliminate all of the major problems associated with using national samples when studying Senate elections, as Hagen, Krasno, and Wolfinger (1986) demonstrated. The overrepresentation of respondents from large states still precludes accurate inferences about *descriptive* information (such as how many Americans can recognize and rate Senate candidates); the data will largely reflect the views of respondents from large states. But for purposes of analyzing the relationship between ideology and the vote among voters from hard-fought versus low-key states, the overrepresentation bias is not a problem, and pooling data is warranted.

6. Also included in these categories are low-key open-seat races; in these cases, the term "incumbent" is intended to refer to the better-known candidate.

7. This possibility was suggested by Goldenberg and Traugott (1984, 111–12).

8. In nearly all cases, there was agreement between the terms used in these sources and the yield of the ratings index. There were two areas where these sources disagreed with the ratings. One was in the South, where descriptions sometimes used the terms "moderate" or "liberal" when the ratings indicated "conservative" or "moderate." The disagreement arises because of the overall conservative atmosphere of southern politics; candidates are sometimes termed "liberal," for example, because they differ from the traditional southern Demo-

crat, when in comparison with the rest of the country they are actually moderate. Similarly, "liberal" Republicans, so described because they were at the liberal end of their party, were actually "moderates" on the basis of the ratings. In such cases, priority was given to the ratings.

9. For possible reasons why Senate opponents tend to be ideologically distinct, see Wright 1978; and Wright and Berkman 1986, 569.

10. The exceptions were the races in Massachusetts in 1972, where Republican incumbent Edward Brooke was considered more liberal than Democratic challenger John Droney; in Maryland in 1974, where Republican Senator Charles Mathias was considered more liberal than Democrat Edward Conroy; and in Alaska in 1978, where Republican Senator Ted Stevens faced archconservative Donald Hobbs.

11. Sabato (1981, 155) observed that most incumbents deliberately avoid touting issue positions in their paid advertising in favor of vague but pleasing slogans, emphasizing "their accomplishments or simply their incumbency."

12. The media tend to focus the vast proportion of their coverage of presidential elections on subjects other than the candidates' issue positions; see, e.g., Patterson and McClure 1976, chap. 1; Patterson 1980, chap. 3; and Robinson and Sheehan 1983.

13. See also Miller et al. 1976.

14. Froman (1966) and Jones (1966) made this point generally. Others have looked at the impact of specific issues. For example, McLeod et al. (1977, 5–6) summarized their literature review of the effects of the Watergate issue on the electorate by noting that some studies "tend to show some effects of exposure to Watergate media coverage in the form of increasing knowledge of the scandal events and accepting Nixon's guilt. There is little evidence, however, that exposure to Watergate generalized to more abstract political attitudes, to behavior in the 1974 election." Their own panel study of Madison, Wisconsin, voters found that except among the very young, Watergate had little impact on voting in the 1974 election. One statement that issues mattered in the 1982 elections came from Mann and Ornstein (1983, 146), although House and Senate elections were not differentiated: "The voters sent many . . . messages during the 1982 election campaign. Among the substantial messages: cut back on defense growth, do something—anything—about unemployment, treat social security as a ticking time bomb and not, certainly, as a budget issue."

15. It should also be noted that the extensive paid advertising in the Brown-Wilson campaign focused on policy issues, such as the nuclear freeze, Reaganomics, and Social Security, as opposed to candidate-oriented questions such as honesty, competence, or experience.

16. All news stories, but not letters to the editor or paid ads (of which there were very few), were examined. Most often the issues were raised by the candidates themselves, but in some cases they were raised by candidates' aides and supporters or by others not associated with the candidates, such as commentators and reporters themselves. All such mentions were counted. While one might object that this improperly inflates the frequency of an issue's mention, my interest is the importance of a particular issue's role in the campaign. Rehash and discussion by third parties often contributes to the general salience level an issue acquires during a campaign. No extra credit was given to issues mentioned on the

front page, to those raised in the lead paragraph, or to those constituting the major topic of a story. Headlines containing the essential message—e.g., "Brown digs at Wilson's no-tax filing" (*San Francisco Chronicle,* 12 October); "Brown Used Judgeships to Get Backing: Wilson" (*Los Angeles Times,* 19 October)—were noted, since a casual reader might more readily absorb a headline message than one raised in the body of an article. However, headline messages were uncommon and were not weighted in the table.

17. In a two-week period in late September and early October 1982 at least 15 different spots were aired. See *Los Angeles Times* Poll 61, questions 77–91, for the subjects of these 15 ads.

18. Since many of the strongest opponents of the nuclear freeze might also have felt that the country was not in danger of nuclear war, the figures for "danger of nuclear war" in table 22 probably underestimate the salience of the nuclear freeze issue debated by Brown and Wilson.

19. Because this issue, unlike the other three, was not a national one and therefore probably would not have reached the electorate except as a result of the Senate campaign, its lower salience might have been partly due to its lesser exposure. Those who heard the message might have found this issue to be as important as the other three, which dominated the Brown-Wilson debate. However, this possibility was not borne out by the California Poll: on measures of interest in politics, media usage, and knowledge about the fall campaigns, the most attuned respondents—presumably those most likely to have heard the "judges and the courts" messages—were only slightly more likely than others to rate this issue as very important, and were, like the others, much more inclined to consider Reaganomics, the nuclear freeze and Social Security very important.

20. When an individual "issue votes," he casts a vote because his candidate is closer to his view on a particular issue than the other candidate. In testing for issue voting, then, we can attribute it only to those voters to whom a particular issue is very important; if an issue is not salient to that voter, any relationship between his own vote and his candidate's position on an issue is surely not causal. In early October the California Poll asked respondents to indicate how important to them a series of issues were, but this question was not asked in the surveys just prior to Election Day. We saw in table 22 that most respondents said that the nuclear freeze, Social Security, and issues central to Reagan's economic policies were very important to them. We cannot, of course, conclude that every voter to whom this (or any other issue) is important is casting his ballot on the basis of the candidates' positions on the issue. But this information allows us to continue to entertain the possibility.

21. Questions might also be raised about the causal direction of these relationships. It is conceivable, for example, that instead of choosing Brown on the basis of his Social Security position, some voters may have responded the way they did to the survey questions because they supported Brown and were persuaded by his stance on the issue.

22. I suggested earlier that self-described ideology is not always the best measure of an individual's ideology. Some individuals are unaware of what the terms "liberal" and "conservative" mean and either call themselves "moderate," even when they are not, or do not respond to the question. Neither of these polls lends itself to the creation of an ideology index, since neither contains many attitude

items, and it was necessary to exclude any items about Reagan's economic policies. It was possible, though, to create an ideology index from items in the California Poll. The index consists of items on "government size vs. government service," cutting services versus raising taxes, whether the government should aid minorities, and attitudes toward welfare, plus the self-designated-ideology item. The substitution of this index for the self-designated item alone produced slightly different coefficients for all variables but did not change any of the general conclusions.

23. Whitaker's personal worth was reported by Wyoming's two largest newspapers on September 29. The spending figures are from the 1982 *Almanac of American Politics* (Barone and Ujifusa 1981).

24. Population statistics were taken from the 1980 *County and City Data Book;* circulation figures are from the *1980 IMS/Ayer Directory of Publications.*

25. It is of course possible for someone to issue vote even if he misidentifies the candidates' actual positions, but two things make such a possibility unlikely here. First, for the issue to affect the voter's choice of candidates, the two candidates must differ, which means that "misidentified" issue voting could occur only when the voter has reversed the positions of *both* candidates. The percentage of respondents who did this was negligible. Second, it is much more likely that those who misidentified one or both of the candidates' stances were guessing due to ignorance. This is borne out by their responses to other items: for example, the guessers were more likely than others not to have been able to identify correctly the candidates' party or ideology.

26. Because there are so few respondents to start with, an ideology control cannot be applied. It is possible that some Democrats did choose the Senate candidate on the basis of these issues, but their numbers would be very small indeed.

27. Those respondents scoring highest on a 7-point campaign/media attentiveness scale, which tapped general newspaper and television news attention as well as attention to the 1978 campaigns, were examined as to their knowledge of the Senate candidates' positions on oil and gas deregulation and right-to-work laws. Fifty-three percent of this group correctly identified Simpson as supporting right-to-work legislation; 34 percent correctly identified Whitaker as opposed. Forty-three percent of this group correctly identified Simpson as favoring deregulation; 22 percent correctly identified Whitaker as favoring continued regulation. This already low knowledge steadily decreased as campaign and media attention decreased. Moreover, on other issues not prominent in the campaign, knowledge levels about the candidates' positions were lower among all categories of attentiveness.

7. The Effect of State-specific Factors on Senate Election Outcomes

1. Ninety-four percent of House incumbents but only 83 percent of Senate incumbents won reelection in the period 1960–84. Over the same period, 70 percent of House incumbents who won reelection received at least 60 percent of the two-party vote, as opposed to only 44 percent of Senate incumbents.

2. See, e.g., Bailey 1970, 5; Jewell and Patterson 1977, 91; Jacobson 1980, 27; Harris and Hain 1983, 91; and Woll 1985, 280.

3. See also Jones 1981; and Uslaner 1981. Jones noted that recent House

staff allowance increases have led to greater personal recognition of representatives by their constituents (91).

4. Wolfinger and Hollinger 1965; Mayhew 1974b; Cover and Mayhew 1981; Ripley 1983, 103–4.

5. It should not be forgotten that the few most heavily populated states do dominate national samples, and the findings here underscore a point made in chapter 5—that it is dangerous to generalize about voting behavior in Senate elections solely on the basis of data from national samples.

6. The regression coefficient on the diversity index was neither substantively nor statistically significant; indeed, the sign was in the "wrong" direction.

7. Other measures relying on past election results have been adopted by Schlesinger (1955), Dawson and Robinson (1963), Ranney (1965), and Pfeiffer (1967), to mention a few. For a review and critique of still other such measures, see Pfeiffer 1967; and Tucker 1982.

8. According to the 1974, 1976, and 1982 editions of the *Almanac of American Politics,* the percentage of registered Democrats and Republicans in New Mexico were 60–33, 63–30, and 64–29.

9. As a check on the general validity of the Wright figures, I compared the party identification figures from all the state-level surveys at my disposal, plus the figures for certain states published by Jewell (1984), Jones and Miller (1984), and Lamis (1984) and appearing in various newspaper surveys. For the large and moderate-sized states, the sources were in very close agreement; for a few of the smaller states, these other sources deviated considerably from Wright's figures. It is noteworthy that the Wright measure placed the Democratic proportion of the two-party vote for New Mexico at 68 percent, 13 points higher than the figure of 55 percent produced by the Hibbing-Brandes technique, and that the six statewide Zia Polls conducted by F. Chris Garcia at the University of New Mexico in 1976 and 1978 yielded proportions quite similar to Wright's.

10. For a list of the figures used for each state, see Westlye 1986, app. 6.

11. Except for the distinction between the states leaning Democratic and those leaning Republican, these breaks are somewhat arbitrary, and the range of "Democrat-ness" is different within each of the five groupings. The states with Democratic majorities were divided into three groups in order to ensure that enough states appear in each category to provide meaningful analysis, while at the same time allowing for any distinction that might turn up between the most Democratic states, the least Democratic, and those in between (termed "solid" Democratic in the tables). The three "solid" Republican states were separated from the "leaning" Republican states because of their notably higher proportion of Republican identifiers. Had equal breakpoints been preselected on the basis of proportion Democratic (e.g., 51 to 60, 61 to 70, 71+) almost all Democratic-leaning states would have fallen into the middle group. Had the 50 states been divided into five groups of 10, half of the "lean Republican" states would have been combined with the three solid Republican states, and half would have been combined with some of the moderately Democratic states.

12. The six Senate races in the period 1968–84 in which a Democrat was unopposed by a Republican in the general election were omitted from this calculation. Had these Democrats encountered token opposition rather than none, the resulting inclusion of their probable margins of victory would have driven this figure of 19 percent even higher.

240

8. The Effect of Primary Divisiveness on Senators' Reelection Prospects

1. To generalize about the impact of divisive primaries nationwide for the period prior to the mid-1960s is difficult, because before the Republican party became strong enough to compete in Senate elections in the South, victory in the Democratic Senate primary in that region virtually guaranteed election; that is, without strong Republican opponents in the general election, divisiveness in primaries tended to have a very different impact on general election outcomes in the South than in other parts of the country. Studies focusing on this earlier period have usually either excluded the South from their analysis or discussed southern primaries as a special case. Since the mid-1960s the growth of the Republican party in the South has eliminated the automatic Democratic general election victory. Therefore, it is no longer necessary to analyze southern states separately; accordingly, the conclusions of this chapter are based on all Senate elections in the period 1968–84 in which an incumbent sought reelection. See Westlye 1986, app. 7, for a description of changes in competitiveness in Senate primaries in the South.

2. In earlier studies, Hacker (1965) and Bernstein (1977) reached different conclusions. Hacker, looking at all senatorial and gubernatorial primaries in the period 1956–64, concluded that what happens in Senate primaries has no bearing on the results of the general election, once incumbency and the distribution of a state's two major parties are taken into account. Bernstein replicated the Hacker study for Senate elections only and also corrected a flaw in Hacker's analysis. His findings are summarized by the title of his study: "Divisive Primaries Do Hurt: U.S. Senate Races, 1956–1972." Bernstein's conclusion with respect to Senate elections was echoed by Lengle (1980) in his examination of presidential primary divisiveness: in both parties "divisive presidential primaries hurt [the] chances of winning those same states in the November general election" (261). However, in a study focusing on gubernatorial races, Pierson and Smith (1975) found that primary divisiveness had no impact on gubernatorial general election outcomes. Born (1981) found that in the period 1962–76, divisiveness in an incumbent House member's primary had at most a slight impact on the general election outcome, and divisiveness in a non-incumbent's primary had no effect.

3. In the period 1956–74, 60 percent of House primaries were uncontested (Schantz 1980, 548). The outcomes of fewer than 10 percent of primaries were as close as a 2-to-1 margin (Schantz 1976, 543). In replicating Turner's (1953) study of House primaries in the 1940s, Schantz looked only at primaries in the dominant party of safe House seats—these being the most likely kinds of primaries to be contested. His figure of 9.1 percent (races where the winner finished with less than a 2-to-1 margin) is thus likely to be even lower for all House primaries. For further evidence of how few House primaries are contested, see Sorauf 1984, 221.

4. Hacker (1965), whose study focused on Senate and gubernatorial primaries, defined primaries as divisive when the winner received less than 65 percent of the total vote. Bernstein (1977) felt that such a definition allowed too many clearly nondivisive contests with three or more candidates to be classified as divisive. Among those contests Hacker's method treats as divisive would be races in which the winner—with, for example, 55 percent of the vote—defeats

several competitors who receive no more than 10 percent each. Bernstein chose to call a race divisive when the winner was held to 20 points or less over the second-place finisher. Born (1981), on the other hand, took issue with Bernstein's reasoning. The important point to consider, argued Born, is not the size of the margin of victory but the proportion of the electorate that supports one of the losing candidates. Any of these disappointed voters, he maintained, "could actually be susceptible to deserting their party or abstaining in the fall" (645). Lengle (1980) also used a 20-percentage-point margin as the cutoff in his study of presidential primary divisiveness, and Piereson and Smith (1975) chose a 30-point margin in their study of gubernatorial primaries. More recently, Born (1981) and Kenney and Rice (1984) did not measure divisiveness dichotomously, yet they adopted margin of victory as the relevant criterion; both developed regression equations that assumed, for both the incumbent's and the challenger's primary, that the lower the winner's proportion of the total vote, the more divisive the primary was.

5. Discussing the prospect of a divisive Republican Senate primary in North Carolina in 1986, a top adviser to Republican Governor James Martin speculated, "You could really wind up with some bad scars, and the problem would be that forces that lined up for the Senate fight would then be in place to go right into the next war, which would be between [New York Congressman Jack] Kemp and [Vice President] Bush for the presidency. . . . It would divert everyone's attention from what we should be about, which is party building" (*Washington Post*, 29 July 1985, national weekly edition, 12).

6. With a few exceptions, this "strong" classification was limited to individuals who had been elected to statewide office or to Congress, who were mayors of large cities in the state, or who had served in a conspicuous position in the national government. Elected leaders of state legislatures, but not other members, were also classified as strong, as were former Senate nominees and two politically inexperienced but highly visible candidates: former professional basketball star Bill Bradley and ex-astronaut Harrison Schmitt.

7. Using a much looser definition of divisiveness— "where the winning candidate received less than 65 percent of the total votes cast"—Hacker (1965, 108) found that in the period 1956–64 five of the six Senate incumbents who had close primaries won in November.

8. A 25-point margin may hardly seem close; it would be widely considered a landslide in a general election. But since most incumbent senators face only token opposition in the primary, a margin of 20–25 percentage points is often considered close. Ornstein (1985, 252) reported, for example, that in 1984, Illinois Republican Senator Charles Percy "faced a stiff primary challenge from the right . . . Percy beat back the challenge from [Congressman Tom] Corcoran by 59 percent to 36 percent, a margin that suggested potential problems in the fall.

9. The degree of divisiveness in the other party's primary was considered important in all but one of the studies on the effects of divisive primaries cited above; in fact, Hacker (1965) and Bernstein (1977) centered their analyses around the interaction of the variables of divisiveness in the incumbent and challenger primaries. They assumed that when both or neither of the parties' primaries were divisive, the parties were, in Hacker's terms, "at an equal advantage" (110). This balanced condition was used as a baseline: to the extent that the victory rate in the general election declined from the baseline when one candidate

had a divisive primary and the other did not, that difference was a measure of the impact of that divisiveness. Bernstein's conclusion that "divisive primaries do hurt" stemmed from his finding that "both incumbents and challengers did worse [in the general election than those in the 'balanced' condition] when they had to face a divisive primary and their opponent did not" (541). Although he acknowledged that some of the cells in his tables were small, he concluded that "these differences show that divisive primaries hurt incumbents, nonincumbents and challengers to some degree" (ibid.).

10. Although the studies listed in note 2 controlled for the possibility of one or more intervening effects, only Born (1981) attempted to account for the possibility that close general election races are due in part to factors that may weaken a candidate *prior to* the primary election. Kenney and Rice (1984) considered this possibility but declined to investigate, partly because they were unable to find a way to test its impact properly and partly because they suspected it had little impact (908–9).

11. In each survey, 20–25 percent were not familiar enough with the senator's performance to give an opinion.

12. Vulnerability on Tunney's part was never mentioned when successive candidates entered the race. When Hayden announced his candidacy on June 3, the press gave no indication that Tunney was viewed as already vulnerable and might be hurt by such a move. Neither in October, when Republican Alphonso Bell announced, nor in November, when Hayakawa and state senator John Schmitz announced, did anyone claim that Tunney was politically vulnerable. Houston Flournoy, who had been the Republican nominee for governor in 1974 and who was "widely regarded in political circles as having the strongest ultimate chance to unseat Tunney" (*Los Angeles Times,* 24 July 1975, 23), took himself out of contention in late July 1975. He was followed by state senator Paul Carpenter, who was considered "a potentially strong challenger," in November and by Barry Goldwater, Jr., in January.

In December, when Tunney lashed out at Hayden for the first time (accusing him of dwelling on "malicious gossip and personal pique"), the *Los Angeles Times* noted that "this first direct clash between the pair . . . was unusually strong for an incumbent, particularly one holding such a lopsided lead" in the primary. *Times* reporter George Skelton wrote that "normally, a front-running incumbent would try to curtail his challenger's publicity by ignoring him" (4 December, 1), but he did not ascribe Tunney's behavior to any nervousness caused by prior vulnerability.

13. In November 1975 the California Poll showed Goldwater as the overwhelming choice for the nomination among Republicans, leading former Lieutenant Governor Robert Finch and eventual nominee S. I. Hayakawa by margins of 46 percent to 26 percent and 23 percent, respectively, with two others claiming the support of the remaining 5 percent. Tunney's own assessment of his opponents was personally communicated to me in April 1973 by a member of Tunney's senior staff.

14. Goldwater had announced in July 1975 that his decision whether to give up his House seat and run for the Senate would be made on the basis of "whether I can beat John Tunney" (*Los Angeles Times,* 24 July 1975, 23). Three months later, Goldwater was still unsure, saying that "it may take weeks or even months to determine" whether he had "a fighting chance." By late October, Goldwater

was quoted as being "terribly unsure that he could beat Tunney" (ibid., 22 October, pt. 2, 1).

15. When asked how vulnerable he thought Tunney was, Hayakawa answered, "Gee, I don't know" (ibid., 15 September 1975).

16. For various reasons, each of the five was vulnerable to attack from within his or her own party.

17. For a discussion of candidate strategies concerning when and when not to run, see Jacobson and Kernell 1981.

18. The other two candidates, a current and a former member of the state legislature, were not as well known statewide as were Stone and Gunter, but one had wrested the endorsement of most labor unions from Stone, and the other had hired nationally prominent media consultant Robert Squier and pollster Pat Caddell and was prepared to pour millions of dollars into television and radio advertising (see "Senate Candidates Wage a TV War," *Miami Herald*, 11 August 1980, 1).

19. Twenty-five percent of respondents gave Stone mixed or negative ratings, and 25 percent were unable to rate him at all. Because rating scales vary in their format from one state poll to another, it is not possible to determine generally just how bad a positive rating of 50 is. But whatever the format, most senators score much higher among voters of their own party.

20. *Los Angeles Times* reporter Richard Bergholz, in an in-depth analysis of the 1968 primary, described the concerted effort by influential conservatives in the state to "get Kuchel" after the senator refused to endorse Ronald Reagan for governor in 1966 (16 June 1968, B-1).

21. These and subsequent survey data on this race are from the California Polls of July, September, and October 1968.

22. The analysis that follows treats (with one exception) any incumbent primary loss as more divisive than a narrow incumbent victory; i.e., the more negative the incumbent's "margin of victory," the more divisive the primary. The exception is the race between Democratic incumbent Paul Hatfield and Congressman Max Baucus in the Montana Senate primary in 1978. In essence, it was Baucus rather than Hatfield who held claim to the seat. Baucus had been shoring up support for over a year in an effort to succeed Democrat Lee Metcalf, who had announced his intention to retire. But Metcalf died in office with less than a year remaining in his term, and Hatfield was appointed to serve it out by a governor who was not enamored of either Metcalf or Baucus. Hatfield, who had no particular following in the party, decided to run for the nomination in spite of united party support for Baucus and was defeated in the primary by 43 percentage points. Under the unique circumstances, the margin in this particular case was scored as 43 rather than −43.

23. Since not all elderly incumbents necessarily *look* old or frail, actual age was not used as a criterion. Also, scoring of this aspect of the variable was based on pre-primary evidence of either notable agedness or scandal; when the issue turns up for the first time during the primary campaign it can hardly be treated as initial vulnerability.

24. CQ regularly produces two ratings: one measuring support for and the other measuring opposition to roll-call votes in which a majority of Republicans and southern Democrats oppose a majority of non-southern Democrats. I created

the "ideological distance" variable by averaging the six yearly scores yielded from the following formula: (Conservative Coalition [CC] support X 100) / (CC support − CC opposition). For those incumbents who had not served a full term, the ratings for the number of years they had served were averaged.

25. To achieve this transformation, I regressed the incumbent ideology variable on the Wright index, producing a slope and an intercept. I subtracted the intercept from the conservative coalition score and then divided this figure by the slope. The ideological distance index ranges from 0.00 to 0.39.

26. For details of the construction of the state party distribution measure, see chapter 7.

27. For example, the Wright mean partisanship score for Mississippi is −.287 (on a scale with a possible range from −1.0, for totally Democratic, to 1.0, for totally Republican). For Democratic incumbents Eastland and Stennis a score of +.287 was entered, indicating the extent of advantage provided by the predominance of Democratic identifiers in the state; by the same token, incumbent Republican Thad Cochran received a score of −.287.

28. It is less clear what perceived incumbent vulnerability might produce in the challenger primary—perhaps a fight among strong contenders, perhaps a consolidation of resources behind a single strong candidate.

29. For each party within a state, scores are based on which candidates received support in the party's presidential conventions (in which ideological choices were available), which presidential candidates received a majority in selected presidential elections, and the average ideological ratings of the party's congressmen in 1978. For details of the construction of each index, see Bartels 1983, 104–6, 157–58.

30. To put the incumbent ideology scores on a scale that is equivalent with the Bartels measure, Republican Conservative Coalition (CC) scores are regressed on the Bartels Republican conservatism index, and Democratic CC scores on his Democratic liberalism index. In each case, the CC value was added to the appropriate intercept and then divided by the slope of the appropriate Bartels coefficient.

31. Born (1981), finding a similar need for excluded variables in his rather differently conceived model of the effect of divisive primaries on House elections, introduced two variables into his first-stage equation. The first was whether or not there had been redistricting. Of course, redistricting is not relevant to the Senate, and this variable is of no use to us here. Born's second variable was the divisiveness in the incumbent's primary (measured by the incumbent's percentage of the two-party vote) two years before. This variable was designed "to control for [the incumbent's] past level of intra-party support" (651). It is difficult to see how this variable could have much of an impact on the primary two years later, and since Born did not report his first-stage coefficients, whether it did or did not is not known.

32. Information in Jewell and Olson 1978 (130) and Price 1984 (128–29) indicates that North Dakota, Massachusetts, Delaware, and the Democratic party in Illinois belong in the "strong" category and that Idaho and Indiana are better placed in the "moderate" category. I adapted the Morehouse index accordingly. Because their endorsements come *after* the primary, Iowa and South Dakota were moved from the "moderate" to the "weak" category. Also, even though

unofficial party organizations sometimes endorse candidates in California, these endorsements are widely perceived as representing the views of only small segments of the parties, which themselves are weak organizations (see Lawson 1980, 116, 123–24). Therefore, California was moved from the "moderate" to the "weak" category. These changes yield an index of 19 "strong," 15 "moderate," and 66 "weak" state parties.

References

Abramowitz, Alan I. 1980. "A Comparison of Voting for U.S. Senator and Representative in 1978." *American Political Science Review* 74, no. 3:633–40.
———. 1981. "Choices and Echoes in the 1978 U.S. Senate Elections: A Research Note." *American Journal of Political Science* 25, no. 1:112–18.
———. 1988. "The Root of All Evil: Campaign Spending in U.S. Senate Elections." Paper delivered at the Hendricks Symposium on the U.S. Senate, University of Nebraska, Lincoln, 6–8 October.
Abramson, Paul R., John H. Aldrich, and David W. Rohde. 1983. *Change and Continuity in the 1980 Elections*. Washington, D.C.: Congressional Quarterly Press.
Alford, John R., and John R. Hibbing. 1981. "Increased Incumbency Advantage in the House." *Journal of Politics* 43, no. 4:1042–61.
———. 1983. "Incumbency Advantage in Senate Elections." Paper delivered at the annual meeting of the American Political Science Association, Chicago, 1–4 September.
The Almanac of American Politics, 1974. See Barone, Ujifusa, and Matthews 1973.
The Almanac of American Politics, 1976. See Barone, Ujifusa, and Matthews 1975.
The Almanac of American Politics, 1982. See Barone and Ujifusa 1981.
The Almanac of American Politics, 1984. See Barone and Ujifusa 1983.
Anderson, Walt. 1970. *Campaigns: Cases in Political Conflict*. Pacific Palisades, Calif.: Goodyear.
Arseneau, Robert B., and Raymond E. Wolfinger. 1973. "Voting Behavior in Congressional Elections." Paper delivered at the annual meeting of the American Political Science Association, New Orleans, 4–8 September.
Arterton, F. Chris. 1978. "The Media Politics of Presidential Campaigns." In *Race for the Presidency,* edited by James D. Barber, 55–78. Englewood Cliffs, N.J.: Prentice-Hall.

Bagdikian, Ben H. 1971. *The Information Machines*. New York: Harper Torchbooks.

Bailey, Stephen K. 1970. *Congress in the Seventies*. New York: St. Martin's Press.

Barone, Michael, and Grant Ujifusa. 1981. *The Almanac of American Politics, 1982*. Washington, D.C.: Barone.

———. 1983. *The Almanac of American Politics, 1984*. Washington, D.C.: National Journal.

Barone, Michael, Grant Ujifusa, and Douglas Matthews. 1973. *The Almanac of American Politics, 1974*. Boston: Gambit.

———. 1975. *The Almanac of American Politics, 1976*. New York: Dutton.

Bartels, Larry. 1983. "Presidential Primaries and the Dynamics of Public Choice." Ph.D. diss., University of California, Berkeley.

Becker, Ted, and Christa Slaton. 1980. "Hawaii *Televote:* Measuring Public Opinion on Complex Policy Issues." Paper delivered at the annual meeting of the American Political Science Association, Washington, D.C., 28 August–1 September.

Bernstein, Robert. 1977. "Divisive Primaries Do Hurt: U.S. Senate Races, 1956–1972." *American Political Science Review* 71, no. 2:540–45.

Bibby, John F., Cornelius Cotter, James Gibson, and Robert Huckshorn. 1983. "Parties in State Politics." In *Politics in the American States*, edited by Virginia Gray, Herbert Jacob, and Kenneth Vines, 59–96. Boston: Little, Brown.

Bibby, John F., and Roger D. Davidson. 1973. *On Capitol Hill*. Hinsdale, Ill.: Dryden.

Bicker, William E. 1978. "Network Television News and the 1976 Presidential Primaries." In *Race for the Presidency*, 79–110. *See* Arterton 1978.

Blumler, J. G., and D. McQuail. 1969. *Television and Politics: Its Uses and Influence*. Chicago: University of Chicago Press.

Bond, Jon R. 1983. "The Influence of Constituency Diversity on Electoral Competition in Voting for Congress, 1974–1978." *Legislative Studies Quarterly* 8, no. 2:201–11.

Born, Richard. 1979. "Generational Replacement and the Growth of Incumbent Reelection Margins in the U.S. House." *American Political Science Review* 73, no. 3:811–17.

———. 1981. "The Influence of House Primary Election Divisiveness on General Election Margins, 1962–76." *Journal of Politics* 43, no. 3:640–61.

Boyd, Richard W. 1972. "Popular Control of Public Policy: A Normal Vote Analysis of the 1968 Election." *American Political Science Review* 66, no. 2:429–49.

Brody, Richard A., and Benjamin I. Page. 1972. "Comment: The Assessment of Policy Voting." *American Political Science Review* 66, no. 2:450–58.

Bullock, Charles S., and David W. Brady. 1983. "Party, Constituency, and Roll-Call Voting in the U.S. Senate." *Legislative Studies Quarterly* 8, no. 1:29–43.

Burnham, Walter D. 1970. *Critical Elections and the Mainsprings of American Politics*. New York: Norton.

Cain, Bruce E., John A. Ferejohn, and Morris P. Fiorina. 1984. "The Constituency Service Basis of the Personal Vote for U.S. Representatives and British Members of Parliament." *American Political Science Review* 78, no. 1:110–25.

"Campaigning on Cue." 1986. Pt. 2. PBS. KQEC-TV, San Francisco. 12 February.

Campbell, Angus, Philip E. Converse, Warren E. Miller, and Donald E. Stokes. 1960. *The American Voter.* New York: John Wiley & Sons.

————. 1966. *Elections and the Political Order.* New York: John Wiley & Sons.

Campbell, James E. 1983. "The Return of the Incumbents: The Nature of Incumbency Advantage." *Western Political Quarterly* 36, no. 3:434–44.

Carey, John. 1976. "How Media Shape Campaigns." *Journal of Communication* 26, no. 2:50–57.

Carter, Richard F., and Bradley S. Greenberg. 1965. "Newspapers or Television: Which Do You Believe?" *Journalism Quarterly* 42, no. 1:29–34.

Clarke, Peter, and Susan H. Evans. 1983. *Covering Campaigns.* Stanford, Calif.: Stanford University Press.

Clarke, Peter, and Eric Fredin. 1978. "Newspapers, Television and Political Reasoning." *Public Opinion Quarterly* 42, no. 2:143–60.

Clarke, Peter, and L. Ruggles. 1970. "Preferences among News Media for Coverage of Public Affairs." *Journalism Quarterly* 47, no. 3:464–71.

Clyde, Robert W., and James K. Buckalew. 1969. "Inter-Media Standardization." *Journalism Quarterly* 46, no. 2:349–51.

Cohen, Bernard. 1963. *The Press and Foreign Policy.* Princeton: Princeton University Press.

Comer, John. 1976. "Another Look at the Effects of the Divisive Primary." *American Politics Quarterly* 4, no. 1:121–28.

Converse, Philip E., Warren E. Miller, Jerrold G. Rusk, and Arthur C. Wolfe. 1969. "Continuity and Change in American Politics: Parties and Issues in the 1968 Election." *American Political Science Review* 63, no. 4:1083–1105.

Cooper, Joseph, and William West. 1981. "The Congressional Career in the 1970s." In *Congress Reconsidered,* edited by L. Dodd and B. Oppenheimer, 83–106. Washington, D.C.: Congressional Quarterly Press.

Cover, Albert D. 1977. "One Good Term Deserves Another: The Advantage of Incumbency in Congressional Elections." *American Journal of Political Science* 21, no. 2:523–42.

————. 1980. "Contacting Congressional Constituents: Some Patterns of Perquisite Use." *American Journal of Political Science* 24, no. 1:125–35.

Cover, Albert D., and Bruce S. Brumberg. 1982. "Baby Books and Ballots: The Impact of Congressional Mail on Constituent Opinion." *American Political Science Review* 76, no. 2:347–59.

Cover, Albert D., and David R. Mayhew. 1981. "Congressional Dynamics and the Decline of Competitive Congressional Elections." In *Congress Reconsidered,* 62–82. *See* Cooper and West 1981.

Cowart, Andrew. 1973. "Electoral Choice in the American States: Incumbency Effects, Partisan Forces, and Divergent Partisan Majorities." *American Political Science Review* 67, no. 3:835–53.

Davidson, Roger D., and Walter J. Oleszek. 1984. "Changing the Guard in the U.S. Senate." *Legislative Studies Quarterly* 9, no. 4:635–63.

Dawson, Paul A., and James E. Zinser. 1971. "Broadcast Expenditures and Electoral Outcomes in the 1970 Congressional Elections." *Public Opinion Quarterly* 35, no. 3:398–402.

————. 1976. "Characteristics of Campaign Resource Allocation in the 1972

Elections." In *Changing Campaign Techniques,* edited by L. Maisel, 93–137. Beverly Hills: Sage.

Dawson, Richard E., and James A. Robinson. 1963. "Inter-Party Competition, Economic Variables, and Welfare Policies in the American States." *Journal of Politics* 25, no. 2:265–89.

Dodd, Lawrence. 1981. "Congress, the Constitution, and the Crisis of Legitimation." In *Congress Reconsidered,* 390–420. *See* Cooper and West 1981.

Drew, Dan, and G. Cleveland Wilhoit. 1976. "Newshole Allocation Policies of American Daily Newspapers." *Journalism Quarterly* 56, no. 3:434–40.

Ducey, Richard V., and Joey Reagan. 1981. "Sources for State Government News." Paper delivered at a meeting of the Association for Education in Journalism, East Lansing, Mich., August.

Dunn, Delmer. 1969. *Public Officials and the Press.* Reading, Mass.: Addison-Wesley.

Eismeier, Theodore J., and Philip H. Pollock. 1986. "Strategy and Choice in Congressional Elections: The Role of Political Action Committees." *American Journal of Political Science* 30, no. 1:197–213.

Epstein, Edward J. 1973. *News from Nowhere.* New York: Vintage.

Erikson, Robert S. 1971. "The Advantage of Incumbency in Congressional Elections." *Polity* 3, no. 3:395–405.

Erskine, Hazel G. 1963. "The Polls: Textbook Knowledge." *Public Opinion Quarterly* 27, no. 1:133–41.

Eubank, Robert B., and David J. Gow. 1983. "The Pro-incumbent Bias in the 1978 and 1980 National Election Studies." *American Journal of Political Science* 27, no. 1:122–39.

Feldman, Stanley, and Pamela J. Conover. 1983. "Candidates, Issues and Voters: The Role of Inference in Political Perception." *Journal of Politics* 45, no. 4:810–39.

Fenno, Richard F. 1982. *The United States Senate: A Bicameral Perspective.* Washington, D.C.: American Enterprise Institute.

Fenton, John H., and Donald M. Austern. 1976. "The Case of the Priestly Zealot: The Fourth District of Massachusetts." In *The Making of Congressmen,* edited by Alan Clem, 93–106. North Scituate, Mass.: Duxbury.

Ferejohn, John A. 1977. "On the Decline of Competition in Congressional Elections." *American Political Science Review* 71, no. 1:166–76.

Fiorina, Morris P. 1974. *Representatives, Roll-Calls, and Constituencies.* Lexington, Mass.: Lexington Books.

———. 1977. *Congress: Keystone of the Washington Establishment.* New Haven: Yale University Press.

———. 1978. "Economic Retrospective Voting in American National Elections: A Micro-Analysis." *American Journal of Political Science* 22, no. 2:426–43.

———. 1982. "Congressmen and Their Constituents, 1958 and 1978." In *The United States Congress,* edited by Dennis Hale, 33–64. New Brunswick, N.J.: Transaction Books.

Foote, Joe S., and David J. Weber. 1984. "Network Evening News Visibility of Congressmen and Senators." Paper delivered at a meeting of the Association for Education in Journalism and Mass Communication, Gainesville, Fla., August.

Freedman, Stanley R. 1974. "The Saliency of Party and Candidate in Congressional Elections." In *Public Opinion and Public Policy,* edited by Norman Luttbeg, 126–31. Homewood, Ill.: Dorsey.

Froman, Lewis A. 1963. *Congressmen and Their Constituencies.* Chicago: Rand McNally.

———. 1966. "A Realistic Approach to Campaign Strategies and Tactics." In *The Electoral Process,* edited by M. Kent Jennings and Harmon Ziegler, 1–20. Englewood Cliffs, N.J.: Prentice-Hall.

Gans, Herbert. 1979. *Deciding What's News.* New York: Pantheon.

Glenn, Norval. 1972. "The Distribution of Political Knowledge in the United States." In *Political Attitudes and Public Opinion,* edited by Dan D. Nimmo and Charles M. Bonjean, 273–83. New York: David McKay.

Goldenberg, Edie, and Michael W. Traugott. 1984. *Campaigning for Congress.* Washington, D.C.: Congressional Quarterly Press.

———. 1985. "The Impact of News Coverage in Senate Campaigns." Paper delivered at the annual meeting of the American Political Science Association, New Orleans, 29 August–1 September.

Gormley, William. 1976. *The Effects of Newspaper-Television Cross-Ownership on News Homogeneity.* Chapel Hill, N.C.: Institute for Research in Social Science.

Graber, Doris A. 1971. "Press Coverage Patterns of Campaign News: The 1968 Presidential Race." *Journalism Quarterly* 48, no. 3 : 502–12.

———. 1976a. "Effect of Incumbency on Coverage Patterns in the 1972 Presidential Campaign." *Journalism Quarterly* 53, no. 3 : 499–508.

———. 1976b. "Press and TV as Opinion Resources in Presidential Campaigns." *Public Opinion Quarterly* 40, no. 3 : 285–303.

———. 1980. *Mass Media and American Politics.* Washington, D.C.: Congressional Quarterly Press.

———. 1984. *Processing the News.* New York: Longman.

———. 1985. "Candidate Images: An Audio-Visual Analysis." Paper delivered at the annual meeting of the American Political Science Association, New Orleans, 29 August–1 September.

Hacker, Andrew. 1965. "Does a Divisive Primary Harm a Candidate's Election Chances?" *American Political Science Review* 59, no. 1 : 105–10.

Hagen, Michael, Jon Krasno, and Raymond E. Wolfinger. 1986. "Pooling Samples to Study Senate Elections." Memorandum to the National Election Studies Board of Overseers, 23 April.

Hale, Jon F. 1985. "A Lot or a Lot of Nothing: Press Coverage of Issues in the 1984 Texas Senate Race." Paper delivered at the annual meeting of the Midwest Political Science Association, Chicago, 18–20 April.

Harris, Fred R., and Paul L. Hain. 1983. *America's Legislative Processes.* Glenview, Ill.: Scott, Foresman.

Herrnson, Paul S. 1985. "Parties, PACs, and Congressional Elections: The View from the Campaign." Paper delivered at the annual meeting of the Midwest Political Science Association, Chicago, 18–20 April.

Hershey, Marjorie R. 1984. *Running for Office.* Chatham, N.J.: Chatham House.

Hibbing, John R., and John R. Alford. 1982. "Economic Conditions and the Forgotten Side of Congress: A Foray into U.S. Senate Elections." *British Journal of Political Science* 12, pt. 4 : 505–13.

Hibbing, John R., and Sara L. Brandes. 1983. "State Population and the Electoral

Success of U.S. Senators." *American Journal of Political Science* 27, no. 4:808–19.

Hinckley, Barbara. 1970. "Incumbency and the Presidential Vote in Senate Elections." *American Political Science Review* 64, no. 3:836–42.

———. 1980a. "The American Voter in Congressional Elections." *American Political Science Review* 74, no. 3:641–50.

———. 1980b. "House Reelections and Senate Defeats: The Role of the Challenger." *British Journal of Political Science* 10, pt. 4:441–60.

———. 1981. *Congressional Elections*. Washington, D.C.: Congressional Quarterly Press.

Hofstetter, C. Richard. 1978. "News Bias in the 1972 Campaign: A Cross-Media Comparison." *Journalism Monographs*, no. 58 (November):1–30.

IMS/Ayer. 1980. *1980 IMS/Ayer Directory of Publications*. Philadelphia: IMS Press.

Jacob, Charles. 1985. "The Congressional Elections." In *The Election of 1984*, edited by Gerald Pomper, 112–32. Chatham, N.J.: Chatham House.

Jacobson, Gary C. 1975. "The Impact of Broadcast Campaigning on Electoral Outcomes." *Journal of Politics* 37, no. 3:769–93.

———. 1978. "The Effects of Campaign Spending in Congressional Elections." *American Political Science Review* 72, no. 2:469–91.

———. 1980. *Money in Congressional Elections*. New Haven: Yale University Press.

———. 1981a. "Congressional Elections, 1978: The Case of the Vanishing Challengers." In *Congressional Elections*, edited by Louis Maisel and Joseph Cooper, 219–48. Beverly Hills: Sage.

———. 1981b. "Incumbents' Advantages in the 1978 Elections." *Legislative Studies Quarterly* 6, no. 2:183–200.

———. 1983. *The Politics of Congressional Elections*. Boston: Little, Brown.

———. 1984. "Money in the 1980 and 1982 Congressional Elections." In *Money and Politics in the United States*, edited by Michael L. Malbin, 38–69. Washington, D.C.: American Enterprise Institute.

———. 1985. "Congress: Politics after a Landslide without Coattails." In *The Elections of 1984*, edited by Michael Nelson, 215–37. Washington, D.C.: Congressional Quarterly Press.

Jacobson, Gary C., and Samuel Kernell. 1981. *Strategy and Choice in Congressional Elections*. New Haven: Yale University Press.

Jamieson, Kathleen, and Karlyn Campbell. 1983. *The Interplay of Influence*. Belmont, Calif.: Wadsworth.

Jewell, Malcolm E. 1984. *Parties and Primaries*. New York: Praeger.

Jewell, Malcolm E., and David M. Olson. 1978. *American State Political Parties and Elections*. Homewood, Ill.: Dorsey.

Jewell, Malcolm E., and Samuel C. Patterson. 1977. *The Legislative Process in the United States*. New York: Random House.

Johannes, John R., and John C. McAdams. 1981. "The Congressional Incumbency Effect: Is It Casework, Policy Compatibility, or Something Else?" *American Journal of Political Science* 25, no. 3:512–42.

Johnson, Donald, and James Gibson. 1974. "The Divisive Primary Revisited: Party Activists in Iowa." *American Political Science Review* 68, no. 1:67–77.

Jones, Charles O. 1966. "The Role of the Campaign in Congressional Politics." In *The Electoral Process*, 21–41. *See* Froman 1966.

———. 1981. "The New, New Senate." In *A Tide of Discontent,* edited by Ellis Sandoz and Cecil V. Crabb, 89–111. Washington, D.C.: Congressional Quarterly Press.

———. 1982. *The United States Congress.* Homewood, Ill.: Dorsey.

Jones, Ruth S., and Warren E. Miller. 1984. "State Polls: Promising Data Sources for Political Research." *Journal of Politics* 46, no. 4:1182–92.

Joslyn, Richard. 1984. *Mass Media and Elections.* Reading, Mass.: Addison-Wesley.

Kayden, Xandra. 1978. *Campaign Organization.* Lexington, Mass.: D. C. Heath.

Kazee, Thomas A. 1983. "The Deterrent Effect of Incumbency on Recruiting Challengers in U.S. House Elections." *Legislative Studies Quarterly* 8, no. 3:469–80.

Keefe, William. 1984. *Parties, Politics and Public Policy.* New York: Holt, Rinehart, & Winston.

Kenney, Patrick J., and Tom Rice. 1984. "The Effect of Primary Divisiveness in Gubernatorial and Senatorial Elections." *Journal of Politics* 46, no. 3: 904–15.

Key, V. O. 1964. *Politics, Parties and Pressure Groups.* New York: Thomas Y. Crowell.

Kirkpatrick, Samuel A., David R. Morgan, and Thomas G. Kielhorn. 1977. *The Oklahoma Voter.* Norman: University of Oklahoma Press.

Kostroski, Warren L. 1973. "Party and Incumbency in Postwar Senate Elections." *American Political Science Review* 67, no. 4:1213–34.

Kuklinski, James H., and Darrell M. West. 1981. "Economic Expectations and Voting Behavior in United States House and Senate Elections." *American Political Science Review* 75, no. 2:436–47.

Lamis, Alexander P. 1984. *The Two-Party South.* New York: Oxford University Press.

Latimer, Margaret K., and Patrick Cotter. 1985. "Effects of News Measure on Selection of State Government News Sources." *Journalism Quarterly* 62, no. 1:31–36.

Lawson, Kay. 1980. "California: The Uncertainties of Reform." In *Party Renewal in America,* edited by Gerald Pomper, 116–38. New York: Praeger.

Leary, Mary Ellen. 1977. *Phantom Politics: Campaigning in California.* Washington, D.C.: Public Affairs Press.

Lemert, James B., William R. Elliott, Karl J. Nestvold, and Galin R. Rarick. 1983. "Effects of Viewing a Presidential Primary Debate." *Communication Research* 10, no. 2:155–73.

Lengle, James I. 1980. "Divisive Presidential Primaries and Party Electoral Prospects, 1932–1976." *American Politics Quarterly* 8, no. 3:261–77.

Linsky, Martin. 1983. *Television and the Presidential Elections.* Lexington, Mass.: Lexington Books.

Luttbeg, Norman R. 1983. "Television Viewing Audience and Congressional District Incongruity: A Handicap for the Challenger?" *Journal of Broadcasting* 27, no. 4:411–17.

Luttbeg, Norman R., and Michael M. Gant. 1985. "The Failure of Liberal/

Conservative Ideology as a Cognitive Structure." *Public Opinion Quarterly* 49, no. 1:80–93.

McAdams, John C., and John R. Johannes. 1983. "The 1980 Elections: Reexamining Some Theories in a Republican Year." *Journal of Politics* 45, no. 1:143–62.

———. 1984. "The Voter in the 1982 House Election." *American Journal of Political Science* 28, no. 4:778–81.

———. 1985. "Congressmen, Perquisites, and Elections." Paper delivered at the annual meeting of the American Political Science Association, New Orleans, 29 August–1 September.

McClure, Robert D. 1983. "Media Influence in Presidential Politics." In *The Presidential Election and Transition, 1980–81*, edited by Paul T. David and David H. Everson, 133–56. Carbondale: Southern Illinois University Press.

McClure, Robert D., and Thomas E. Patterson. 1974. "Television News and Political Advertising." *Communication Research* 1, no. 1:3–13.

McDowell, Charles. 1986. "Television Politics: The Medium Is the Revolution." In *Beyond Reagan: The Politics of Upheaval*, edited by Paul Duke, 235–61. New York: Warner Books.

McLeod, Jack M., Jane D. Brown, Lee B. Becker, and Dean A. Ziemke. 1977. "Decline and Fall at the White House: A Longitudinal Analysis of Communication Effects." *Communication Research* 4, no. 1:3–23.

McLeod, Jack M., C. Bybee, J. Durall, and Dean A. Ziemke. 1977. "The 1976 Debates as Forms of Political Communication." Paper presented at the annual meeting of the Association for Education in Journalism, Madison, Wis., August.

MacNeil, Robert. 1968. *The People Machine.* New York: Harper & Row.

Manheim, Jerol B. 1974. "Urbanization and Differential Press Coverage of the Congressional Campaign." *Journalism Quarterly* 51, no. 4:649–53, 669.

Mann, Thomas E. 1978. *Unsafe at Any Margin: Interpreting Congressional Elections.* Washington, D.C.: American Enterprise Institute.

———. 1981. "Elections and Change in Congress." In *The New Congress*, edited by Thomas Mann and Norman Ornstein, 32–54. Washington, D.C.: American Enterprise Institute.

Mann, Thomas E., and Norman J. Ornstein. 1983. "Sending a Message: Voters and Congress in 1982." In *The American Elections of 1982*, by Thomas E. Mann and Norman J. Ornstein, 133–52. Washington, D.C.: American Enterprise Institute.

Mann, Thomas E., and Raymond E. Wolfinger. 1980. "Candidates and Parties in Congressional Elections." *American Political Science Review* 74, no. 3: 617–32.

Mansfield, William. 1976. "Florida: The Power of Incumbency." In *Campaign Money*, edited by Herbert E. Alexander, 39–77. New York: Free Press.

Markus, Gregory B., and Philip E. Converse. 1979. "A Dynamic Simultaneous Equation Model of Electoral Choice." *American Political Science Review* 73, no. 4:1055–70.

Matthews, Donald. 1960. *U.S. Senators and Their World.* Chapel Hill: University of North Carolina Press.

———. 1978. "Winnowing: The News Media and the 1976 Presidential Nominations." In *Race for the Presidency*, 55–78. *See* Arterton 1978.

Mayhew, David R. 1974a. *Congress: The Electoral Connection.* New Haven: Yale University Press.

———. 1974b. "Congressional Elections: The Case of the Vanishing Marginals." *Polity* 6, no. 3:295–317.

Meadow, Robert G. 1976. "Issue Emphasis and Public Opinion: The Media during the 1972 Presidential Campaign." *American Politics Quarterly* 4, no. 2:177–92.

Mezey, Michael. 1970. "Ambition Theory and the Office of Congressmen." *Journal of Politics* 32, no. 3:563–79.

Miller, Arthur H., and Warren E. Miller. 1975. "Issues, Candidates and Partisan Divisions in the 1972 American Presidential Election." *British Journal of Political Science* 5, pt. 4:393–434.

Miller, Arthur H., Warren E. Miller, Alden S. Raine, and Thad A. Brown. 1976. "A Majority Party in Disarray: Policy Polarization in the 1972 Election." *American Political Science Review* 70, no. 3:753–78.

Miller, Warren E., and Donald E. Stokes. 1963. "Constituency Influence in Congress." *American Political Science Review* 51, no. 1:45–56.

Mullen, William F., and John C. Pierce. 1985. "Political Parties." In *Political Life in Washington,* edited by Thor Swanson, William F. Mullen, John C. Pierce, and Charles Sheldon, 55–73. Pullman: Washington State University Press.

Murray, Richard, and Kent L. Tedin. 1983. "The Divisive and Non-Divisive Primary: Voter Choices in Two Gubernatorial Elections." Paper delivered at the annual meeting of the Southern Political Science Association, Birmingham, Ala., 3–5 November.

Nelson, Candice J. 1978–79. "The Effect of Incumbency on Voting in Congressional Elections." *Political Science Quarterly* 93, no. 4:665–78.

Orman, John. 1985. "Media Coverage of the Congressional Underdog." *PS* 18, no. 4:754–59.

Ornstein, Norman J. 1985. "The Elections for Congress." In *The American Elections of 1984,* edited by Austin Ranney, 245–76. Washington, D.C.: American Enterprise Institute.

Ostroff, David. 1980. "A Participant-Observer Study of TV Campaign Coverage." *Journalism Quarterly* 57, no. 3:415–19.

Ostroff, David, and Karin Sandell. 1984. "Local Station Coverage of Campaigns." *Journalism Quarterly* 61, no. 2:346–51.

Page, Benjamin I., and Calvin Jones. 1979. "Reciprocal Effects of Policy Preferences, Party Loyalties, and the Vote." *American Political Science Review* 73, no. 4:1071–89.

Paletz, David L., and Robert Entman. 1981. *Media Power Politics.* New York: Free Press.

Parker, Glenn R. 1980a. "Sources of Change in Congressional District Attentiveness." *American Journal of Political Science* 24, no. 1:115–24.

———. 1980b. "The Advantage of Incumbency in House Elections." *American Politics Quarterly* 8, no. 4:449–64.

———. 1981. "Incumbent Popularity and Electoral Success." In *Congressional Elections,* edited by Louis Maisel and Joseph Cooper, 249–79. Beverly Hills: Sage.

Parker, Glenn R., and Roger H. Davidson. 1979. "Why Do Americans Love

Their Congressman So Much More Than Their Congress?" *Legislative Studies Quarterly* 4, no. 1:53–61.

Parker, Glenn R., and Suzanne L. Parker. 1985. "Correlates and Effects of Attention to the District by U.S. House Members." *Legislative Studies Quarterly* 10, no. 2:223–42.

Patterson, Thomas E. 1980. *The Mass Media Election.* New York: Praeger.

Patterson, Thomas E., and Robert D. McClure. 1976. *The Unseeing Eye.* New York: G. P. Putnam's Sons.

Perkins, Jerry, and Randall Guynes. 1976. "Partisanship in National and State Politics." *Public Opinion Quarterly* 40, no. 3:376–78.

Pfeiffer, David. 1967. "The Measurement of Inter-Party Competition and Systemic Stability." *American Political Science Review* 56, no. 2:457–67.

Piereson, James E., and Terry B. Smith. 1975. "Primary Divisiveness and General Election Success: A Re-examination." *Journal of Politics* 37, no. 2:555–62.

Polsby, Nelson W., and Aaron Wildavsky. 1984. *Presidential Elections.* New York: Charles Scribner's Sons.

Powers, Ron. 1977. *The Newscasters.* New York: St. Martin's Press.

Price, David E. 1984. *Bringing Back the Parties.* Washington, D.C.: Congressional Quarterly Press.

Quarles, Rebecca C. 1979. "Mass Media Use and Voting Behavior." *Communication Research* 6, no. 4:407–36.

Ragsdale, Lyn. 1981. "Incumbent Popularity, Challenger Invisibility, and Congressional Voters." *Legislative Studies Quarterly* 6, no. 2:201–18.

Ranney, Austin. 1965. "Parties in State Politics." In *Politics in the American States,* edited by Herbert Jacob and Kenneth N. Vines, 61–100. Boston: Little, Brown.

———. 1984. *Channels of Power.* New York: Basic Books.

Ranney, Austin, and Wilmoore Kendall. 1954. "American Party Systems." *American Political Science Review* 48, no. 2:477–85.

Reagan, Joey, and Richard V. Ducey. 1983. "Effects of News Measure on Selection of State Government News Sources." *Journalism Quarterly* 60, no. 2:211–17.

Ripley, Randall B. 1983. *Congress: Process and Policy.* New York: Norton.

Robinson, John P. 1978. "Daily News Habits of the American Public." *ANPA News Research Report,* no. 15 (22 September):1–6.

Robinson, Michael J. 1975. "A Twentieth-Century Medium in a Nineteenth-Century Legislature: The Effects of Television on the American Congress." In *Congress in Change,* edited by Norman Ornstein, 240–61. New York: Praeger.

Robinson, Michael J., and Kevin R. Appel. 1979. "Network News Coverage of Congress." *Political Science Quarterly* 94, no. 3:407–18.

Robinson, Michael J., and Margaret A. Sheehan. 1983. *Over the Wire and on TV.* New York: Russell Sage Foundation.

Rohde, David W. 1979. "Risk-Bearing and Progressive Ambition: The Case of the United States House of Representatives." *American Journal of Political Science* 23, no. 1:1–26.

Roper, Burns W. 1983. *Trends in Attitudes toward Television and Other Media: A Twenty-four Year Review.* New York: Television Information Office. April.

Rosenbloom, David. 1973. *The Election Men.* New York: Quadrangle Books.

Rubin, Richard L. 1981. *Press, Party and Presidency*. New York: Norton.

Ryan, Michael, and Dorothea Owen. 1976. "A Content Analysis of Metropolitan Newspaper Coverage of Social Issues." *Journalism Quarterly* 54, no. 4: 634–40, 671.

Sabato, Larry. 1981. *The Rise of Political Consultants*. New York: Basic Books.

Salmore, Stephen A., and Barbara G. Salmore. 1985. *Candidates, Parties, and Campaigns: Electoral Politics in America*. Washington, D.C.: Congressional Quarterly Press.

Salzman, Ed. 1977. "Metropolitan Newspapers." *California Journal* 8, no. 4: 123–25.

Sasser, Emery, and John T. Russell. 1972. "The Fallacy of News Judgment." *Journalism Quarterly* 49, no. 2:280–84.

Schantz, Harvey L. 1976. "Julius Turner Revisited: Primary Elections as the Alternative to Party Competition in 'Safe' Seats." *American Political Science Review* 70, no. 2:541–45.

———. 1980. "Contested and Uncontested Primaries of the U.S. House." *Legislative Studies Quarterly* 5, no. 4:545–62.

Schlesinger, Joseph A. 1955. "A Two-Dimensional Scheme for Classifying the States According to Degree of Inter-Party Competition." *American Political Science Review* 49, no. 4:1120–28.

Shaw, Donald L., and Maxwell E. McCombs, eds. 1977. *The Emergence of American Political Issues*. St. Paul: West.

Sinclair, Barbara. 1983. "Purposive Behavior in the U.S. Congress: A Review Essay." *Legislative Studies Quarterly* 8, no. 1:117–31.

Sorauf, Frank. 1984. *Party Politics in America*. Boston: Little, Brown.

———. 1988. *Money in American Elections*. Glenview, Ill.: Scott, Foresman.

Stempel, Guido H. 1961. "The Prestige Press Covers the 1960 Presidential Campaign." *Journalism Quarterly* 38, no. 2:157–63.

———. 1965. "The Prestige Press in Two Presidential Elections." *Journalism Quarterly* 42, no. 1:15–21.

———. 1969. "The Prestige Press Meets the Third-Party Challenge." *Journalism Quarterly* 46, no. 4:699–706.

———. 1973. "Effects on Performance of a Cross Media Monopoly." *Journalism Monographs*, no. 29 (June):1–30.

Stempel, Guido H., and John Windhauser. 1984. "The Prestige Press Revisited: Coverage of the 1980 Presidential Campaign." *Journalism Quarterly* 61, no. 1:49–55.

Sterling, Christopher. 1984. *Electronic Media*. New York: Praeger.

Stevenson, Robert L., and Kathryn P. White. 1980. "The Cumulative Audience of Television Network News." *Journalism Quarterly* 57, no. 3:477–81.

Stokes, Donald E., and Warren E. Miller. 1962. "Party Government and the Salience of Congress." *Public Opinion Quarterly* 26, no. 1:531–46.

Sullivan, John L. 1973. "Political Correlates of Social, Economic, and Religious Diversity in the American States." *Journal of Politics* 35, no. 1:70–84.

Sundquist, James L., and Richard M. Scammon. 1981. "The 1980 Election: Profile and Historical Perspective." In *A Tide of Discontent*, 19–44. *See* Jones 1981.

Swerdlow, Joel. 1981. "The Decline of the Boys on the Bus." *Washington Journalism Review*, January/February 15–19.

Tidmarch, Charles M., and Brad Karp. 1981. "The Missing Beat: Press Coverage of Congressional Elections." Typescript, Union College, Schenectady, N.Y.

Tipton, Leonard, Roger D. Haney, and John R. Basehart. 1975. "Media Agenda-Setting in City and State Election Campaigns." *Journalism Quarterly* 52, no. 1:15–22.

Traugott, Michael, and M. Vinovskis. 1980. "Abortion and the 1978 Congressional Elections." *Family Planning Perspectives* 12 (September/October): 238–46.

Tuckel, Peter. 1983. "Length of Incumbency and the Reelection Chances of U.S. Senators." *Legislative Studies Quarterly* 8, no. 2:283–88.

Tucker, Harvey J. 1982. "Interparty Competition in the American States." *American Politics Quarterly* 10, no. 1:93–116.

Tufte, Edward R. 1973. "The Relationship between Seats and Votes in Two-Party Systems." *American Political Science Review* 67, no. 2:540–54.

Tunstall, Jeremy, and David Walker. 1981. *Media Made in California*. New York: Oxford University Press.

Turner, Julius. 1953. "Primary Elections as the Alternative to Party Competition in 'Safe' Districts." *Journal of Politics* 15, no. 2:197–210.

Uslaner, Eric M. 1981. "The Case of the Vanishing Liberal Senators: The House Did It." *British Journal of Political Science* 11, pt. 1:105–13.

Vermeer, Jan Pons. 1982. *"For Immediate Release": Candidate Press Releases in American Political Campaigns*. Westport, Conn.: Greenwood.

Wanat, John. 1974. "Political Broadcast Advertising and Primary Election Voting." *Journal of Broadcasting* 18, no. 4:413–22.

Westlye, Mark C. 1986. "The Dynamics of U.S. Senate Elections." Ph.D. diss., University of California, Berkeley.

Winter, James P. 1982. "The Public and Local News." *ANPA News Research Report*, no. 37 (27 October):1–4.

Wolfinger, Raymond E., and Joan H. Hollinger. 1965. "Safe Seats, Seniority, and Power in Congress." *American Political Science Review* 59, no. 2:337–49.

Wolfson, Lewis W. 1985. *The Untapped Power of the Press*. New York: Praeger.

Woll, Peter. 1985. *Congress*. Boston: Little, Brown.

Wootton, Graham. 1985. *Interest Groups: Policy and Politics in America*. Englewood Cliffs, N.J.: Prentice-Hall.

Wright, Gerald C. 1978. "Candidates' Policy Positions and Voting in U.S. Congressional Elections." *Legislative Studies Quarterly* 3, no. 3:445–64.

Wright, Gerald C., and Michael B. Berkman. 1986. "Candidates and Policy in United States Senate Elections." *American Political Science Review* 80, no. 2:567–88.

Wright, Gerald C., Robert S. Erikson, and John P. McIver. 1985. "Measuring State Partisanship and Ideology with Survey Data." *Journal of Politics* 47, no. 2:469–89.

Yiannakis, Diana E. 1981. "The Grateful Electorate: Casework and Congressional Elections." *American Journal of Political Science* 25, no. 3:568–80.

Index

Abramowitz, Alan I., 22, 99, 112, 225 n, 226 n, 234 n, 236 n
Aldrich, John H., 236 n
Alford, John R., 5, 225 n
American Conservative Union, 8, 117
Americans for Democratic Action, 8, 117, 177
Amlong, William, 182
Anaya, Toney, 234 n
Anderson, Walt, 124
Andrews, Mark, 56
Appel, Kevin R., 226 n
Arseneau, Robert B., 225 n, 234 n
Arterton, F. Chris, 228 n
Ashbrook, John, 41
Attendance records, of incumbents, 71–72, 177
Austern, Donald M., 122

Bagdikian, Ben H., 229 n
Bailey, Stephen K., 239 n
Baker, Howard, 72
Barone, Michael, 41, 124, 226 n
Bartels, Larry, 191, 245 n
Basehart, John R., 230 n
Baucus, Max, 244 n
Bayh, Birch, 47, 79, 124, 231 n
Beall, J. Glenn, 124
Bell, Alphonso, 243 n
Bell, Jeffrey, 184
Bentsen, Lloyd, 47, 52, 83, 233 n
Bergholz, Richard, 244 n
Berkman, Michael B., 111, 112, 236 n, 237 n

Bernstein, Robert, 171, 175, 192, 195, 241 n, 242 n
Bibby, John F., 124, 191
Bicker, William E., 229 n
Bird, Rose, 128
Blumler, J. G., 230 n
Bond, Jon R., 158–59
Born, Richard, 241 n, 242 n, 243 n, 245 n
Bradley, Bill, 28, 31, 103, 184, 242 n
Bradley, Tom, 84
Brady, David W., 226 n
Brandes, Sara L., 6, 153, 157, 160, 161, 226 n
Brekke, Gerald, 87
Brian, Earl, 64, 65
Brody, Richard A., 147
Brooke, Edward, 102, 166, 235 n, 237 n
Brown, Cooper, 47, 52–54, 70, 79, 87
Brown, Edmund G. (Jerry), Jr., 35, 47, 50, 73–77, 80, 81, 83, 84, 125–38, 141, 142, 149, 150, 231 n, 238 n
Brumberg, Bruce S., 225 n
Buckalew, James K., 36
Buckley, James, 31
Bullock, Charles S., 226 n
Burdick, Quentin, 8, 47, 56
Burnham, Walter D., 160
Busch, Pete, 79, 87
Bush, George, 85, 233 n, 242 n
Byrd, Harry, Jr., 22

Caddell, Pat, 244 n
Cain, Bruce E., 225 n

Composed by G & S Typesetters, Inc.
in Sabon text and display.
Printed on 50-lb. BookText Natural
and bound in Holliston Roxite B
by Bookcrafters.